Designing for Behavior Change

Applying Psychology and Behavioral Economics

Stephen Wendel

Beijing • Cambridge • Farnham • Köln • Sebastopol • Tokyo

Designing for Behavior Change
by Stephen Wendel

Printed in the United States of America.

Published by O'Reilly Media, Inc., 1005 Gravenstein Highway North, Sebastopol, CA 95472.

O'Reilly books may be purchased for educational, business, or sales promotional use. Online editions are also available for most titles (safaribooksonline.com). For more information, contact our corporate/institutional sales department: (800) 998-9938 or corporate@oreilly.com.

Editor: Mary Treseler
Production Editor: Kara Ebrahim
Copyeditor: Jasmine Kwityn
Proofreader: Amanda Kersey
Indexer: Angela Howard
Cover Designer: Randy Comer
Interior Designers: Ron Bilodeau and Monica Kamsvaag
Illustrator: Leo Fonseca
Compositor: Kara Ebrahim

October 2013: First Edition.

Revision History for the First Edition:

2013-10-25	First release
2013-12-02	Second release
2015-01-09	Third release

See *http://oreilly.com/catalog/errata.csp?isbn=0636920030201* for release details.

[LSI]

[Contents]

[*Foreword*]

On the first day of class at Stanford, I never know which of my students will change the world.

When student Mike Krieger turned in his first few projects, I saw his potential. He masterfully applied concepts learned in class to his designs. A few years later Mike drew from a class project called "Send the Sunshine" to create a global phenomenon called Instagram.

The success of Instagram wasn't an accident. Mike had the skills to follow a winning formula: He tapped existing motivation, and he kept things simple. This is the same formula that students in my Facebook course used to engage over 24 million people with their class projects.

Many thousands of people can write code. But only a relative few can get the psychology right. And when it comes to behavior change, the right psychology makes all the difference.

If you're confused about how human behavior works, I say there's a reason. The problem is not you. The problem comes from traditional theories and models about human psychology. We've inherited some approaches that rarely help design for behavior change in the real world.

Even our language about behavior can mislead. For example, you don't "break" a habit. That's the wrong verb. It implies you exert sudden force and the habit goes away. A better verb would be "untangle" because it sets the right expectations of how to get rid of such behaviors. It requires persistence.

Because I saw how often traditional approaches led to failure, at one point I decided to ignore what I'd learned about psychology. I decided to start fresh. With nothing to muddy my view, I explored basic questions: What are the components of human behavior? What are the different types of change? How do you design behavior solutions that really work?

Over time I mapped out 15 ways behaviors can change (the Behavior Grid). I discovered that behavior occurs only when three elements converge at the same moment: motivation, ability, and a trigger (the Behavior Model). And I created a new way to form habits (now called Tiny Habits). My conclusion: Behavior is systematic. And all the pieces fit together.

I began sharing my new insights and methods at Stanford. And I started guiding innovators who enrolled in my Boot Camps. That's how I met Steve Wendel, the author of this book. He joined me for two days of learning about behavior design.

A common reaction after learning my stuff: *Wow, why didn't I see that before? It all makes sense.* With the right insights and methods, innovators can reliably design products that change behavior. It's not as complicated as many believe.

In my personal life and my professional work, I'm fascinated with this challenge: Design the simplest solution that has the biggest impact. I call this the "Feather Principle." Why? Because a feather seems simple, yet it can do so much: insulate, propel, tickle, adorn, and amuse.

You can see a combination of simplicity and power in art and music. Those are the creations I admire most. In our digital world, Twitter and Instagram are paragons of the Feather Principle. You can also find feathers in architecture, food, fashion, and more.

When well designed, a simple thing can have a big impact.

During my Boot Camp, I teach people to explain the Behavior Model (B=MAT) in less than two minutes. You learn to stand up at a white board and map out how human behavior works. I get you ready to teach clients and colleagues. Simple and powerful, this feather changes the game because it changes how people think.

As I talk with innovators in my 15-minute phone chats, I focus them on the essential elements of designing for change. This is a feather I call the Fogg Method. It has three steps:

1. Select the right target behavior.
2. Make the target behavior easy to do.
3. Ensure a trigger will prompt the behavior.

In many cases, people who phone me are stuck in abstractions. I help them understand these three steps and get started on the right path.

When I first shared Tiny Habits in 2011, I didn't expect that years later I'd still be coaching people, day by day, to create new habits in their lives. The method works, and people like to share it with friends. So I keep teaching it.

Not only is Tiny Habits a feather, it also follows my three steps. First, people pick a specific new behavior they want in their life, such as flossing. In Step 2, they make the behavior easier in two ways: They scale back the behavior itself (floss one tooth), and they redesign their environment to make the behavior easier (setting floss on the counter). The third step is to find a trigger for the new behavior. In Tiny Habits, the breakthrough is to have your existing routine (brushing your teeth) prompt you to do the new behavior (flossing).

When you put the right pieces together, the habit forms quickly. Some people say it feels like magic. But of course it's not magic: It's good design.

Knowing how to design for behavior change gives you power. The methods I teach, the content in this book, and the insights you find elsewhere—all this boosts your ability to change people's lives. That's a big deal. I strongly believe the best approach is to *help people do what they already want to do.* In other words, as a behavior designer, you are not manipulating people or transforming them into someone else. You are helping people become a better version of themselves.

The author of this book is the type of person I like to join my Boot Camp. He's smart and motivated. He asks good questions. He knows how to synthesize and how to extrapolate. And just as important, he wants to use his skills to make people's lives better. I'm proud of Steve's work in this book, and he should be proud too. You'll soon see why...

But before you turn the page, I have a challenge for you. It's the same one I give to students on the last day of my Stanford classes. My challenge is that you'll use what you learn about behavior design to do three things: to make individuals happier, to make households stronger, and to make communities more vibrant.

To achieve these worthy goals, the author and I have invested some of the best days of our lives. We are using our skills to benefit other people and to change the world in good ways. I invite you to join us.

—BJ Fogg, PhD
Healdsburg, California
October 2013

[*Preface*]

- The Nike+ FuelBand, a wristband that automatically tracks your movement and helps you exercise more (one of a dozen new, wearable computing devices on the market)
- Nest, a thermostat that learns your home heating schedule, reinforces good energy usage with a simple phone app, and automates saving money on electricity bills
- GlowCap, a cap for prescription bottles that flashes when it's time to take medication and automatically reorders the medication online when you need it
- Clocky, an alarm clock that jumps off your nightstand and rolls around the room, so you can't turn it off without getting out of bed (Figure Preface-1)
- Barack Obama's highly successful online volunteer platform that enabled volunteers to call potential voters from home, whenever they had a few minutes to spare (Figure Preface-2)
- Lift, the habit-building application; 401(k) auto-escalation programs for saving for retirement; and the QuitNow! mobile app to stop smoking with peer support[1]

FIGURE PREFACE-1. Clocky, the clock that runs away from you

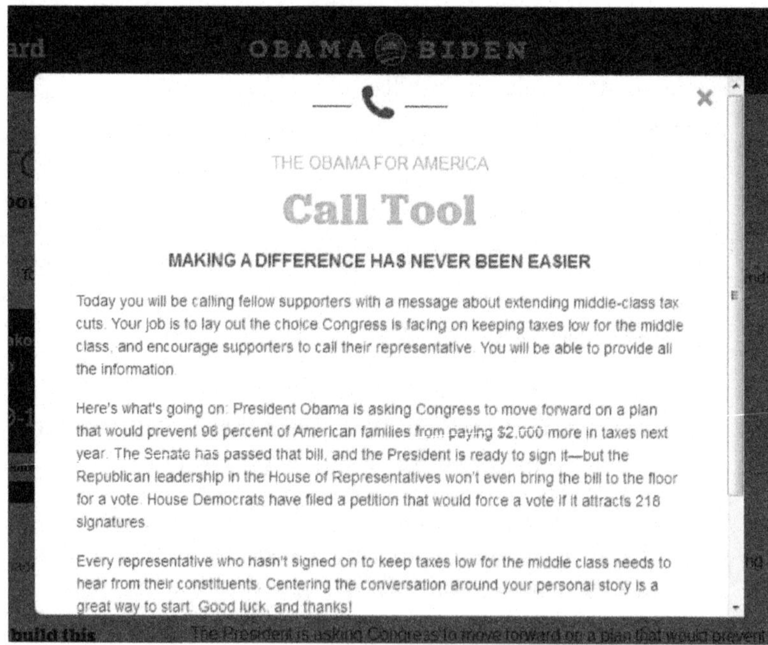

FIGURE PREFACE-2. Obama's volunteer mobilization site, *call.barackobama.com*, during the 2012 campaign

Each of these products was designed to help individuals take action in their lives. Companies have developed a slew of new and innovative products in this space over the past few years—inspired by behavioral economists like Richard Thaler and psychologists like Daniel Kahneman and BJ Fogg.

This book is about how to design, implement, and test such products. Traditional product design is about building *good* products—products that work well and people like using. Designing for behavior change is about building products that are both *good* and *behaviorally effective*—products that help people change their behavior. The goal is to help people do things that they want to do but have struggled with in the past.

The method I discuss here comes, in large part, from our daily experiences at HelloWallet, where I serve as the head researcher. Over the past few years, we've successfully built (and experimentally tested) products that help people take control of their finances—after much trial and error and learning along the way. This method also builds upon the experiences of countless other companies and researchers that we've been talking to and sharing notes with about behavior change. So, let's get started.

What Does It Mean to Design for Behavior Change?

Within the last decade, there has been a tremendous flowering of research in behavioral economics, psychology, and persuasive technology. This research helps us understand how people make decisions in their daily lives, and how those decisions are shaped by people's prior experiences and their environment. Throughout this book, you'll see how to methodically and rigorously apply the lessons from psychology and behavioral economics to the practical problems of product design and development.

Applying that literature is the *first* part of designing for behavior change. The overall process entails four phases, which inform and enhance how we build products (Figure Preface-3):

1. *Understand* how the mind decides to act and what that means for behavior change.

2. *Discover* the right behaviors to change, given your goals and your users' goals.
3. *Design* the product itself around that behavior.
4. *Refine* the product's impact based on careful measurement and analysis.

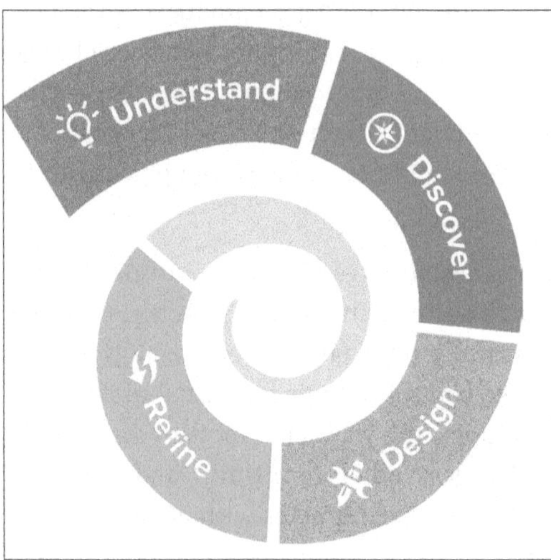

FIGURE PREFACE-3. Designing for behavior change is four stages: start with a core understanding of the mind, discover the right behavior, design the initial product, and then iteratively refine it

In fact, that's the basic outline of the book—we'll cover each of these topics in detail, along with additional information and techniques that will help you along the way.

The "Design" Part of Designing for Behavior Change

Of these four phases, designing the product itself is the sexiest part, so I devote the single largest chunk of the book to that. Our natural inclination is to jump straight to the product and say, "What should the product do to drive behavior change?" But that's actually not the best place to start. Instead, we'll start with the action or behavior that we're trying to change. We'll ask how we can reimagine the action, based on what we learned in the first two phases, to make it more feasible and more palatable for the user *even before we build anything.*

From there, we'll talk about how to construct the decision-making environment—both the product itself and the surrounding context that the person is in—to support action. And, we'll talk about how to prepare users to take action with the product.

Here's a quick outline of the design process:

1. *Action.* Structure the target action to make it feasible and inviting.
2. *Environment.* Construct the decision-making environment to support the target action.
3. *User.* Prepare users to take the target action.

We'll use this three-step design process for both the *conceptual design* (figuring out what the product should do) and the *interface design* (figuring out how the product should look).

Designing for Behavior Change in an Agile or Lean World

Designing for behavior change doesn't require a specific product development methodology—it is intended to layer on top of your existing approach, whether it is agile, lean, Stage-Gate, or anything else. But to make things concrete, Figure Preface-4 shows how the four stages of designing for behavior change can be applied to a simple iterative development process. At HelloWallet, we use a combination of lean and agile methods, and this sample process is based on what we've found to work.

Figure Preface-4 shows you the specific outputs that the team will generate within each stage of the process.

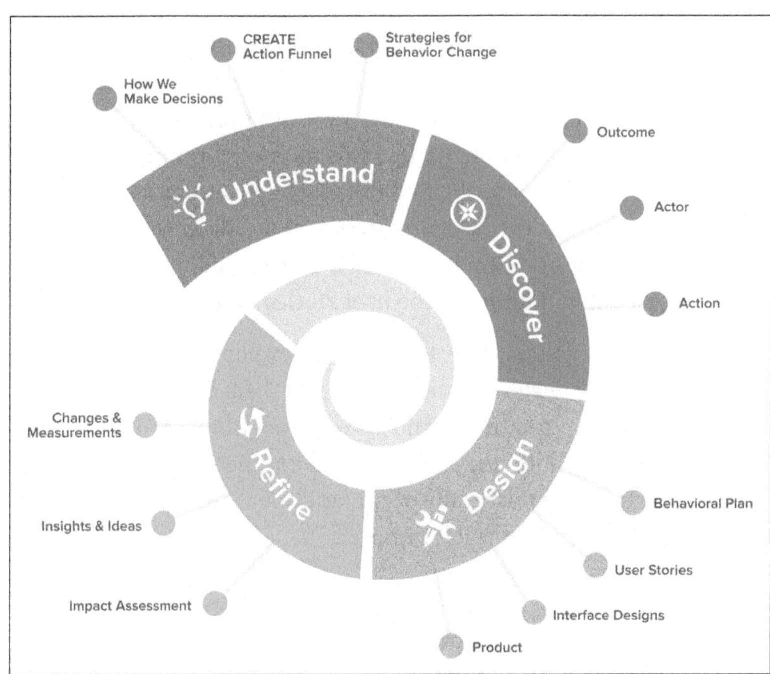

FIGURE PREFACE-4. The outputs generated by designing for behavior change at each stage of the process, using a simple iterative product development cycle

Let's assume that a company (or NGO, government body, or individual entrepreneur; I use "company" as a convenient shorthand for any individual and organization making behavior change products) is developing a new product. Here is how this sample process works, and the outputs the team will generate at each stage:

1. *Understand.* To start things off, the company gains an understanding of how we make decisions and how our cognitive mechanisms can support (or hinder) behavior change. The two main topics to cover are the prerequisites for action, which are summarized in the *Create Action Funnel*, and the three *strategies for behavior change* that companies can use.

2. *Discover.* With that knowledge in hand, it clarifies what, specifically, the company wants to accomplish with the product, and for whom. Perhaps the company seeks a world full of (newly) healthy people. The company then identifies the particular group it wants to make healthier (let's say it's office workers), and the action it wants to encourage (let's say it's walking more); that's the *actor* and *action*.

3. *Design.* It's convenient to think of the design stage in terms of two subtasks—designing the overall concept for the product, and then designing the specific user interface and actually building the product.

   a. *Conceptual design.* The company develops a *behavioral plan*, a story about how the user will interact with the product. That's the high-level conceptual design of the product. The behavioral plan is incrementally built up by examining the *action* itself, the *environment*, and the *user's preparation* to act. Then, the company extracts *user stories*: short statements that capture the spirit of each piece of the behavioral plan. The product team will flesh out the user stories in greater detail.

   b. *Interface design.* The team then develops *interface designs*, which are reviewed and revised for their behavioral content (action, environment, and user preparation). Next, it's time to actually build *the product*. Some engineering compromises and trade-offs naturally occur, and the team reviews them as well for their behavioral impact.

4. *Refine*. Once a version of the product is ready for field testing, the team starts to gather quantitative and qualitative data about user behavior to form an initial *impact assessment* of how the product is doing. A careful, structured analysis of that data leads to *insight and ideas* for improving the product. That could lead the team members to revise their underlying conception of whom they are helping and how, and generate a new behavioral plan and new user stories accordingly. The new user stories turn into designs, the designs into product revisions, and so on. The spiral continues inward until the desired level of impact is achieved. With each revision, the team makes *changes and measurements* of how those changes impacted user behavior.

If the company already has an existing product and wants to refine it, the process is similar but starts at a different place. After establishing the desired outcome, actor, and action, the company jumps directly to refinement: measuring user behavior and the product's current impact, and comparing it against the company's behavioral goals for the product. Then the team uses that information to drive insights that inform the product's target actor and actions, behavioral plan, and user stories.

As I mentioned, this particular process follows a simple iterative approach. Of course, you're not required to follow it (well, you might hurt my feelings). In this book, I also discuss how to employ these methods using a sequential development (aka "waterfall") process. The key is that you can slot in the tools of designing for behavior change where you need them.

Behavioral Plan? User Stories?

Throughout the book, you'll find terms to express new ideas—like the behavioral plan. They are defined in the text, and in a quick-reference glossary (Appendix A). There is also a smattering of special terms from particular product development processes—like user stories—with suggestions on where to learn more about them. For example:

Behavioral plan
: A detailed "story" of how the user progresses from being a neophyte to accomplishing the action while using the product. The "story" can be narrative, visual, verbal, whatever—as long as it gets the job done. See Chapter 6 for how to develop it.

User story
: A term used in product development (especially agile development) for a plain-English statement about what the user needs. It captures the "who," "what," and "why" of a product requirement. For example: "As a user, I want to <take an action>, in order to <reason for action>." See *http://en.wikipedia.org/wiki/User_story* for more information.

Who This Book Is For

As you can probably tell by now, this book is aimed at practitioners—the people who design and build products with specific behavioral goals. Teams that design for behavior change should generally include the following roles, and individuals in each of these roles will find practical, how-to instructions in this book:

- Interaction designers, information architects, user researchers, human factors experts, human-computer interaction (HCI) practitioners, and other user experience (UX) folks
- Product managers, product owners, and project managers
- Behavioral social scientists (behavioral economists, psychologists, judgment and decision-making experts) interested in products that apply the research literature

The person doing the work of designing for behavior change could be any one of these people. At HelloWallet, we have a dedicated person with a social science background on the product team (that's me). But this work can be, and often is, done wonderfully by UX folks. They are closest to the look and feel of the product, and have its success directly in their hands. Product owners and managers are also well positioned to seamlessly integrate the skills of designing for behavior change to make their products effective. Finally, there's a new movement of behavioral social scientists into applied product development and consulting at organizations like ideas42 and IrrationalLabs. So, the people designing for behavior change probably wear other hats as well.

In addition, this book is for entrepreneurs and managers. If you've ever read *Nudge*, *Blink*, or *Predictably Irrational*,[2] and wondered how you could apply them to your own product and users, read on. While the book is about helping users take action in their lives, that doesn't mean that designing for behavior change is incompatible with a for-profit business model. Businesses make a profit; that's how they exist. So you'll find suggestions in Chapter 15 for building a successful business model on voluntary behavior change. If in addition to making a profit, you are helping your users take action and change their behavior, this book can help you do it.

Nonprofit entities and some government agencies often explicitly focus on helping users change their behavior; *Designing for Behavior Change* can help. For example, the United Kingdom government's Behavioural Insights Team is widely applying behavioral research to UK public policy and the provision of services.[3] Where relevant, I'll note parts that are particularly important for nongovernmental organizations (NGOs) and government agencies. Because it's more compact to write, I'll refer primarily to "companies" here. In almost all cases, I really mean companies, organizations, and relevant government agencies.

Finally, my expertise is software development, so I'll use the terminology that I use in my day-to-day life—applications, software, and programs. You don't need to be in software development to find this relevant to you. In fact, some of the most innovative work in persuasive design, one of the fields that this book draws inspiration from, is in the design of everyday objects.[4] As you apply *Designing for Behavior Change* to your work, whether in software or beyond, I'd love to talk with you and share notes!

Combining Research, Data, and Product Expertise

One of the book's recurring themes is that understanding how the mind works is not enough to build behaviorally effective products.

In addition to behavioral science research, we need two sets of skills to support the process. First, we need to plan for data analysis (both qualitative and quantitative) and for refinement and iteration based on that data. That means adding metrics to the application and conducting user research to understand individual behavior, analyzing the data, and making improvements over time based on it. Why do we need to plan for iteration? The research literature is invaluable, but we're just starting to understand how to best apply it to practical product development. There are no magic formulas for behavior change: we're all unique people, with different histories and personalities. This book will help you take your first, best shot, then fine-tune your product based on what the data tells you about your real-life users and their behavior.

Second, we need to build products that people actually enjoy using. I know it sounds obvious, but it's something that's often forgotten as we build products designed to educate, motivate, or otherwise help our users. We tend to focus on the behavior change (and how important it is, etc.), and forget the fact that people still have to *choose* to use our products. Users avoid boring, frustrating, ugly applications, so we should remember the lessons of good product design: from identifying user needs and frustrations to designing an intuitive, beautiful user interface.

When you bring these raw ingredients together—behavioral research, product design expertise, and data analysis—you have what's needed to design for behavior change (Figure Preface-5).

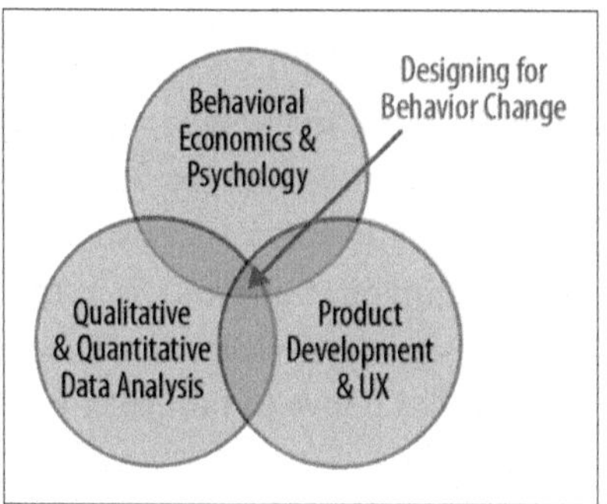

FIGURE PREFACE-5. Designing for behavior change integrates behavioral research, pragmatic product development, and rigorous data analysis

What Do You Need to Know to Benefit from This Book?

This book gives you enough knowledge in each of these three areas to get oriented and to start working on concrete products. It covers most of the behavioral research you'll need to finish the products as well, but at some point along the way, you'll need people who are experts in qualitative or quantitative data and in product design.

If you *are* an expert in one of these areas, all the better. The book will show you how designing for behavior change builds upon and complements your existing expertise. You'll find out how to leverage your existing skills to play a leading role in the development of behaviorally effective products within your organization.

What Types of Behaviors Can This Help With?

The techniques I'll talk about here assume that the product will support an action that people aspire to but have had difficulty taking. Learning a language. Sticking to a diet. Meeting new people. This may seem like it applies only to a narrow set of products, but I've found that there are two big groups of behaviors that fit this criteria. Both groups of behaviors (and products that work with them) can use this method:

- Behaviors that users want to change *within their daily lives*
- Behaviors *within the product itself* that are part of using the product

The first group, behavior change within people's daily lives, includes:

- Controlling diabetes
- Paying off credit card debts
- Getting back in shape
- Getting involved in their communities

Often these behaviors relate to big-picture social issues, like health and wellness. When we design products that support these behaviors, we help the individual and impact our society at the same time. Opower and Nest, for example, are companies that help individuals decrease individual energy usage: saving people money and helping the environment at the same time. Other products that change behavior in this way are Fitbit (exercise) and Weight Watchers (diet).

In the second group, individuals often seek to change behavior for more mundane purposes. Let's say a user wants to learn a new language, and gets a software package to help do it. Simply learning how to effectively use the software can take some substantial changes in behavior *within the product*—building new habits to log in daily and practice the language, overcoming fears about looking foolish while doing it, and so on. The user wants to take an action (learning the language) but struggles. A well-designed product can help the user make those personal adjustments.

This second type of behavior change, and the products that require it, is much broader than the first type. It covers the sweep of voluntary changes in behavior that people might make to benefit from products they've already chosen to use. It touches upon a huge swath of the consumer product space, from Yelp to Square to Rosetta Stone. Here are some examples of behaviors that occur *within software products* that one might try to improve:

- Organizing email contacts
- Drawing decent flowcharts
- Formatting documents

These two types of behavior change also differ from the perspective of the company making the product. Companies can think of these two categories like this:

- Behavior change is the core value of the product for users; or
- Behavior change is required for users to extract the value of the product.

In the first case, users have some behavioral problem in their daily lives and buy the product to help them with it. In the second case, users have some other need that the product solves, but they must adapt and change their behavior in order for the product to deliver on its promise.

In both cases, the goal of designing for behavior change is to develop products that help users take action, and to deliver the value that the company offers. This voluntary, transparent support for behavior change helps companies be successful as well.

What it's not designed for is persuasion, trickery, or coercion (for both practical and ethical reasons).

What This Book Is Not About

If you're looking for a book on how to make people do something *you* want them to do (even if they don't want to do it), you're in the wrong place. I'm not necessarily judging your motives or aims; I just can't help you much. Here is what this book won't cover, and why:

Persuading people
: Designing for behavior change doesn't seek to persuade people to take action, for two reasons. First, it relies on the fact that people already want to act. Second, it's fundamentally about *action* and not about beliefs or intentions; the goal is to help people do something physical in the real world. It's in the real world of action where good intentions often fail.

Trickery
: This involves *tricking people* into doing something they don't want to do. In many cases, taking a "hard" action takes numerous small steps. Putting aside the morality of manipulating people, it's simply impractical in this scenario—people wise up somewhere along the process of small steps. It's hard to build a *sequence* of actions around trickery.

Coercing people
: Few products can *force* people to do something. And, to be frank, the techniques in this book are largely ineffective when the person is being coerced. Thankfully, people find creative ways to resist coercion.

For different reasons, there are a couple of other things that I don't focus on here:

Clicking a button on a single page
: We'll certainly talk about how to support that action, because that's a basic building block of online applications, including those that change behavior. But if that's all you're trying to do, get a book on testing web designs, run dozens of experiments, and then go with the best one. This book focuses on more complex and challenging behaviors.

Addiction
: Many of the habits that people want to stop are tied to a chemical addiction (i.e., drugs or alcohol) or an underlying disorder. The neurobiology of addiction and of psychological disorders that cause

> deeply ingrained and undesirable habits are beyond the scope of this book. I do provide a section on how to avoid triggering existing habits and how to build new habits that seek to *displace* existing ones, but those sections are geared for less intractable behaviors.

Because we're not focusing on stopping addiction, and because most of the ways to stop a (less pernicious) habit involve overcoming the habit with a *different* action, I'll often refer to "behavior change" and "taking action" interchangeably here. That makes writing and reading this a bit more interesting, too.

Behavior Change and the Dark Arts

While the goal here isn't persuasion or coercion, there's no escaping it—this book builds upon research into what I half-jokingly call "the Dark Arts": using products to change people's behavior when they aren't aware of what you're doing, or when it's explicitly against their will. Many of the cognitive mechanisms that I reference in this book have been studied in the fields of consumer behavior, marketing, and sales for decades. Some of the research in these fields has been laudable, and used to better understand what people really want. But much of it has been used to push products that people don't want, don't need, and can't afford. In 1957, Vance Packard's book *The Hidden Persuaders* (Pocket Books) decried the tricks that advertisers used at the time; the techniques have only gotten more advanced since then.

THE DARK ARTS ARE SIMILAR...

To drive sales, companies have invested heavily over the last few decades in understanding how the mind works. Books such as Paco Underhill's *Why We Buy* (Simon & Schuster, 2000) and Martin Lindstrom's *Buyology* (Crown Business, 2010) detail how companies have used everything from randomized control trials about product placement to fMRI brain scans of brand exposure to understand how we, as consumers, tick.[5] Behavioral economics and the psychology of judgment and decision making, both of which I rely heavily upon here, study many of the same cognitive mechanisms but in different contexts. The brain is the brain, whether it's telling the body to buy soap or to exercise more.

What's been lacking, I believe, in the study of "stuff that's good for you" (exercise, good diet, financial control, etc.) has been an honest assessment that we're actually doing some similar things as companies selling products—we just aren't doing it as well. Realistically, most diet programs, personal finance tools, political advocacy campaigns, and Bible study groups have always been about changing people's behavior. Marketers already know this, and some of them apply their craft to pursue explicit social goals (aka "social marketing").[6] But the rest of us have just tried to hide from that fact, and so we've been ineffective.

I figure that if you say that you want to build a product that's designed to help someone, don't dance around the issue: get off your butt and actually do it. There's just no point to designing these products if they are ineffective. That's not to say that we should start moral crusades in the name of helping people whether they like it or not. We need to be cautious and humble, check our assumptions about our products, and verify that our products are voluntary, transparent, and beneficial. If they are, excellent. Use human psychology to help people take control of their own lives.

...BUT NOT IDENTICAL

On the other hand, if we can learn so much from the manipulative side of sales and consumer research, why do we need something new? Why not just provide a list of books on effective sales techniques and call it a day? There are some key differences between designing products for behavior change and marketing/sales. Products that engender different types of behavior look and act differently. We'll build upon their research, but apply it in a very different context.[7]

Focusing on *voluntary* change helps one scale back the unmanageable topic of behavior change into something more digestible and practical. For example, pushing someone to buy a product that he wouldn't otherwise buy is a very different task than helping a recovering alcoholic avoid cues in the environment to drink. Also, if you assume people want to take a particular action (but haven't been able to), you can focus on the relevant research and dispense with discussions of preference generation, dissonance, manipulation, and so on. Similarly, focusing on software applications and digital-physical tools like the Nike+ FuelBand allows us to avoid tangents about person-to-person coaching, therapy, and the like. It usefully narrows the range of possible psychological mechanisms and approaches to a reasonable set that one can work with.

AND HOPEFULLY, THIS IS MORE SUSTAINABLE

I also firmly believe that designing for voluntary and transparent behavior change is also the most sustainable path, from a product development perspective. This isn't the first time that behaviorism has taken hold of the social sciences and of businesses practices—it flowered in the early to mid-1900s under researchers such as John Watson and B.F. Skinner. Behaviorism eschewed internal mental states as primary causes of behavior, and looked to environmental factors to explain and ultimately change behavior. This approach dominated psychology and strongly influenced behavioral research in other social sciences, but a backlash against the external, mechanistic view of behavior finally overcame behaviorism. Behaviorism's fall had many causes, but one enduring critique is that viewing people as mechanical devices led to an atheoretical, soulless view of humanity, and one in which researchers sought to control or manipulate us.

When I see books about "how you can get people to do anything," first I laugh—since most of those books tremendously exaggerate the real research that's out there. Their authors are deceiving themselves, their readers, or both. But I also cringe—because I know that that manipulative approach invites a backlash.

So this book takes a middle path—using the tools of behaviorism, along with other traditions within psychology and economics, to be effective at changing behavior, but being transparent about it and focusing on voluntary action, to avoid that backlash. I think we can do something new and different with the research. We'll see how it goes.

How This Book Came About

I'm the head research guy at HelloWallet, and the idea for this book started with my own experience, and the experiences of all of us at HelloWallet. For many years now, we've sought to help our users take control of their finances and make the best use of their employee benefits. For some people, that means saving up money for emergencies, so they don't fall deep into credit card debt when someone gets sick or the car breaks down. For others, that means getting free of debt. And, for some, it means saving money for retirement, their kids' education, or a really cool vacation they've always wanted to take.

The basics are simple—we provide online and mobile applications to help people understand their current financial situation and then help them take action. Our members are primarily the employees of large companies who buy our software to help their workers get ahead financially. We're currently serving the employees of some of the best-known companies in the country—from retail workers at your local outlet mall to the investment bankers handling your 401(k) at T. Rowe Price, and from the people that put ketchup into Heinz bottles to the ones who designed the Black Hawk Helicopter at Sikorsky. At these companies and others, we're helping their employees take control of their finances.

The details are much more complex. We started out building software that *told people what do to.* We looked up the relevant mathematical models for optimal financial behavior and piped them into the application as marching orders for our users. We quickly found out that no one listened. They didn't want to be yelled at.

So we started looking for models that worked. Around that time, Richard Thaler and Cass Sunstein's book *Nudge* came out, showing how behavioral economics was being applied to nudge people into better behavior. We dug into the literature in behavioral economics and related fields, and assembled an academic advisory board of great researchers from across the country. They helped us parse the academic literature, and put it into practice in our applications.

We found that the translation process—from academic research into real products—was far from straightforward and easy. Our first attempts flopped, to put it bluntly. We designed features on the cutting edge of academic knowledge, with all indications that if people used the features, we would transform their lives. Well, we found that people just didn't use those features. A product that *could* change behavior is useless if no one *wants* to use it. So, we hired good people with real expertise building consumer-facing products (something we had lacked, unfortunately). We tested the heck out of our app. We fixed the parts that were broken, and developed a user experience that people enjoyed using.

After all of this, we've finally crossed the threshold. We're helping our users take control of their finances. For example, we ran an experimental study with a set of independent researchers, and found that one feature (the "Guided Approach") caused our users to put aside

$100–$200 more in a month than they otherwise would have. To put that in context, for the median US family earning about $50,000 a year, that represents an additional 5% of their salaries saved for the future. That means more than doubling the US savings rate (about 4%, on average).

Along the way, we learned that in order to make behaviorally effective products, you need three things:

1. The product and design expertise to build something that people will actually like
2. A clear understanding of user behavior and how to influence it
3. A commitment to testing the heck out of your product and listening to what the data tells you

My personal story has been intertwined with that of HelloWallet for the last four years. I'm a political scientist by training, and my research focused on how people change their political behavior by interacting with their local environment over time. In 2007, I cofounded a micro-targeting company that employed machine learning and simulation modeling to find new volunteers for political advocacy groups—and then (successfully) encouraged them to get involved. The math worked, but the business model didn't. So, a year later, I started looking around for other options. My cofounder and I happened upon HelloWallet, and were inspired by the promise of democratizing access to financial guidance for everyone. I quickly joined HelloWallet as its first full-time employee.

Initially, I was HelloWallet's (only) software engineer, designing and developing a highly detailed (and, in hindsight, completely unrealistic) simulation model of financial behavior over an individual's lifetime. Later on, I ran the engineering team, and then headed up the quantitative analysis of our application. Along the way, I attended BJ Fogg's Behavior Design Bootcamp, and applied the behavioral economics and psychology literatures to develop new ideas for the product.

I'm currently HelloWallet's principal scientist, and my job entails digging through the academic literature for product insights, running experiments on how to improve financial behavior, and coordinating our academic advisory board. I've also had the fun privilege of organizing Action Design D.C., a Meetup group of behavior change practitioners in Washington, D.C., that focuses on learning from one another's efforts to support behavior change.[8]

So, when I mentioned the mistakes and lessons that HelloWallet learned—about mathematically correct but behaviorally unrealistic models and academically interesting but unengaging product features—those were, to a large extent, my own mistakes and lessons. At HelloWallet, we've run the gauntlet and come out the other side with a product that's both beautiful and effective. This book comes from our experiences, and from the lessons we've learned through Action Design D.C. and conversations with like-minded groups around the country.

It's my sincere hope and belief that this book can help you skip over some of the mistakes I've made along the way, and jump straight to the fun part—learning how to best help your users take action.

The Chapters Ahead

In the following pages, I walk you through each of the skills you need to design for behavior change, starting with a firm foundation in how the mind makes decisions. Then, I show each step that's required to develop a new product, using the simple iterative product development process shown previously in Figure Preface-4: moving from discovery to design to implementation to refinement. I introduce each concept where it is first needed. In the concluding chapters, I step back and give some additional tips on how to use these skills in practice, how to apply these techniques to refine existing products, and likely problems you'll face along the way. That's it.

However, if you're looking for a more formal chapter outline, here you go:

Part I: Understanding the Mind and Behavior Change

Chapter 1 arms you with your first skill: an understanding of how the mind makes decisions. You'll get an overview of the current literature on decision making, as well as a dozen key lessons and their implications for the design process.

Chapter 2 describes the five high-level factors that must come together at the same time for a person to take action. They form the Create Action Funnel, which shows you what needs to be addressed in your app and where users usually drop off. The funnel will help you diagnose and fix problems in your products.

Chapter 3 develops three specific strategies for changing behavior. In short, you can focus on our conscious mode of thinking or on our habits, or you can shift the burden of work from the user to the product (what I call "cheating"). You'll reuse these three strategies throughout the product development process.

Part II: Discovering the Right Actor, Action, and Outcome

Chapter 4 starts charting your course by discovering the overall outcomes you hope the product will deliver and who it seeks to help. From there, it demonstrates how to brainstorm potential ideas for behavior change—how, specifically, your users will get fit or take control of their finances, for example.

Chapter 5 gathers knowledge about your users, and then evaluates the various behaviors they *could* change in light of their needs, interests, and prior experience. It shows how to analyze the (behavioral) cost-effectiveness of various actions, and how they affect the bottom line of a company. It also demonstrates how to make a decision and select the specific behavior that the product will support.

Part III: Developing the Conceptual Design

Chapter 6 introduces you to the meat of the process: designing the product itself. You start by structuring the action so people will actually take it! This task includes breaking the problem down into component steps, tailoring it based on your user research, and making it understandable and feasible. To make the discussion concrete, this section also starts the idea of a conceptual design or behavioral plan: a narrative of how the product team envisions user interaction with the product and how users will change their behavior.

Chapter 7 covers the second part of the design: how to construct the environment—especially the product itself—so that the user is encouraged to take the action. Naturally, this involves motivation, but I discuss how that is often not the core issue with behavior change products. You can encourage action with an immediate cue to act, a feedback loop, removing distractions, and avoiding user-specific obstacles.

Chapter 8 completes the design process with a discussion of how a product can prepare users for action ahead of time. I talk about how to help users rewrite their personal narrative to weave in action, how to build a behavioral bridge between the new action and other things they are familiar with, and how to provide users with information and education, especially about the task ahead.

Part IV: Designing the Interface

Chapter 9 moves from the behavioral plan, or conceptual design, to the interface design. I discuss how to convert the behavioral plan into user stories or written specs, and then into wireframes and graphic designs.

Chapter 10 delves into how to review a set of interface designs for their behavioral impact. I show you how to reapply the core design process (gather knowledge, structure the action, construct the environment, and prepare the user) at a more detailed, tactical level.

Chapter 11 is about implementation: how to build the product from the designs. I talk about the collaboration between the product team and the engineering team, and how to evaluate the behavioral impact of design revisions. Early user feedback on the product (hopefully in a prototype phase) can help immensely.

Part V: Refining the Product

Chapter 12 focuses on assessing the product's impact: its success or failure. I cover how to instrument the application to track essential data, and how to use experimental methods and statistical models to gain insight. I talk about the challenges of gauging the causal impact of software on real-world behavior, and how to overcome them.

Chapter 13 delves into another aspect of data gathering and analysis: finding the problems that limit impact. I also discuss how proper instrumentation can identify bottlenecks in the application that are limiting impact. This chapter also discusses how qualitative and quantitative analyses are both needed, and work hand in hand.

In Chapter 14, I talk about how the lessons from the measurement process can be reapplied in later versions of the application. I also discuss how designing for behavior change fits into the product development processes, and how it can be applied to retrofit existing products.

Part VI: Putting It into Practice

Chapter 15 covers some of the questions that can arise when putting these lessons into practice, such as how to build a sustainable business around behavior change, and how to sustain engagement with your product.

Finally, Chapter 16 wraps things up with a quick review of the designing for behavior change process and key takeaways on how to make it happen in your organization.

In the appendixes, there's information for those who are looking to dive even deeper into these topics:

- A glossary of key terms, like "behavioral plan" and "data bridge"
- An annotated list of resources for learning more about psychology and product design
- The book's bibliography

Each of the core chapters ends with a quick summary of the approach, if you only have a few minutes. It's a useful wrap-up and also gives advice if you're just looking for an informal process to sketch things out before you jump in head first. In honor of the many people coming up with exciting ideas to start new companies based on a concept sketched on a cocktail napkin, the summary sections of each chapter are titled "On a Napkin."

Let's Talk

My hope with this book is to further the conversation about voluntary behavior change and help build up the tools needed to develop behaviorally effective products. However, I have no illusions about the completeness of this work—there's still a tremendous amount to figure out. We're all going to learn as we go along.

Personally, I'm always looking to learn, share, and collaborate, so please don't hesitate to reach out to me if you have a cool story to share, an idea for a research project that would further develop the field, or just an idea for a behavior-changing project that you'd like to bounce off someone. In most places, you can find me under "sawendel" (Twitter, LinkedIn, AngelList); you can also find my up-to-date contact information at *http://about.me/sawendel*.

If you think there's something that can be improved in this book or something that is inaccurate, please reach out to me and tell me about it. One of the many benefits of working with O'Reilly Media as a publisher is that a lot of you will be reading this book in an electronic format and can quickly get an updated version of the book if corrections need to be made. For those who are reading this in paper form, I'll keep a list of corrections, additions, and other updates online at my blog, *actiondesign.hellowallet.com*.

Acknowledgments

I am pleasantly indebted to dozens of people who have encouraged my writing this book, given feedback and comments, or sparked new ideas during one of the many workshops and talks I've held with unsuspecting audiences to iron out these concepts. At HelloWallet, where I work, I'm particularly thankful for the support, encouragement, and feedback of Paul Ballas, Aaron Benway, Jaime Dalbke, Matt Fellowes, Matt Garza, Katherine Kendall, Rajesh Nerlikar, Rob Pinkerton, Evan Samek, and, especially, Michael Yoch. Also, a number of the graphics in this book come from the expert hands of Heyjin Kang, Alisa March, and Katie Palermo.

Beyond HelloWallet, the list is long and diverse (with my apologies to those I've missed): Dave Aidekman, Denis Baranov, John Beshears, Danny Boice, Cameron Breslin, Julia Brown, Jim Burke, Anna Cash, Chris Daggett, Nir Eyal, BJ Fogg, Spencer Gerrol, Zach Goodwin, Peter Jackson, Erik Johnson, Warren Jokinen, Panayiotis "Dr. Voodoo" Karabetis, Keri Kettle, Shreya Kothaneth, Maxim Leyzerovich, Ronnie Lipton, Neale Martin, Katy Milkman, Michael Mentzel, Enio Ohmaye, Anastasiya Pocheptsova, Brendan Robinson, Justin Thorp, Remi Trudel, Anna Tulchinskaya, Katya Vasilaky, Marko Vasiljevic, Jonathan Zinman. My editor, Mary Treseler at O'Reilly, has been a pleasure to work with, and I appreciate the help and thoughtfulness of my technical reviewers: Tom Boates, Sebastian Deterding, Randy Farmer, Karl Fast, and Samantha Starmer. And, most of all, I'd like to thank Alexia Muchisu, for putting up with me while I was writing and for taking care of our entertaining and surprisingly energetic son.

Research and Inspiration

There's a great excitement and flurry of activity around beneficial behavior change, and throughout this work, I cite researchers with studies that are particularly relevant or that I'm directly building upon. But I should thank five people for their inspiration above and beyond their printed words and research studies:

- Joe Oppenheimer—theorist, experimentalist, chair of my dissertation committee, coauthor, friend, and sourdough baker
- Jon Zinman—behavioral economist, advisory board member, and unofficial, unpaid mentor in all things behavioral economics
- John Beshears—behavioral economist, advisory board member, discussion partner, and sounding board
- Nir Eyal—entrepreneur, thinker, master storyteller, and co-traveler trying to level the playing field for beneficial behavior change
- BJ Fogg—social psychologist, innovator, behavior change leader, and teacher of the Persuasion Bootcamp, which spurred my journey into product-mediated behavior change

Like many researchers, I believe that there are no truly new ideas—only new ways to present and organize old ideas. If you see a compelling idea in this book, without a specific citation next to it, the odds are good that one of these five people originally inspired it. I am deeply grateful for their leading the way.

[*Part I*]

Understanding the Mind and Behavior Change

- Doctors were 34% more likely to opt for a surgical treatment for cancer when they were presented with the surgery's survival rate instead of the surgery's death rate *(note: they are exactly the same thing)* (McNeil et al. 1982).
- Simply moving bottles of water (instead of soda bottles) so that they were at eye-level in the kitchens at Google, a place not known for its dullards, increased water uptake by a whopping 47% (Kuang 2012).

You've probably come across similarly surprising cases of how the mind works, either in your own life or in the news. The examples given here are from research studies in psychology and behavioral economics on how changing small aspects of our environment, like the framing of questions, can radically affect our behavior.

Part I focuses on how the mind makes decisions—and what that means for products that drive behavior change. In our daily lives, we're often on autopilot, and we aren't making conscious "decisions" at all. Even when we are making decisions, our minds sometimes work in ways that seem rather odd—at least until one understands a set of simple principles about how decision making works.

The goal for this part is to provide an overall understanding of how the mind decides, what's required for people to take action, and how we can use this knowledge to think strategically about behavior change.

[1]

How the Mind Decides What to Do Next

The Deliberative and Intuitive Mind

Our society has a polarized, contradictory view of how the mind works—either we think we're careful, rational people, or we're just emotional wrecks that are lucky to get through the day alive. Sometimes we even hold both views at the same time—we consider ourselves to be rational, but those in opposing political parties or in different departments at work are blinded by their emotions.[9]

Well, the truth is that both are absolutely true—and they are true at the same time, in every single one of us. That fact is essential to understanding how to design products that change behavior.

We have two modes of thinking in the brain—one is deliberative and the other is intuitive. Psychologists have a well-developed understanding of how they work, called dual process theory.[10] Our intuitive mode (or "emotional" mode; it's also called "System 1"), is blazingly fast and automatic, but we're generally not conscious of its inner workings. It uses our past experiences and a set of simple rules of thumb to almost immediately give us an intuitive evaluation of a situation—an evaluation we feel through our emotions and through sensations around our bodies like a "gut feeling" (Damasio et al. 1996). It's generally quite effective in familiar situations, where our past experiences are relevant, and does less well in unfamiliar situations.

Our deliberative mode (aka our "conscious" mode or "System 2") is slow, focused, self-aware and what most of us consider "thinking." We can rationally analyze our way through unfamiliar simulations, and handle complex problems with System 2. Unfortunately, System 2 is woefully limited in how much information it can handle at a time (we struggle holding more than seven numbers in short-term memory at once! [Miller 1956]), and thus relies on System 1 for much of the real work of thinking. These two systems can work independently of each other, in parallel, and can disagree with one another—like when we're troubled by the sense that, despite our careful thinking, "something is just wrong" with a decision we've taken.[11]

Making Sense of the Mind

The distinction between deliberative and intuitive thinking is just one of the many findings that researchers have discovered about how the mind works. In fact, there are literally hundreds of such lessons, many of which describe quirky mechanisms that lead us to behave in unexpected ways.[12] Each one describes a piece of how the mind works, and often, how that piece can push individuals toward one action or another. To give you an idea of their breadth, here are just some of the mechanisms that start with the letter "A":[13]

Ambiguity effect

We're intuitively uncomfortable with actions in which the potential effects have unknown probabilities. This makes us avoid otherwise preferred options when uncertainty is added (Ellsberg 1961).

Anchoring

We automatically use an initial reference point (anchor) as basis for estimates, even if the estimate is wrong. For example, the initial listing prices for houses, even if completely invalid, strongly affect how much buyers (and real estate agents) think the house is worth (Northcraft and Neale 1987)!

Attentional bias

We pay attention to particular cues in our environment based on our internal state. For example, people who are addicted to a drug are extra sensitive to cues related to their addiction. They effectively see things that relate to the drug more often than everyone else, whether they want to or not (Field and Miles 2008).

Availability cascade

Incorrect (and correct) ideas can become increasingly believed and widespread because of (a) repetition by well-meaning people who don't want to appear wrong, and (b) manipulation from interested parties. Kuran and Sunstein (1999) cite the example of the Love Canal toxic waste scare in New York—which, from expert accounts, was vastly overblown and was later discredited.

Availability heuristic

We estimate the likelihood of events based on how easy they are to remember. For example, people incorrectly believe that the names of famous people to be more common than normal names (Tversky and Kahneman 1973).

Various authors provide lists of mechanisms, and ways that those mechanisms can affect our behavior.[14] What's lacking are good guidelines on how to use these scattered bits and pieces of research in actual products.

Ironically, one of the phenomena that researchers have studied is choice overload (Iyengar 2010; Schwartz 2004). In short, we are drawn to big lists like these, but once we actually try to use them and pick out the "best" or the "most useful" one, we are paralyzed and unable to choose! This occurs with everything from 401(k) plans (Iyengar et al. 2003) to buying jam at a supermarket (Iyengar and Lepper 2000). We're just not good at handling choices among lots of complex options. We need fewer options, or a better way to organize them that doesn't overwhelm us.

This book provides one way to organize the research literature, focusing on the most important lessons for practical product development. The distinction between System 1 and System 2 is a good place to start, so let's build on that.

A Note to My Fellow Researchers

In this chapter and the next two, you'll see an overview of current research on how our minds make decisions. To accomplish that, I necessarily take a broad-brush strokes approach. Each of the concepts mentioned here has a vast line of research behind it, with theoretical models, divergent opinions, potential counterevidence, and special cases.

I won't exhaustively discuss the literature and its many facets, as we can become accustomed to doing in academic research. Instead, I will only provide core lessons that are most relevant to products and behavior change. As a researcher, I apologize for glossing over theoretically important differences and for extracting high-level lessons from a broad array of studies. However, as a practitioner, this approach is necessary.

This book is about building products in the real world, and making the best use of the powerful, though still quite limited, knowledge that's available on behavior and decision making. My aim is to provide a practitioner's framework for experimentation and learning—and not to claim that anyone fully understands the decision-making process. This framework gets the product design effort started in the right direction, and prepares the resulting product for rigorous testing, evaluation, and refinement. So, bear with me: we'll get to the process of testing and refining the products later on.

Most of the Time, We're Not Actually "Choosing" What to Do Next

At least, we're not choosing consciously. Most of our daily behavior is governed by our intuitive mode. We're acting on habit (learned patterns of behavior), on gut instinct (blazingly fast evaluations of a situation based on our past experiences), or on simple rules of thumb (cognitive shortcuts or heuristics built into our mental machinery).[15] Researchers estimate that roughly half of our daily lives are spent executing habits and other intuitive behaviors, and not consciously thinking about what we're doing (see Wood et al. 2002; Dean 2013). Our conscious minds usually only become engaged when we're in a novel situation, or when we intentionally direct our attention to a task.[16]

Unfortunately, our conscious minds *believe* that they are in charge all the time, even when they aren't. Jonathan Haidt (2006) and Chip and Dan Heath (2010) build on the Buddha's metaphor of a rider and an elephant to explain this idea: the elephant is our immensely powerful but uncritical, intuitive self. The rider is our conscious self, trying to direct the elephant where to go. The rider thinks it's always in charge, but it's the elephant doing the work; if the elephant disagrees with the rider, the elephant usually wins.

There are fascinating studies of people whose left and right brains have been surgically separated and can't (physically) talk to one another. The left side makes up convincing but completely fabricated stories about what the right side is doing (Gazzaniga and Sperry 1967). That's the rider standing on top of an out-of-control elephant crying out that everything is under control![17] Or, more precisely, crying out that every action that the elephant takes is absolutely what the rider wanted him to do—and *the rider actually believes it.*

Even though we're not necessarily choosing what we do, we're always *thinking*—even when we're watching TV or daydreaming. The point is that what we're *doing* is sometimes quite different. We might be walking to the office, but we're actually thinking about all of the stuff we need to do when we get there. The rider is deeply engaged in preparing for the future tasks, and the elephant is doing the work of walking. In order for behavior change to occur, we need to work with both the rider and elephant (Heath and Heath 2010).

In each part of this section, I include some basic Lessons for Behavioral Products. These are top-level comments, and they are only the beginning—the next few chapters build upon these lessons to think strategically about behavior change, and undertake the design process itself.

Lessons for Behavioral Products

If you design a product to appeal to someone's conscious, rational decision-making process, you might educate the rational mind, but not actually affect behavior (because it is often intuitive or automatic). Be very clear about the *type* of behavior you are trying to encourage—a conscious choice or an intuitive response.

While the mind consciously thinks about what needs to be done at work, the subconcious mind keeps the body walking (habits and skills), avoids shadowy alleys (intuitive response), and follows the sweet smell of a bakery (habit).

Our Prior Experiences Guide Our Intuitive Reactions and Behavior, Without Us Necessarily Knowing It

We are constantly learning, and our experiences teach us whether something is worthwhile or not—that's a key part of how we decide what to do at each moment of our lives. Our deliberative mind can carefully analyze experiences and find complex relationships. However, to a large extent, *our intuitive responses are grounded in simple associations between things that we've experienced in the past.* Like an association between a certain subtle perfume and romance, or between a stormy sky and impending rain.[18]

We build these associations constantly in everyday life, and they guide our actions. We learn, for example, that greasy pizzas are strongly associated with tasting good and satisfying hunger—and rice cakes are not. When we're hungry and confronted with a pizza, our behavior (eating quickly and with great gusto) isn't a conscious deliberation about the merits of pizza as a nutritional source. Instead, it's based on the fact that we've eaten it before, and we have a positive association for it. The origins of those associations are often invisible once formed (you "just like" pizza), but something in our past experience actually formed them.

Importantly, our intuitive mind learns, and responds, even without our conscious awareness. Participants in a famous study were given four biased decks of cards—some that would win them money, and some that would cause them to lose. When they started the game, they didn't know that the decks were biased. As they played the game, though, people's bodies started showing signs of physical "stress" when their conscious minds were about to use a money-losing deck. The stress was an automatic response that occurred because the intuitive mind realized something was wrong—long before the conscious mind realized anything was amiss (Bechara et al. 1997).[19]

And, once formed, these associations have a life of their own. Our intuitive minds sometimes use them well beyond their original context—we apply them to "similar" situations and experiences even if they aren't really justified. For example, when someone sees something new, like a new product, he will rapidly and automatically judge it based on the associations he's built up for similar things. He may have no idea why he reacted the way we did; the answer is buried in his web of learned associations.

Lessons for Behavioral Products

The first time that users try out your application, they immediately judge it based on their prior experiences and associations. You don't have time to convince them logically; the judgment is made in an instant. Instead, you must proactively gain insight into their prior associations to avoid land mines and find positive hooks that help people change their own behavior. That's one role of user research.

Habits Drive Intuitive Behaviors in Predictable Ways

We use the term "habit" loosely in everyday speech to mean all sorts of things, but a concrete way to think about them is this: a habit is a repeated behavior that's triggered by cues in our environment. It's *automatic*—the action occurs outside of conscious control, and we may not even be aware of it happening.[20] Habits save our minds work; we effectively *outsource* control over our behavior to cues in the environment (Wood and Neal 2007). That keeps our conscious minds free for other, more important things, where conscious thought really is required.

Habits arise in one of two ways (Wood and Neal 2007).[21] First, we can build habits through simple repetition: whenever you see X (a *cue*), you do Y (a *routine*). Over time, your brain builds a strong association between the cue and the routine, and doesn't need to think about what to do when the cue occurs—it just acts. For example, whenever you wake up in the morning (cue), you get out of bed at the same spot (routine). Rarely do you find yourself lying in bed, awake, agonizing over which exact part of the bed you should exit by. That's how habits work—they are so common, and so deeply ingrained in our lives, that we rarely even notice them.

Sometimes, there is also a third element, in addition to a cue and routine: a *reward*, something good that happens at the end of the routine. The reward pulls us forward—it gives us a *reason* to repeat the behavior. It might be something inherently pleasant, like good food, or the completion of a goal we've set for ourselves, like putting away all of the dishes (Oullette and Wood 1998). For example, whenever you walk by the café and smell coffee (cue), you walk into the shop, buy a double mocha espresso with cream (routine), and feel chocolate-caffeine goodness (reward). We sometimes notice the big habits—like getting coffee—but other, less obvious habits with rewards (checking our email and receiving the random reward of getting an interesting message) may not be noticed.

Once the habit forms, the reward itself doesn't directly drive our behavior; the habit is automatic and outside of conscious control. However, the mind can "remember" previous rewards in subtle ways; intuitively wanting (or "craving") them.[22] In fact, the mind can continue wanting a reward that it will never receive again, and may not even enjoy when it does happen (Berridge et al. 2009)![23] I've encountered that strange situation myself—long after I formed the habit of eating certain potato chips, I still habitually eat them even though I don't enjoy them and they actually make me sick. This isn't to say that rewards aren't important after the habit forms—they can push us to consciously repeat the habitual action and can make them even more resistant to change.

The same characteristics that make habits hard to root out can be immensely useful. Thinking of it another way, once "good" habits are formed, they provide the most resilient and sustainable way to maintain a new behavior. Charles Duhigg, in *The Power of Habit* (Random House, 2012), gives a great example. In the early 1900s, advertising man Claude C. Hopkins moved American society from being one in which very few people brushed their teeth to a majority brushing their teeth in the span of only 10 years. He did it by helping Americans form the habit of brushing:[24]

1. He taught people a cue—feeling for tooth film, the somewhat slimy, off-white stuff that naturally coats our teeth (apparently, it's actually harmless in itself).
2. When people felt tooth film, the response was a routine—brushing their teeth (using Pepsodent, in this case).
3. The reward was a minty tingle in their mouths—something they felt immediately after brushing their teeth.

Over time, the habit (feel film, brush teeth) formed, strengthened by the reward at the end. And, so did a craving—wanting to feel the cool tingling sensation that Pepsodent caused in their mouths that people associated with having clean, beautiful teeth (Figure 1-1).

Stepping back from Duhigg's example, let's look again at the three pieces of a reward-driven habit.

1. The *cue* is something that tells us to *act now*. The cue is a clear and unambiguous signal in the environment (like the smell of coffee) or in the person's body (like hunger). BJ Fogg and Jason Hreha categorize the two ways that they work on behavior into "cue behaviors" and "cycle behaviors" (Fogg and Hreha 2010): based on whether the cue is something else that happens and tells you it's time to act (brushing teeth after eating breakfast) or the cue occurs on a schedule, like at a specific time of day (preparing to go home at 5 p.m. on a weekday).
2. The *routine* can be something simple (hear phone ring, answer it) or complex (smell coffee, turn, enter Starbucks, buy coffee, drink it), as long as the scenario in which the behavior occurs is consistent. Where conscious thought is not *required* (i.e., consistency allows repetition of a previous action without making new decisions), the behavior can be turned into a habit.

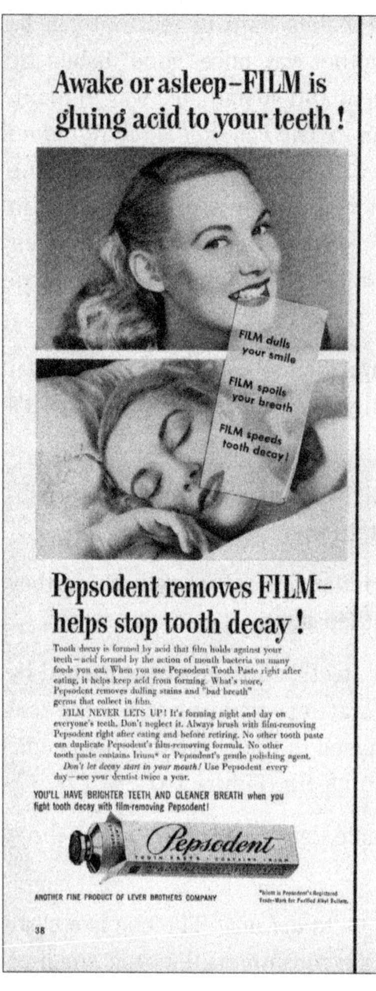

FIGURE 1-1. Pepsodent advertisement from 1950, highlighting the cue for the habit of brushing teeth: tooth film (courtesy of *Vintage-Adventures.com*)

3. The *reward* can occur every time—like drinking our favorite brand of coffee—or on a more complex "reward schedule." A reward schedule is the frequency and variability with which a reward occurs each time the behavior occurs. For example, when we pull the arm of (or press the button on) a slot machine, we are randomly rewarded: sometimes we win, sometimes we don't. Our brains *love* random rewards. In terms of timing, rewards that occur immediately after the routine are best—they help strengthen the association between cue and routine.

Researchers are actively studying exactly how rewards function, but one of the likely scenarios goes like this: when these three elements are combined, over time, the *cue* becomes associated with the reward.[25]

When we see the cue, we *anticipate* the reward, and it tempts us to act out the routine to get it. Nir Eyal (2012) has a great phrase for this process: *the desire engine.* The process takes time, however—varying by person and situation from a few weeks to many months (Lally et al. 2010). And again, the desire for the reward can continue long after the reward no longer exists (Berridge et al. 2009).

> **Lessons for Behavioral Products**
>
> We're hardwired to build habits—they save our minds work. It's difficult to overcome existing habits, but we can intentionally create new habits or change existing ones. Once formed, they are resilient. To build them: identify a specific, unambiguous cue, a stable routine, and, ideally, a reward that occurs immediately after the person takes action.

How We Respond and Interact with the World Is Malleable

How our intuitive minds react to a situation *isn't* predetermined—it isn't even predetermined how a single person will react, given full knowledge of prior experience, personality, and other traits. The particular mindset we're in at the moment of action matters immensely.

We have multiple frames of reference, or mindsets,[26] for interpreting and responding to the world, which shape how we act. You can think of these mindsets as facets of our selves, which are built up in different contexts. We often have distinct mindsets for when we're at work, when we're home with our family, and when we're joking with friends. In each of these contexts, we have *different behavioral routines* as well. For example, we'd respond differently to someone making fun of us in each of these different contexts. We'd also respond very differently to someone asking us to exercise more in each of these contexts.

We always have an active mindset, shaping our choices. That mindset is usually appropriate to the situation we're in, helping us make sense of environment. However, our mindsets aren't as fixed and clear cut as we might think—they can be accidentally (or even intentionally) *activated* based on small cues in our environment. These cues "prime" us to act in a way that is appropriate for that frame of reference. The following is a famous study about what happens when we're primed to think about stereotypes.

Researchers divided a set of Asian American women into three groups, each of whom were asked a set of questions about their lives, and then subsequently took a math test. The group that received questions relating to race later answered 54% of the math questions correctly; the group that received questions relating to gender later answered only 42% correctly, and those with generic questions were in between, with 49% correct (Shih et al. 1999).

In the United States, the common stereotype of women is of bad performance in math, and the common stereotype of Asian Americans is of good performance. Merely being prompted to think about these stereotypes led participants to respond accordingly.[27]

Another example I love comes from a related body of research, on how we build up internal stories or "self-concepts" (also known as self-narratives) about who we are. These self-concepts guide our future behavior: when we're not sure what to do, we implicitly ask ourselves, "Is this something that fits with whom I am?" They help us interpret the world by focusing our attention and making sense of ambiguous information. We also have multiple self-concepts that become active based on cues in our environment. This particular study changed how students saw themselves:

Randomly selected students who were given a positive interpretation of their early problems in college came to see themselves as capable and performed better on tests than their randomly selected fellows (Wilson 2011).

With respect to behavior change, you can think of activating or "priming" a particular mindset as a way to change behavior in the short term, and building a supporting self-concept as a way to change it in the long term.

Lessons for Behavioral Products

It is especially important to understand the mindset that individuals are in, as it shapes how they respond to your application. These different facets of self can be selectively activated, and shape our behavior in different contexts. Similarly, if a product can change how a person sees herself (i.e., her self-concept), it can have profound impacts on long-term behavior.

Even When We "Choose," Our Minds Save Work

Our minds avoid work whenever possible. Habits and other intuitive reactions are some of the ways of avoiding conscious work. Another way that our minds avoid work, even when we're consciously thinking something through, is by using rules of thumb or "heuristics." Heuristics are shortcuts that save our minds effort; they work well in most situations, but occasionally lead us astray (Newell and Simon 1972; Kahneman 2011).

For example, we employ a "scarcity heuristic": things that are difficult to obtain are often seen as more valuable than things that aren't. It's a very good rule of thumb to go by: platinum is rare and valuable. Dirt isn't. But sometimes it causes us to make bad decisions, and can be intentionally manipulated. When retailers mark something as "limited time only" or "only five left!" often it's just a ruse to make us think the item is more valuable. The scarcity heuristic, and indeed most mental heuristics, are examples of a simple shortcut that our minds take: instead of solving the problem at hand, we find an easier problem to solve.[28]

We Find Easier Problems

When our mind is confronted with hard problems it can't immediately solve, it often substitutes a different, easier problem, solves that, and acts like it was the original one! There are a slew of humorous examples in the research literature; one of my favorites is the following:

> *A group of randomly selected German students were asked first whether they were generally happy, then asked how many dates they had had in the last month. There was no relationship (pun intended) between the two answers.*
>
> *Another group of randomly selected German students were asked the exact same questions, in reverse order. Suddenly, they judged how happy they were based on the number of dates they'd had!*

Remembering how happy you've generally been is tough. When you've just been asked how many dates you've had, it's easy for the mind to subtly substitute that answer for the harder question (Strack et al. 1998).[29]

Another less humorous example occurs in our everyday life—in how we judge people based on how they look. Holding other things the same—like competency—we vote for politicians according to how attractive the candidates are, their gender, and their race (Olivola and Todorov 2010). Our intuitive minds have a hard time processing the complex set of positions and competencies of candidates. So, we use a shortcut: does the person look like us? Are they attractive? Unfortunately, this phenomenon has been well documented in corporate job interviews and salaries as well. Physical beauty does pay (e.g., Hamermesh and Biddle 1993).

> **Lessons for Behavioral Products**
>
> When you ask users questions, they may not answer the question you think. In many cases, they'll answer a simple quick version of your question. This undermines some of the answers we get from surveys (especially), and it reminds us that we should not take responses too seriously when we ask people whether they will commit to changing their own behavior. Also, if you have a sense of the simple shortcuts people are using, you can target those shortcuts directly. In the preceding example, if you have pictures of people in your app to make it feel more human, ensure the people are attractive and look similar to the users.

Our Peers Provide Answers

One of the most important and common ways that our minds save work is by looking at what other people are doing. If we don't know what to do, for example, we:

- Judge the value of a product or action by whether other people seem to like it—it's called social proof. That's why TV shows use canned laughter—we know it's fake, but it still makes us laugh more (Chapman 1973).[30]
- Judge the value of a product or action by whether "experts" recommend it—even without knowing if they were paid to recommend it! That's why we hear "9 out of 10 experts recommend" so darned often; it actually works (Till and Busler 1998).

- Judge whether we *should* take an action based on whether we perceive the action is common in our social group—via the many flavors of social conformity (Cialdini 2001).[31]

There are multiple processes going on underneath these socially determined behaviors and judgments, and their impacts are widespread. Peer influence, for example, has been studied in countless domains, from voting (Gerber and Rogers 2009) to diet and obesity (Christakis and Fowler 2007). But at a high level, the lesson is the same—if you want to guess what people will do, look at what others around them are already doing. Usually, we follow what we believe others we trust or others like us are doing. Sometimes we try to explicitly avoid what they are doing. But either way, we're reacting to our perception of what others around us are doing.

> **Lessons for Behavioral Products**
>
> People are more likely to take an action if they think other people are as well—for a wide range of reasons. It is *our perception* of other people's behavior that matters the most; that perception can be (and has been) shaped for good and for ill.

Our Mental Resources Are Sorely Limited

A frequent, if somewhat depressing, topic for researchers is just how limited our minds really are. Yes, there are numerous lines of research on the mind's many constraints. Not only do we avoid work, we really don't have the mental horsepower to tackle certain difficult problems head-on, due to the following limitations:

Memory

George Miller famously studied how limited our immediate memory is—we can generally hold seven (plus or minus two) numbers or other chunks of information in our heads at one time (Miller 1956).

Attention

Christopher Chabris and Daniel Simons's studies showed how limited our attention is: how we can literally fail to notice a big gorilla in the middle of our visual field. They had people watch a basketball game, and count the number of times the ball was passed in a certain way. During the game, the gorilla guy walked right into the middle of the game, beat his chest, and walked on (see Chabris and Simons 2009 for a summary). Half of the participants in the study (and many subsequent ones) failed to notice such "obvious" things because they were looking for something else.

Willpower and mental energy

Roy Baumeister has shown, in gory detail, how our willpower is fundamentally limited, and varies from moment to moment in startling ways (Vohs and Baumeister 2011; Baumeister and Tierney 2011). Our ability to concentrate, perform well on mentally challenging tasks, and to resist temptation are all linked to how "tired" our brains are—how much work we've recently been asked to do, and how recently we've eaten or rested. Researchers have found, for example, that the proportion of inmates granted parole by Israeli judges varies roughly from 65% down to 0% based on how long judges had been working since a break (Danziger et al. 2011). Our ideal of an impartial judicial system is sadly at odds with our basic human frailties.

When we're tired, and our willpower is drained, we increasingly rely on our intuitive processing. We tend to go with the status quo (hence the Israeli judges not granting parole). Each choice we make, and especially each temptation we resist, temporarily tires us. For product design, there's a special lesson—not only do we need to consider how much willpower people have coming into our apps, but we need to think about how our products, and the choices and temptations they present, sap our users of willpower. It's not all bad news, however—willpower is a skill that people can build up, and something that our products can invest in (Baumeister and Tierney 2011).[32]

Decision making

Another line of research shows the limitations of our decision-making processes, at least compared with strategies that would find us the "optimal" answer. When we pick a movie from Netflix or Amazon Instant Video to watch, we don't read the reviews for every single movie in their catalogs, nor could we. We don't have the mental power to handle all of that information, nor the time.

We "satisfice" (Simon 1982), or are satisfied with the first movie that looks sufficiently interesting to watch.[33] Instead of optimizing, we go with the first option we find that is good enough.

> **Lessons for Behavioral Products**
>
> Your users have busy lives and limited mental resources to devote to your product. You can't assume they have a lot of available attention, willpower, or memory. Build your interfaces to respect our limitations as people, and try to take into account the other demands on the user's brain.

The Obvious, Simple Stuff Is Really Important

Whole bodies of research in psychology and behavioral economics are devoted to the lesson that simple, seemingly trivial stuff affects behavior. It affects behavior for some of the reasons previously mentioned—because something in the environment activates a different facet of our selves, or because our minds are trying to avoid work and take the easy option. But there are six other *really blazingly obvious* things that are worth drawing out, because we too often forget them when developing software:

Easier really is better

The easier something is to do (i.e., the less mental and physical effort required from the perspective of the user), the more likely the user is to do it. Psychologists study these as "channel factors," behavioral economists talk about using "nudges" to overcome the small frictions blocking action, and BJ Fogg argues strongly for simplicity—but the lesson is the same. We like to have some challenge in our lives, but we still (usually) take the easy route, all else being equal.

Familiar really is better

We're just more comfortable with things we've seen before and actions that we've taken before. Again, there are lots of reasons—because of the "mere exposure effect" (we like stuff we've seen before—Zajonc 1968; Bornstein 1989), or because we've built up skill and a sense of self-efficacy (a belief in our ability to successfully tackle the task)—but the lesson is the same. We take the familiar route, all else being equal.

Beauty really is better

We're more comfortable with things (including products) that are easy on the eyes, shall we say. In part, it's because of the "halo effect" (Nisbett and Wilson 1977)—if we really like one aspect of something, we tend to like it overall. In part, it's because our minds fundamentally mix the ease of viewing, the ease of remembering, and the ease of using something with the value we ascribe to it (Schwarz 2004).[34] Either way, we like stuff that looks good. Not avant garde and incomprehensible, but good.

Rewarding experiences really do make us want to come back

Our routines are often built around the expectation of a reward we've received in the past. Our intuitive responses, based on prior experiences, guide us to avoid things that are like previous bad experiences and toward things like previous good experiences. And, when we think consciously, we clearly weigh the costs and benefits of action. Either way, conscious or not, we like rewarding experiences (i.e., you must have a good product that provides value to the user).

We really don't want to fail

We avoid activity that we think we'll be unsuccessful at. If we think we'll fail, we foresee two problems—we won't get the reward for completing the action, and we'll feel stupid (or be judged harshly by our peers, fail to meet our commitments, etc.). So, another obvious point that bears repeating: don't make people fail (frequently), or even make them expect that they'll fail. A challenging experience can be good, but failure is bad.

We do urgent things first

If your toddler is about to touch a hot stove, and the college savings account you've set up for him is underfunded, which one will you act on first? Urgency matters. It's so obvious that we often forget about it when we build our products—we assume that people have nothing else going on in their lives.

There are always exceptions, and that's why we test out products in the field to see what is working and what isn't. But these are six useful rules of thumb.

> **Lessons for Behavioral Products**
>
> Don't forget the basics. Yes, there's a huge amount of research literature. The previous sections highlight nonobvious lessons from that literature. But there's no point if you have a product that is needlessly hard to use, foreign, ugly, painful, lacking urgency, and makes users feel like failures. We all know this, and yes, there's research to back it up, too.

A Map of the Decision-Making Process

We've talked about a range of ways by which the mind decides what to do next—from habits and intuitive responses to heuristics and conscious choices. Table 1-1 lists where each of these decision-making processes often occurs.

TABLE 1-1. The various tools the mind uses to choose the right action

MECHANISM	WHERE IT'S MOST LIKELY TO BE USED
Habits	Familiar cues trigger a learned routine
Other intuitive responses	Familiar and semi-familiar situations, with a reaction based on prior experiences
Active mindset or self-concept	Ambiguous situations with a few possible interpretations
Heuristics	Situations where conscious attention is required, but the choice can be implicitly simplified
Focused, conscious calculation	Unfamiliar situations where a conscious choice is required or very important decisions we direct our attention toward

As you look down this list, they are ordered in terms of how familiar the situation is in our daily lives, and how much thought is required. That's not accidental; the mind wants to avoid work, and so it likes to use the process that requires the least thought. Unfamiliar situations (like, for most people, math puzzles) require a lot of conscious thought. Walking to your car doesn't.

But that's doesn't mean that we always use habits in familiar situations, or we only use our conscious minds in unfamiliar ones. Our conscious minds can and do take control of our behavior, and focus very strongly on behaviors that otherwise would be habitual. For example, I can think very carefully about how I sit in front of the computer, to improve my posture; that's something I normally don't think about because it's so familiar. That takes effort, however. Remember that our conscious attention and capacity is sorely limited. We only bring in the big guns (conscious, cost-benefit calculations) when we have a good reason to do so: when something unusual catches our attention, when we really care about the outcome and try to improve our performance, and so on.

You can think about the range of decision-making processes in terms of the *default, lowest energy* way that our minds would respond, if we didn't intentionally do something different. Those defaults occur on a spectrum from where very little thinking is required to where intensive thinking is needed (Figure 1-2).

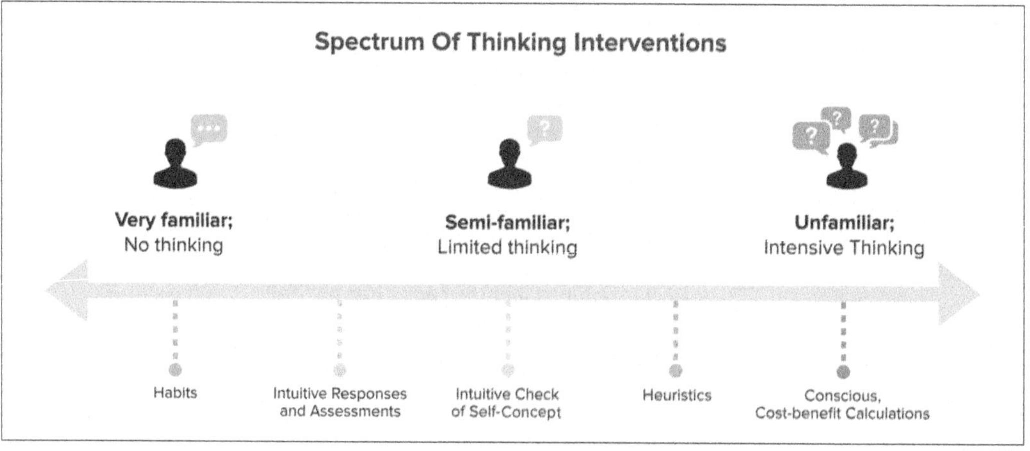

FIGURE 1-2. In familiar situations, our minds can use habits and intuitive responses to save work

Here are some simple examples, using a person who is thinking about going on a diet and doesn't have much past experience with diets:

Eating potato chips out of a bag
Very familiar. Very little thought. Habit.

Picking out what to get at your favorite buffet bar
Familiar. Little thought. Intuitive response or assessment.

Signing up for dieting workshops at the office

Semi-familiar. Some thought. Self-concept guides choice.

Judging whether a cheeseburger will violate your diet's calorie limit for the day

Unfamiliar. Thought required, but with easy ways to simplify.[35] Heuristic.

Making a weekly meal plan for the family based on the individual calorie and nutrient counts of hundreds of foods

Unfamiliar. Lots of attention and thought. Conscious, cost-benefit calculations.

As behavior change practitioners, it's a whole lot easier to help people *take actions* that are near the potato chip side of the spectrum, rather than the meal plan side. But it's much harder for people to *stop actions* on the potato chip side than on the meal plan side. The next two chapters dig deeper into the research to show how you can use the mind's decision-making process in each case, to help users change their behavior.

On a Napkin

That was a lot to take in, I know. Here is a quick snapshot of the most important lessons about how the mind works:

- Most of the time, we're not consciously deciding what to do next.
- We often act based on habits. They can be created, but are hard to defeat.
- We often make intuitive, immediate decisions based on our past experiences.
- When consciously thinking, we often avoid hard work. We "wing it" with rough guesses based on similar, but simpler, problems.
- We look to other people, especially peers and experts, for what we should do.
- The obvious stuff really matters: making things easy, familiar, rewarding, beautiful, urgent, and feasible.

[2]

Why We Take Certain Actions and Not Others

> *I'm sitting at my computer, and I just decided to drink some orange juice. You're sitting somewhere reading this book, and probably didn't. Our basic cognitive machinery is the same. So why do we do different things?*

Our actions depend on our environment (I have a big, tempting bottle of orange juice in front of me, and you probably don't), our needs and desires (I'm thirsty), our prior experiences (I generally like orange juice), and many other factors. But there's no magic formula that says if you do A, B, and C, people will take the action *you want* them to take, even when they want to take the action themselves. We're all unique individuals embedded in uniquely different environments, and our decision-making processes are complex, messy, and full of surprises.

Despite the messiness of our decision-making process, there's an odd sort of logic to how we decide to take one action instead of another. That logic can't tell us how to force someone to take a different behavior, but it can help us set up the right conditions for action, if the person chooses to do so. Designing for behavior change requires embracing the quirky ways in which our minds work, and how we interact with our environment, to better understand how products can help us change our behavior.

In Chapter 1, we asked how the mind decides what do to next. In this chapter, we'll turn that question around, and ask: specifically, what can our products do to help users take a particular action? What's different about the actions that we do decide to take versus those that we don't? Let's start with a high-level view of what it takes for a particular action to go from a mere possibility to something that we actually do.

A Simple Model of When, and Why, We Act

From moment to moment, why do we undertake one action and not another? There are five preconditions for action that must occur, at the same time, before someone will act. Behavior change products encourage action by influencing one or more of these preconditions: cue, reaction, evaluation, ability, and timing.

To illustrate the five preconditions to action, let's say you're sitting on the couch, watching TV. There's an app on your phone you downloaded last week that helps you plan and prepare healthy meals for your family. When, and why, would you suddenly get up, find your mobile phone, and start using the app?

It's an odd question, I know. We don't often think about user behavior in this way—we usually assume that somehow our users find us, love what we're doing, and come back whenever they want to. But researchers have learned that there's more to it than that, based on how the mind makes decisions. So, imagine you're watching TV. What needs to happen for you to use the meal planning app *right now*?

1. *Cue*. The possibility of using the app needs to somehow cross your mind. Something needs to cue you to think about it: maybe you're hungry or you see a commercial about healthy food on TV.

2. *Reaction*. Second, you'll intuitively react to the idea of using the app in a fraction of a second. Is using the app interesting? Was it a good experience last time you used it? What other options come to mind, and how do I feel about them?

3. *Evaluation*. Third, you might briefly think about it consciously, evaluating the costs and benefits. What will you get out of it? What value does the app provide to you? Is it worth the effort of getting up and working through some meal plans?

4. *Ability*. Fourth, you'll check *whether* actually using the app now is feasible. Do you know where your mobile phone is? Do you have your username and password for the app? If not, you'll need to solve those logistical problems first, and then use the app.
5. *Timing*. Fifth, you'd gauge *when* you should take the action. Is it worth doing now, or after the TV show is over? Is it urgent? Is there a better time? This may occur before or after checking for the ability to act. Both have to happen though.

If all five of these check out, then you actually *execute the action.*

These five mental processes—detecting a cue, reacting to it, evaluating it, checking for ability, and deciding on the right timing—are the preconditions to action. You can think of them as "tests" that any action must pass: all must complete successfully in order for you to consciously, intentionally, engage in the action. And, they all have to come together at the same time.[36] For example, if you don't have the urgency to stop watching TV and act now, you certainly could do it later. But when "later" comes, you'll still need these five factors. You'll reassess whether the action is urgent at that point (or whether something else, like walking the dog, takes precedence). Or maybe the cue to act will be gone and you'll forget about the app altogether for a while.

So, products that encourage us to take a particular action have to somehow cue us to think about the action, avoid negative intuitive reactions to it, convince our conscious minds that there's value in the action, convince us to do it now, and ensure that we can actually take the action. That's a lot to do! Much of this book talks about how to organize, simplify, and structure that process (and then test whether you've got it right).

For habitual actions, the process is mercifully shorter. The first two steps (cue and reaction) are the most important ones, and, of course, the action still needs to be feasible. Evaluation and timing can play a role, but a lesser one, because the conscious mind is on autopilot. I'll talk a lot more about habits later.

Why We Need a New Model of Behavior Change

Researchers and philosophers have studied why we take the actions we do for centuries (millennia, even). A large portion of the contemporary research on behavior change focuses on what goes on inside of people's heads as they consciously decide to act. For example, two of the most prominent models are:[37]

Ajzen's Theory of Planned Behavior
: Focuses on how our intentions to act are formed as a product of attitudes, norms, and perceived control over the behavior (Ajzen 1991).

Prochaska and Velicer's Transtheoretical Model
: Looks at the stages of change that a person goes through from starting to contemplate an action to changing the behavior and maintaining it (Prochaska and Velicer 1997).

These authors, and many others, provide valuable insights that can inspire and inform work in behavior change. Personally, though, I haven't found this literature to be practical for the daily tasks of building products. It doesn't tell us what, specifically, our products can do to support action and what barriers our products should help people overcome.

Fogg's Behavior Model (2009a) is one of the few exceptions. His model looks at three factors that are required for intentional action: motivation (pleasure/pain, hope/fear, acceptance/rejection), ability (how easy or hard a behavior is to do), and a trigger (a cue to act now). Over the last decade, BJ Fogg has led the way in practical applications to software products with his Persuasive Technology Lab at Stanford.

I build upon BJ Fogg's model, along with other models in the field, but have a somewhat different focus. Here are some of the reasons why:

- Much of our daily behavior isn't intentional. When designing products, we need to consider how habitual and other intuitive behaviors occur.
- Behavioral economics and psychology have much to teach us that isn't in current models. I draw upon the tremendous explosion of recent work in these fields: from how our intuitive system works, to how it interacts with our conscious minds, to how ideas bubble up to our awareness in the first place.
- The role of urgency (or *when* to take the action) is rarely discussed in existing models. For example, using Fogg's Behavior Model: I have motivation, ability, and numerous triggers to do my taxes at any point in the year. But I'm sure not going to do them well in advance of April 15! Before April, taxes lack urgency.[38]

My goal is to show how products, specifically, can set up the preconditions for action. This chapter starts that process, by outlining what those five preconditions are.

Let's go into more detail about the five preconditions for conscious action.

Cue

At every moment of every day, we're deciding what to do next. But the universe of things we might do with our time is truly infinite. Our minds can't handle that much information, and they protect us from being overloaded by using a set of mental filters. For example, *inattentional blindness* means we simply don't see things we aren't looking for when we're concentrating heavily. That's what happened in Chabris and Simons's famous studies (2009) where half of the people watching a basketball game failed to see a guy in a gorilla outfit walking across the screen! Our mental filters, out of necessity, only let us consider a fraction of what's possible.

Thinking about an action arises in two ways:[39]

External cues

Something in our environment can trigger us (like an email or text message) to think about it. It could be a pair of running shoes that makes us think of running, or something more overt, like a friend calling us on the phone and asking us why we aren't out running in the park with them.

Internal cues

Our minds can drift into thinking about the action on its own, through some unknown web of associated ideas (which may themselves have been cued externally, or by an internal state like hunger).[40]

Sometimes, cues can capture our attention no matter what—like a car that's about to hit us. Other times, we are explicitly looking for cues to act—like scanning over subject lines in our inbox or looking for notifications on our mobile phones. It's even possible that we honestly have no idea why an action bubbles up in our minds.

Lessons for Behavioral Products

When users are just starting to undertake a new action, external cues are vital. For example, if you're beginning to run each morning, placing your running shoes by the door is a good cue. Here are a few strategies products can use for external cueing:

- Placing the product in the user's daily environment
- Using a slightly different cue each time to avoid being ignored
- Building strong associations with parts of a person's existing routines

As the action becomes more familiar, products can help users build strong associations between an internal cue—like hunger or boredom—and the action (Eyal 2013).

When designing for behavior change, you should also avoid, or co-opt, distracting cues that seek the users' attention at the same time. Email inboxes are very crowded in the morning with lots of cues to act, for example.

Reaction

Once the mind starts thinking about a potential action, there is an automatic reaction from "System 1"—the lightning fast, intuitive, and largely nonconscious part of the brain discussed in Chapter 1, Kahneman's *Thinking, Fast and Slow* (Farrar, Straus and Giroux, 2011) and Gladwell's *Blink* (Back Bay Books, 2005). In some cases, it is startling and powerful, like the desire to run the heck out of a building when you smell gas. In more common situations—like removing our running shoes or using an app—the automatic reactions are less jarring but still guide our behavior. Our conscious minds don't really have insight into what goes on within our automatic response system (nor do researchers fully understand it). Social norms, prior experiences, our mood—all of these things shape our intuitive processing. For our purposes, a few important *outputs* come from that automatic response:

A verdict or "gut feeling" about the action

Is this action relevant now? Will it be enjoyable? Is it dangerous? Recall from Chapter 1 that these intuitive feelings are strongly based on our prior experiences. If we're thinking about taking 10 flights of stairs, the last time we took the stairs and almost had a heart attack will color how we feel about doing it again (and this can occur *before* we consciously think about whether or not to act).

Other possible actions and ideas

Our minds are built on associations. So, when we start thinking about one action, we also activate memories and thoughts about other related concepts. If we're thinking of a particular *need* (like hunger), then our minds will search for other possible answers to the need, and evaluate them as well. For example, if I'm looking at the stairs, my mind will automatically, and without my control, also activate thoughts about using the elevator or escalator.[41]

Action

In the case of habitual behaviors, the reaction might automatically initiate the action, based on the cue. Let's say I take the elevator every day. Once I walk in the building, I may go to the elevator and press the button without conscious thought.

The gut feeling we get doesn't necessarily determine our behavior. Our conscious minds can override (or ignore) what our intuitive system tells us—but it will feel wrong. And it's hard to sustain a change in behavior if it intuitively feels wrong.

Lessons for Behavioral Products

Users evaluate your product, and the action it supports, in the blink of an eye. As we discussed in Chapter 1, you can't avoid this, and it happens automatically. But from a behavior change perspective, there are particular aspects of this automatic assessment you should be paying attention to:

Trust.

Your product is encouraging your users to do something. Even when they want to take the action, they will be hesitant if they don't trust the company behind that encouragement. Whether or not a user trusts the product, and company, is often an intuitive sense.

Watch where you get your product signal.

If you ask people what they want to do, or whether they have the motivation to use your app, you're engaging their conscious minds. But it's their intuitive minds you have to pass first, and that isn't something people articulate on surveys. Ideally, watch their behavior, and don't listen to their mouths.

The first-time user experience really matters.

You may be able to convince or entice someone to try out your product and action the first time. But the more your action requires repeated use, the more that you rely on intuitive reactions. And those reactions build on what they've actually experienced, the associations they've made, and the emotions they felt about your product and action.

Evaluation

After the mind is cued to think about a particular action, and assuming it hasn't been derailed by its intuitive reaction, then the action may rise to conscious awareness. This happens especially when we're facing novel situations, and we don't have an automatic behavior to trigger. The conscious mind kicks in and evaluates whether the person should take the action, given the various costs and benefits.

This stage is the one that we tend to think about first, when we're trying to change behavior. We try to educate people about the benefits of the action, increase their motivation with money or other rewards, and reduce the (perceived) cost of taking the action.

For example, again consider people who have the choice of taking the stairs to go up a few flights or taking the elevator. Let's say that their conscious mind is engaged. The common approach to encouraging people to take the stairs would be to focus on:

Highlighting benefits

Taking the stairs will get you in shape, and may lengthen your life.

Minimizing costs

Taking the stairs will only cost you three more minutes, and if you go slowly, you won't sweat like a pig.

Downplaying alternatives

The elevator is slow and crowded at this time of day.

While the subconscious mind might see the stairs and think "Ugh, that's work," the conscious mind thinks about costs and benefits. "Benefits: Good exercise. Cost: Just three minutes. And the elevator is crowded anyway. Done!"

There is, of course, tremendous complexity behind the deliberations we make over whether to act. How much do we really know about the costs and benefits of the action? Where did we get that information, and do we trust it? Is it worth the effort to seek out more information, or should we simply use what we have? What motivations weigh upon us most strongly at the moment we're deciding?

These are vital questions. For now, though, let's leave it at this: if we deem the action worth the effort, *and better than the alternatives,* then we're in business. The choice to act has been made.

Note, the "thinking" that occurs here may be extremely limited and rapid. If the action isn't very important, or is very familiar, then the conscious mind may decide to go ahead without much effort. It's when the action is unfamiliar, or the mind decides to pay a lot of attention, that more intensive thinking occurs.

A product that promotes an important action that users "should" take (and some part of them wants to take) isn't enough. The product must give users something they actually want, right now, more than the alternatives. Like any product, a behavior changing product must solve a problem for its users. Otherwise, the rest of this discussion won't help. If the conscious mind doesn't see value that's worth the effort, then it won't intentionally use the product and won't take the action. That value needn't be purely instrumental—it can be something social, emotional, or an intrinsic enjoyment of the activity (we'll talk more about types of motivation later)—but it needs to be there.

Remember, for habitual behaviors, this conscious awareness and evaluation usually doesn't occur at all. *But* our conscious minds are happy to make up stories about why we do habitual things. Those stories are just noise, and aren't real reflections of our actions.[42]

> **Lessons for Behavioral Products**
>
> The conscious evaluation phase is what most people who are designing products naturally target—making the benefits of the application clear, and removing frustrations and frictions (costs). It's all about the conscious, quantifiable value that the product provides.
>
> The trick when designing for behavior change is to remember that the value that matters most is the value that *the user ascribes to the product and action*, and not the value that *you ascribe to it*. If your company and your product see taking the stairs instead of the elevator as the start to massive changes in long-term health (i.e., huge benefits), and the user doesn't see it that way, you're misaligned.

Ability

Let's say the choice to act has been made, after weighing the costs and benefits. Is it actually *feasible* to undertake the action? If you've decided to finally put aside some money for your retirement, can you actually do it, right now? The individual must be *able* to immediately take the action; the ability to act has four dimensions:[43]

Action plan

The person must know what steps are required to take the action. For example, he must know that setting up a retirement account requires going to a particular website, entering information provided by his employer, and so on.

Resources

The person must actually have the resources required to act. For example, the person must have money available and access to a computer to go to the retirement website and set up an account.

Skills

The person must have the necessary skills to act. For example, in order to sign up for a retirement account online, he must know how to use a computer and navigate its (too often impenetrable) user interface.

Belief in success

No one wants to feel like a failure. The person needs to feel reasonably sure that he can be successful at the action, and not end up looking like an idiot. That's known as a feeling of *self-efficacy*.

If the person doesn't have a clear action plan, doesn't have the necessary resources for immediate action, or is hesitant because the action is daunting, those challenges are surmountable. But that means delay. It means that the person isn't taking the action *right now*. And that, from the perspective of behavior change, is a partial failure.

After those problems are resolved, the person could take the action later. If the other preconditions for action are in place now, it's likely they will also be in place when the person has the ability to act. But the situation may change—other distractions could arise, the cost of action may go up, and so on.

> ### Lessons for Behavioral Products
>
> This step poses four possible barriers to action, which a good product must avoid. Products can readily help users by providing a clear action plan; specific plans grease the pathway to action. They can address self-doubt and anxiety about failure head-on as well by talking about other users that were successful, for example. Resources and skills are trickier. With good user research, you can identify the resource constraints that particular user groups face and their current skills. You can then either accept that some users won't be served well by the product or plan around them.

Timing

You have their attention, and the action is appealing and feasible. But *when* should you take the action? Why not do it a bit later? (And why not later, and later...) That's a major problem with many "beneficial" actions we want to take, like exercising, getting control of our finances, or planting a garden. We can always do them later. Even if we want to take the action, if our minds feel that there is something that's likewise desirable, but more urgent, we're out of luck. We could take the action later. However, as we saw with ability barriers, if there isn't a decision that *now* is the right time to act, there's a problem. By the point the person does feel the timing is right, circumstances may have changed, and the person won't take the action for other reasons.

The decision of *when* to take action (i.e., its timing), can be driven both by a sense of clear and present urgency, and by other, less forceful but still important factors. Urgency can come from a variety of sources (Beshears and Milkman 2013):

External urgency
: In the United States, we really do need to put in our taxes (or file for an extension) by April 15. Otherwise, the IRS comes after us. That's a true, external urgency that results in something bad if we delay.

Internal urgency

Very rarely, changes in behavior are urgent because we have a biological need that we can't ignore (hunger, thirst, etc.). However, these needs just don't apply to most actions and products. Negative mental states like boredom may provide a lesser, but still potent, urgency to act.

Similarly, we can decide that now is the right time to act (even when it doesn't feel strictly urgent) for a variety of reasons:

Specificity

Think about these two statements: "I should save for retirement" versus "I should set up a retirement account on Thursday night, at 8 p.m., right after dinner." The latter one feels more real, right? Simply by putting a specific time on an action, that can settle the issue of "when" to act. It also helps us *remember* to act then, too!

Consistency

Another way to help us decide when to act (and to follow through on it) is to pre-commit to a specific time in the future, especially if we tell others about our commitment. That moves the action from the domain of something that we might do sometime, to an issue of personal consistency with our word. Our desire to be consistent with our prior statements means that the right time to act is exactly when we said we'd act.

The decision to act at a particular time also arises, in part, from our motivation (emotional and deliberative) to take the action. An action that's really exciting and promises to be enjoyable also can feel more urgent, and prompt someone to decide to act now rather than later. I've distinguished between the two concepts to analyze and address them separately, but in reality there can be a significant blurring between them when the action is highly motivating.

When is eating chocolate cake urgent? Top left: When you're hungry! Top right: When the waiter yells "Last chance for cake!" Bottom left: When it's New Years Eve, and it's time to indulge a little. Bottom right: When you've promised yourself cake after finishing your work.

Lessons for Behavioral Products

You can think about the timing of action in terms of two factors: what the product actively does to *make* the timing ripe for action, and what it does to *align* with the times when a person is naturally inclined to take action. To make action urgent, products can use time-sensitive content like news, which is inherently timely (if you care about the content at all). NPR provides this, and so does Facebook (the latest news about your friends). Products can also construct urgency—by creating pre-commitments or using specific dates for planned action.

Instead of making something urgent, products can wisely align themselves with events in a user's life that already provide that urgency. The user may need to take a similar action as part of her work, for example, and the product can hook into and build on that opportunity. This is similar to the ancient Greek concept of "Kairos" or the opportune time—it's the product's job to be there when the opportune time for action arises.[44]

> Products can use internal states like boredom to drive action, but those internal states are a double-edged sword. On one side, they can drive the particular target action, if the person thinks that the product will relieve the negative feeling. On the other side, they could drive a different action that also relieves boredom. Which do you think is more likely—your users surfing the Internet to relieve boredom, or playing with a mobile phone application that helps them plan healthy meals?

The Create Action Funnel

These five mental events—a *cue*, which starts an automatic, intuitive *reaction*, potentially bubbling up into a conscious *evaluation* of costs and benefits, the *ability* to act, and the right *timing* for action—are prerequisites for people to *execute* the action. You may have noticed that they also form an acronym: CREATE. That's because these five elements are what we need to *create action.*[45]

Let's say you have 100 people, all of whom are trying to better organize their email and respond to messages in a more timely manner (remember, not all behavior change is sexy!). All of them have set to-do reminders to go through their old messages and delete or respond to them—on the path to a zero-message inbox. Most of the people will see the reminder, but some of them will quickly and intuitively close it, because they don't want to deal with that annoying task. A subset will think about it for a second, and decide that cleaning up their inbox really is worthwhile (the rest decide it's not worth it).

Among those who do decide to clean up their inbox, a few will realize they don't have enough mental energy and time to do it now, and will postpone. Others will decide that it's important to do, but it can wait because there are more pressing matters; they, too, postpone. In the end, only a handful of the original 100 people actually respond to the cue, and follow all the way through to action.

Another way of thinking about this process is as a leaky funnel: a group of people start the process, and some leak out at each step, leaving only a few of them who make it all the way. The funnel metaphor is a common one for salespeople, marketers, and product folks focused on converting potential clients into actual clients on their website.

Figure 2-1 shows what the Create Action Funnel looks like.

Each section of the funnel has two leaky holes in it. On one side, people can reject the action (or the cue) because it's not valuable or urgent enough. On the other side, they can be distracted into doing something else—either because they think of something else to do with the same effect (like surfing the Internet to relieve boredom instead of using a meal planning app) or because they are pulled into something completely different (like answering the phone).

For habitual actions, the basic funnel is the same, but there is very little drop-off in the conscious evaluation of the action (unless the person is intentionally trying to be aware of her habitual actions and stop them), and in the urgency stage.

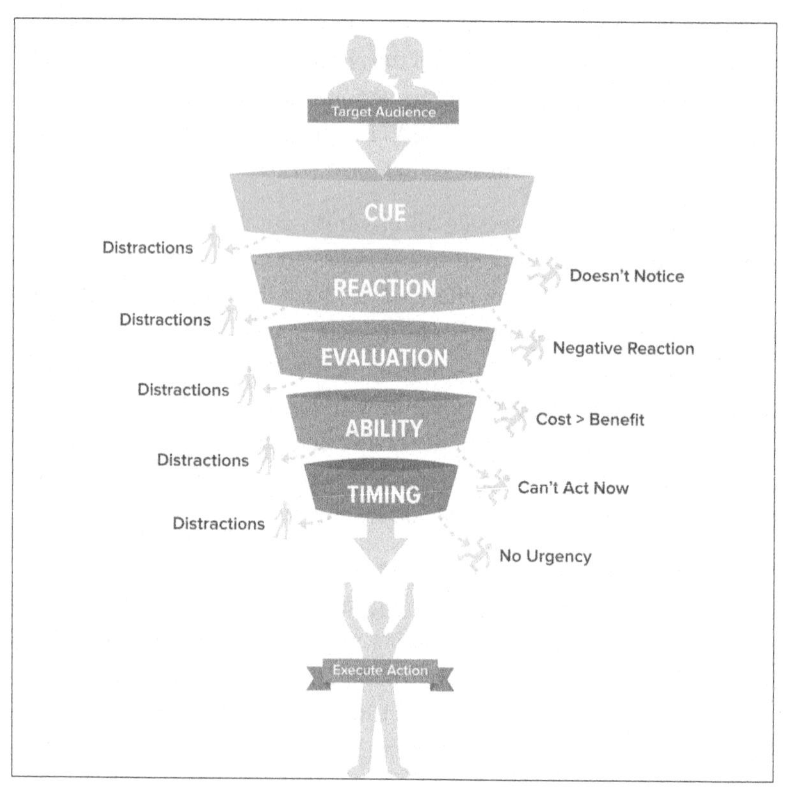

FIGURE 2-1. The Create Action Funnel—the five stages that a potential action has to pass in order to be undertaken. People drop out at every step of the way!

Each Stage Is Relative

An important thing to remember about the funnel is that at each stage, the person only continues on if the action is more effective or *better than the alternatives*. There are always alternatives, including other cues that seek to grab us, other actions we're intuitively and consciously assessing, or other priorities that could be urgent.[46]

From a product design perspective, that means you should consider not only how well the product guides the user through these stages, but what else is competing for the individual's scarce time and mental resources. Removing distractions is a key part of structuring the individual's environment (as discussed in Chapter 7).

A Guide for Debugging Behavior

One way to think about the Create Action Funnel is as a *guide for debugging*.

People are too complex (and our knowledge of behavior is too limited) to build a perfect application that helps every user change behavior every time. Instead, we need good tools to help us put the right pieces in place, then figure out where problems are after we've built the first version of the product. These tools—the tools of debugging—are what allow software developers to create applications that are solid and reliable.

The chapters of this book that cover how to design the application (Chapters 6–11) help companies take their first best shot. The Create Action Funnel will help them debug their product's behavioral impact afterward (Chapters 12–14). It will tell us where to gather feedback when we test the product in the field.

It also means thinking about what the user is currently doing with respect to the action. Let's say the product seeks to promote dieting in order to lose weight. What is the person currently doing? Avoiding any thought about dieting? Trying something and failing? Asking friends for advice, but never acting? *Whatever the user is currently doing, that's the main behavioral competition for the product.* One shouldn't assume that products interact with a user who's a blank slate. Rather, the product needs to beat an existing behavior, and do so at each stage of the Create Action Funnel. Each stage is relative to the alternatives.

Each Stage Is Personal

Whether or not a particular action passes a stage of the action funnel depends on the person, and on the particular situation. The decisions are, ultimately, very personal. One person may intuitively love the idea of walking to work—because it makes him think about showing off his calves. Another person, in equally good shape, may intuitively hate it—because she associates walking to work with poverty, and not having the money to afford to drive.

This serves as a reminder that there simply aren't any universal prescriptions on how to change behavior. The action funnel is a guide, to show where people are dropping off. It doesn't provide a ready-made solution to prevent that drop-off. That requires additional work and analysis.

The Stages Can Interact with One Another

I've presented a nice, neat model with five stages of processing. At a high level, that's correct. The details are much more complex, however. One issue we haven't talked about much is how these different processes interact with one another.

While all five stages must occur at some level for conscious actions, weakness in one area can be counterbalanced by strength in another area. For example, things that are really easy to do (like grabbing a bottle of olive oil out of the cabinet instead of an unhealthy hydrogenated oil blend) don't need to have significant conscious benefits (it might make you a little healthier) or positive intuitive feeling. This is one of the lessons that BJ Fogg incorporates in his Behavior Model (2009a)—in economic terms, the factors are partial substitutes for one another.

In terms of the ordering, the funnel is a useful way to remember the activities the mind performs, but it isn't a perfect representation of sequence of processes. The first two steps generally come before conscious awareness, as shown, but sometime intuitive reactions can occur after (or as part of) conscious deliberation.[47] For the next three, there's some evidence that the evaluation of an idea (e.g., value, timing, and ability) is pursued simultaneously by different parts of the mind (Brass and Haggard 2008), and there can be some interaction between them. These complexities don't affect the central lesson though: intentional actions need to pass all five stages, and there is often a significant drop-off at each step.

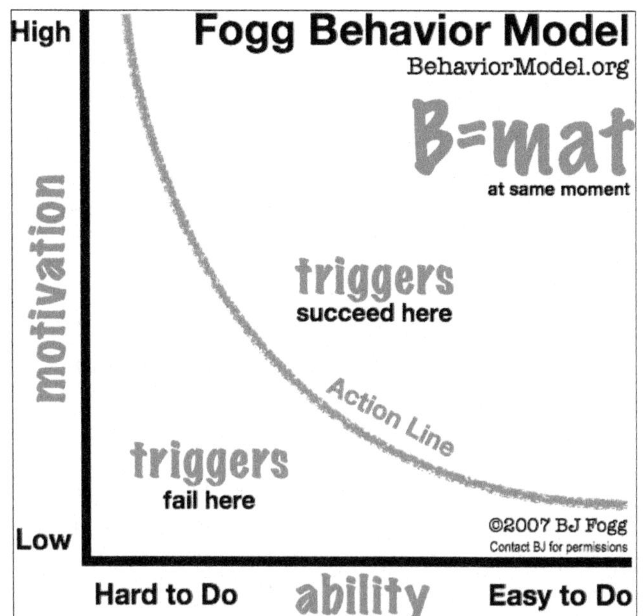

FIGURE 2-2.
Fogg's Behavior Model (2007), showing the diminishing marginal returns that happen with extra motivation or increased ability to act

More Effort Won't Buy You Much

One of the many lessons that BJ Fogg built into his Behavior Model is that making the action easier or making the user more motivated won't buy you as much as you might think. Remember that his model has three factors: motivation, ability, and trigger (Fogg 2009a). Motivation is defined as pleasure/pain, hope/fear, acceptance/rejection (which has elements of an emotional reaction and a conscious evaluation), and ability roughly corresponds to the lack of costs (as the term is used in his model); he includes both intuitive and deliberative elements in both. The trigger part of his model corresponds to the "cue" in the model presented here. His model is displayed in Figure 2-2.

Fogg argues that in order for an intentional action to occur, you need all three elements. You can encourage an action by increasing a person's ability to act (decreasing costs) or increasing motivation.

In each case, the boost it provides to the person decreases as the action becomes easier and more motivating (i.e., when the action is very difficult, a bit of help to make it easier is very powerful). When the action is already easy, making it even easier isn't going to change behavior as much. In economic terms, this is known as diminishing marginal returns.

It's a good practical lesson for product designers.

The Funnel Repeats Each Time the Person Acts

People don't stay in the funnel over time. They drop out somewhere, or they take the action—either way, they're out very quickly. Each time people think about taking the action, the process repeats: a cue leads them to think about it, they react intuitively, and so on. Thus, repeated actions require multiple passes through the Create Action Funnel.

Each Time Through the Funnel Is Different

Each time a person thinks about taking a target action, he passes through the Create Action Funnel. But the Funnel is subtly different each time. This is especially true when the person is deciding whether to take the action a second (or third, etc.) time.

Let's say you've gone to the gym for the first time. Here are some of the things that change from the first time you planned on going, to the second time you're thinking about going:

Your relationship to the action has changed
: You now know how the gym operates, where the equipment is, and so on. So your "cost" to use it decreases. But you also know more clearly whether you like going to the gym or not. So, your intuitive reaction and conscious evaluation change, too.

You've changed
: If you did well your first time exercising, you have more confidence (increasing the perceived feasibility); if you weren't able to do the exercises you had hoped, you have less confidence.

Your environment may have changed
: You may set reminders for ourselves to go back to the gym (creating cues), or set expectations among your family that you will continue going (creating urgency and increasing benefits). You may have friends at the gym who expect you to return.

What's Stopping Your Users?

Here's another way of thinking about the Create Action Funnel and the five stages that a potential behavior passes through: what *blocks* your users from taking action? What are the cognitive and practical barriers they face?[48]

Problems with cues

The user forgets to act, or has limited attention. Nothing in the environment reminds the user to act.

Problems with the intuitive reaction

The user doesn't trust the product or the company behind it. The action is unfamiliar and feels foreign.

Problems with the conscious evaluation

The user just isn't very motivated to act. The costs of taking the action are too high.

Problems of ability

The user doesn't know how to actually do it, or doesn't have what he needs to act. The user fears failure.

Problems of insufficient urgency

The user procrastinates, and puts off the action until another day, which never comes. Or, other urgent issues block the user from the action.

Whether you look at it from the perspective of what's required for action (the Create Action Funnel) or from the perspective of barriers to immediate action, the same factors are required for individuals to successfully act.

On a Napkin

In order for someone to take an action, five things need to happen immediately beforehand:

1. The person responds to a *cue* that starts her thinking about the action.
2. Her intuitive mind automatically *reacts* at an intuitive level to the idea.
3. Her conscious mind *evaluates* the idea, especially in terms of costs and benefits.

4. She checks if she has the *ability* to act—if she knows what to do, has what she needs, and believes she can succeed.
5. She determines if the *timing* is right for action—especially whether or not the action is urgent.

These five events can be visualized as a funnel, like a conversion funnel in ecommerce websites. If the person passes all five stages, then she will *execute* the action.

A quick way to remember the preconditions for action is the acronym CREATE: cue, reaction, evaluation, ability, timing, execute! At each step of the way in the Create Action Funnel, people drop off—because they fail to see the cue, don't consider the action worthwhile, or don't find it urgent. Each step of the way, they can also become distracted and diverted into taking other actions.

If the action requires conscious thought (System 2), our minds go through all five steps. If the action doesn't require conscious thought (System 1 only), then the conscious evaluation and timing check are usually short-circuited.

[3]

Strategies for Behavior Change

A Decision or a Reaction: Three Strategies to Change Behavior

How can a product help its users pass all the way through the Action Funnel and actually take action? There are three big strategies that a company can choose from, to change behavior and help users take action. Two of them come straight from the research literature and from the difference between deliberative and intuitive actions. The third is less obvious, but immensely powerful—it's called cheating.

The conscious, deliberative route is the one that most of us are familiar with already—it entails encouraging people to take action, and them consciously deciding to do it. Users have to pass through all five stages of the Action Funnel, and often spend considerable time on the conscious evaluation stage.

The intuitive route is a bit more complex. Recall from Chapter 1 that our lightning-fast, automatic, and intuitive reactions arise from a mix of various elements: associations we've learned between things, specific habits we've built up, our current mindset, and a myriad of built-in shortcuts (heuristics) that save our minds work but can lead us astray. Of these, habits are the most promising route to developing a sustainable path to behavior change because there are clear, systematic ways to form them.[49] And once they are formed, they allow the user to pass effortlessly through two of the stages of the Action Funnel—the conscious evaluation and the assessment of the right timing for action.

The third strategy takes a lesson from Chapter 1, that our minds are usually on autopilot, to the extreme: it decreases users' need to act altogether, so they simply need to give consent if they wish the target action to occur. This strategy—to "cheat"—I'll argue is the most effective and desirable of all.

In the following sections, I'll go into detail about each of these strategies, and when each of them is most appropriate, but in short, here are the guidelines:

Cheat
: If what you really care about is the action getting done, and it's possible to all but eliminate the work required of the user beyond giving consent, then do it.

Make or change habits
: If the user needs to take an action multiple times (like eating better or spending less), and you can identify a clear cue, routine, and reward, then use the "habits" strategy. Also use this strategy if the user is fighting an existing habit—to cleverly undercut it, rather than using brute force to stop it directly.

Support conscious action
: If neither of the other two is available, then you must help the user consciously undertake the target action. There are ways to make this process nicer and easier, but it's still the hardest path to follow.

In each case, the individual makes a conscious choice; what's different is *what is being chosen* and *what happens afterward*. In the first strategy, the person chooses whether to give consent to the action occurring on her behalf. In the second strategy, the person chooses whether to set up the conditions for habit formation (or for stopping an existing habit), and chooses whether to repeat the behavior until the habit is formed (or broken). In the last strategy, the person chooses whether or not to take the original target action. If the action is to be repeated, so is the choice. There's no (ethical) way to avoid having the user consciously choose whether or not to act, but products can change the nature of that choice by selecting among these three strategies.

How can you help users take better pictures with your camera? Provide a manual ("support conscious action"), provide a frequently used and easy menu system ("build habits"), or set intelligent defaults ("cheat").

These *behavioral strategies* provide high-level direction for how the product should be designed: how it accomplishes the process of behavior change. *Behavioral tactics* (such as comparing users to their peers, highlighting the pain of losing an opportunity, or priming them to think about particular topics) don't provide much overall guidance on how the product should work. Instead, they can be slotted in at various junctions in the product to make each piece of the product more effective. Throughout this book, we'll talk about both high-level strategies and lower-level tactics. This chapter is all about strategy, though, so let's get started with the first one: cheat.

Strategy 1: Cheat!

While you can make an action rewarding, easy, familiar, socially acceptable, or any of the other things we talked about in Chapter 1, the activity still involves *work* for the user. Ideally, the company should find ways to shift the user's burden onto the product, by identifying clever ways to make active participation by the user unnecessary beyond giving informed consent. That's what I call cheating—substituting the user's nasty problem with a much simpler one: deciding whether he wants the product to take the action for him. As you'll see, this strategy is only available in certain cases, but when it is feasible, it is immensely powerful.

Exactly how a company can "cheat" depends on whether the target action is undertaken once or infrequently (like buying running shoes) or repeatedly (like going running each morning). I'll talk about each of these two situations in turn.

Strategies to Cheat at One-Time Actions

DEFAULT IT

To default an action, the company first finds a way to take the action on the user's behalf. Then, it gives the user a choice about whether the product should take the action on his behalf, where the default answer is "yes." The user can say "no" if he so chooses.

Most defaults are invisible—you don't even think about them as defaults; they just happen. In fact, we're not used to seeing the defaults that are all around us, and so we rarely think of it as a solution. To that point, the most common reaction I get to proposing defaults is, "That's great, but there's no way that will work here. You can't default this behavior." Well, maybe. Here are some examples to show how defaulting works in real life:

Behavior change sought: have users save for the future.

Two of the greatest success stories in the recent history in helping users save money are 401(k) auto-enrollment and auto-escalation.[50] (For non-US readers, 401(k)s are retirement savings plans provided by an employer to employees.) Under auto-enrollment, individuals who are eligible to participate in their company's 401(k) plan are defaulted into contributing to the plan, but are given the option to not contribute if they wish. Similarly, auto-escalation automatically increases the contribution rate over time, but the individual can opt out at any time.

The initial action that users take is often quite minimal—signing their name on a package of new-employee documents—and afterward, contributions to the 401(k) plan are automatically deducted from their paychecks and placed into their retirement account on their behalf. Instead of requiring that an individual choose to contribute to the retirement plan each month (or choose to find the HR representative with the necessary paperwork required to enroll in the plan), this process effectively removes the work required by the user.

401(k) auto-enrollment is a powerful example of increasing savings, but it also can skirt the line between *voluntary* behavior change and trickery. Some employers strive to inform employees about their retirement plans and default contributions. In other cases, the employees don't know about their accounts until they leave their job and get a check—which they quickly spend on non-retirement needs, since they weren't informed and invested in the process in the first place.

The impact of defaults is significant in this case: defaulted (auto-enrolled) plans have nearly *twice* the participation of non-defaulted plans (Nessmith et al. 2007).

Behavior change sought: have users take high-quality photos, rather than crappy ones.

High-end camera manufactures have a problem: many consumers want lots of features, but those same features make the camera sensitive to user mistakes and result in bad pictures.

Good cameras have a simple solution that help people take quality pictures, but still provide power options (and a premium price): the cameras have default settings that are dirt simple and would provide a good picture in most scenarios. In addition, they have all of the fancy bells and whistles that make the product more attractive and expensive than a bargain-basement camera.

Similar defaults are common in computer software ("Would you like the standard install or the scary customized one?")—the options are there, but the software makers have provided intelligent defaults so most people don't have to worry about them and install the software without getting themselves in trouble.

Impact of the defaults: apparently, cameras still can't help us take *interesting* pictures. More seriously, though: do any mass market cameras *exist* anymore that don't have intelligent defaults for things like contrast, white balance, and F-stop?

MAKE IT INCIDENTAL

If the action can't simply be defaulted away, there's another clever option—have the action come along for the ride with something else that users are going to do anyway. In other words, don't have them think about doing the action at all. Make the action happen automatically when the user does something else—something that is inherently more interesting or engaging—but leave the option for the user to decline the action if he so chooses.

Here are two examples:

Behavior change sought: improve people's intake of vital vitamins and minerals.

> OK, before I go into the solution, what's the most effective way to improve the amount of vitamins and minerals people get? Convince them of the benefits? Pay them to eat well? Run a public campaign with celebrities endorsing vital minerals? How about this: put it in the food people already eat—with their consent, and without removing other food options. For example, put iodine in salt.
>
> Iodine deficiency is the leading preventable cause of mental retardation (McNeil 2006).[51] It causes stunted growth, infant mortality, lower IQ, goiter (big lumps in the neck), and more (International Council for the Control of Iodine Deficiency Disorders 2013). Two billion people suffer from insufficient iodine. Iodine costs virtually nothing to produce and add to salt.
>
> The story of iodized salt also shows that defaulting can't be allowed to turn into coercion, either practically or ethically. At various times, people around the world have objected to iodine being added to their salt without their consent, causing these iodization campaigns to fail (and iodine deficiency to continue). When there is no way to opt out (non-iodized salt) and no consent, it's not "defaulting"—it's just an ethically problematic mandate. There must be consent among the population *first*.
>
> Impact of making iodine incidental: in many of the places where iodized salt has been used (with consent), the problem of iodine deficiency simply ceases to exist; that's the ideal outcome of any behavior change strategy. In the United States, iodine deficiency is rarely an issue anymore, except where it hasn't been made incidental.

Behavior change sought: have people (voluntarily) contribute money to savings.

One solution in this case is a savings lottery, aka prize-linked savings accounts. A prize-linked savings account is like a lottery in which a person can "buy" multiple tickets.[52] Each ticket is a contribution to their savings account. Like any lottery, there's a jackpot—a big pool of money that one (or more) winners get. Unlike a normal lottery, the participant doesn't lose the cost of their ticket: it's just deposited into their savings account (Tufano 2008). There's a significant upside, but little downside, to participating.

Prize-linked savings makes contributing money to a savings account incidental because some users have a strong preference for playing lotteries (Filiz-Orzbay et al. 2013); the fact that they don't lose the money they use to play is a nice added bonus, but incidental.

Impact of making it incidental: prized-linked savings programs have been highly popular around the world for centuries, starting in Britain (Murphy 2005). They have recently gained traction in the United States through the tireless work of Doorways to Dreams, a Massachusetts-based NGO.[53, 54]

And there are many more examples that we rarely think about in our daily lives. If you want your toddler to take a pill, you crush the pill up and put it in some juice that he likes. The toddler doesn't care or know (and if he doesn't know, he can't complain) about the pill; it's incidental. The juice is what matters.

Strategies to Cheat at Repeated Actions

With repeated actions, you can use both of the last two approaches (defaulting and making the action incidental). For example, with prize-linked savings programs, the savings lottery can be repeated each month to encourage sustained savings contributions. Each time the person acts, savings is incidental. Similarly, each time the person uses an application, she can encounter the same (configurable) defaults.

In addition to these two approaches, another approach becomes possible with repeated actions: you can turn the repeated action into a one-time action by *automating the act of repetition*.

AUTOMATE THE ACT OF REPETITION

Taking an action repeatedly is inherently more difficult than taking that action once, even when the person learns how to do it better over time. So, why not turn a repeated action into a one-time action?

In this scenario, the individual takes a one-time action to set up or accept the automated process, and then the rest is handled without her intervention by the product itself. The principle is simple, and is very similar to defaulting a one-time action: use behind-the-scenes magic to shift the work from the user to the product.

Some great examples of automating repeated behaviors in the health space are exercise trackers that people carry with them throughout the day. These include devices such as the Nike+ FuelBand, Jawbone Up, and Fitbit One; and apps (e.g., RunKeeper) that use GPS or a phone's accelerometer to accomplish this without a separate device (see Figure 3-1). These apps and devices automatically log and compare exercise against a user's target. They've successfully taken something that is annoying but beneficial (logging exercise in a journal, comparing it to one's daily goals), and made the work magically disappear. Once *exercise tracking* was automated away, companies could focus on more interesting (and user-beneficial) target actions—like helping users *exercise more*.

Another example of automating behavior comes from the personal finance space, with software that automatically categorizes transactions and tracks spending—such as HelloWallet (where I work), Mint, and numerous bank websites. In the "old" days (i.e., the 1980s), if you wanted to know how much you had in your checking account, you had to track your spending and balance your checkbook (remember checks?). When ATMs become popular in the 1990s, you also had to track your cash withdrawals. If you had a credit card, it would send you a monthly statement, but before that arrived, you were out of luck.

With personal finance applications, tracking expenses can happen automatically. Each individual transaction is automatically logged, categorized, and, where relevant, compared against a goal or budget item. As with many other forms of automation, once the action is automated for the user, the product team is then free to focus on more interesting and difficult-to-change behaviors—like helping users stay within their budget. But that wouldn't be feasible for most users if they are wasting their time tracking their spending first.

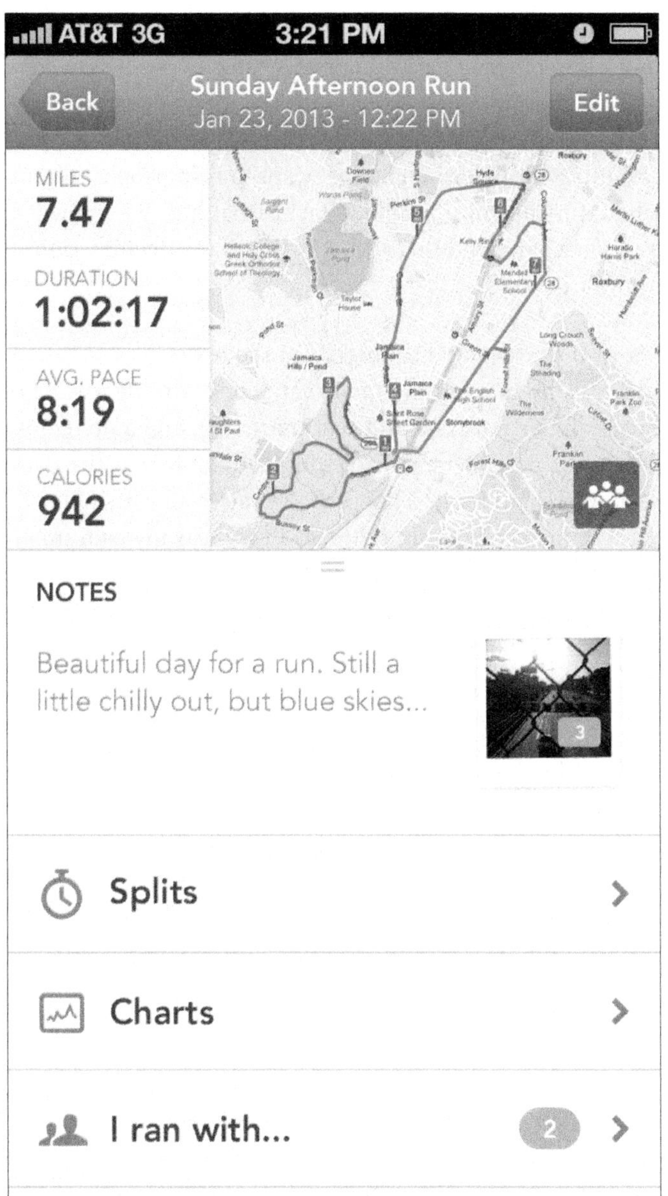

FIGURE 3-1.
RunKeeper, an example of automated exercise tracking

The most powerful combination of all is to combine automation with defaulting—automation makes it a one-time action, and defaulting makes it little more than an acceptance of that automation. I didn't go into detail about this earlier, but 401(k) auto-enrollment is such an example—the savings contributions are automatically deducted, and the default is to enroll in the program.

But Isn't Cheating Well, Cheating?

Before I move on to other behavior change strategies, I'd like to confront an implicit assumption that I've seen in many do-good products—that doing good requires making our users work hard. If we, as people designing for behavior change, want to help people take an action, we should be pushing people to tackle that hill! We know it's hard, they know it's hard, and that's what makes it worthwhile, right?

Well, no.

If the goal is to make people healthier, and the action is consistent with that goal (say, by making the food that people already eat magically become healthier but taste and cost the same), and automation doesn't have nasty side effects, does it inherently matter if the user doesn't have to work hard for it? This probably raises all sorts of hackles. In the case of magically healthier food, I can hear my own inner do-gooder say, "Well, that misses the point—we want people to make wise choices, learn about the wonders of nutrition, be grateful for all the energy we put in to help them, etc.!"

That's why it's vital to be clear about the *end goal* of the product. For example, educating people about health is a laudable goal. But do we really only want to educate people? Or, do we educate in order to help people change their eating habits, which then makes them healthier in the long term? If we could jump ahead, solve this *very particular problem*, and move on to something else, wouldn't that be a good thing? Maybe making food healthier helps with the goal of decreasing vitamin deficiencies, but it doesn't solve the issue of cardiovascular disease. Great—once the food solution is in place, then you can devote your energies to the next problem: helping people decrease cardiovascular disease.

Any product will have multiple aims. But there should be one clear thing that you gauge its success against—a final outcome or goal (that one thing can be a composite of multiple smaller things). I'll talk about how to identify and fine-tune the product's goal in a later chapter, but let's assume you know what it is. When you're clear about what exactly is being sought, go for it. Even if it feels like cheating because it doesn't make people suffer. There are no martyrs in beneficial behavior change. The point of making work magically disappear is that you can move on and help your users with other, more intractable problems.

There's good behavioral science behind this point too. In short, our self-conceptions are constantly adapting based on our own behavior. We often forget or ignore the reasons why we do things and develop a story of who we are based on what we observe about our own behavior (Wilson 2011).[55] For example, if we successfully contribute money to a retirement plan, even if we were defaulted into it, we suddenly feel that that's something we can do—we're savers! The pride that people feel at saving money through automatic enrollment is real, and should not be discounted. That self-conception as a saver then has knock-on effects for other related behaviors—we're prepped for future action.

A classic study in this field is Freedman and Fraser (1966), in which the researchers started by asking homeowners to put a small sticker in their window encouraging safe driving. Weeks later, this randomly selected group was far more likely to accept a large lawn sign about safe driving than other homeowners; a whopping 76% of them accepted the large sign, compared to 17% who hadn't been asked to show the small sticker. In other studies, homeowners were also more likely to accept *other* non-driving related lawn signs. The homeowners started to see themselves as people active in their community, which had broad effects on their behavior.

There are cases when this doesn't work, of course. When people don't know the action occurred at all, then the self-conception doesn't change—but in that case it isn't a voluntary behavior change at all: it's behind-the-scenes trickery.

Cheating at the Action Funnel

Remember the Create Action Funnel from the last chapter? It's difficult for a user to pass all of the way through the funnel from the initial cue to a conscious choice to act with sufficient urgency. The *cheating* strategy takes the funnel, and changes its meaning. With a conscious choice to take a hard action, "success" occurs when the user passes through the funnel. When the product cheats, "success" occurs when the user agrees to the action occurring, but *doesn't* pass through the funnel to stop it from occurring.

Strategy 2: Make or Change Habits

Habits are widely used in products that change behavior. For example, the Nike+ FuelBand builds the habit of checking progress throughout the day with a simple cue (the band itself), routine (checking NikeFuel points), and reward (seeing the points increase). That habit of checking progress is an essential part of the feedback loop used to encourage additional exercise. The mobile phone application Lift builds user-selected habits by cueing people each day to take their action, and then recording it and rewarding them.[56] Before talking about how to build them, let's look at the role they play in behavior change.

Habits Simplify Behavior

Our minds are built to form habits because they are essential—they free our conscious minds from handling mundane details, for everything from thinking about how to prepare our breakfast in the morning to how to properly greet a friend we meet frequently. Without habits, our conscious minds would be overloaded with the minutiae of daily decisions—it would be like we were always moving to a new house, a new job, a new city, and trying to consciously maneuver our way around, every single day of our lives.

Before a habit is formed, however, the user still needs to choose to act. Just like with automation and intelligent defaults, using habits doesn't remove the need for the mind to think; it simply shifts the task to a simpler problem. With habits, the simpler problem is to help the person "get into the groove"—to start taking the action, so that the mind can make it habitual. I'll talk about how to consciously *start* taking an action in the next strategy; for now, we'll focus on how to build the habit given the user's initial commitment to act.

From a behavior change perspective, habits are both a boon and a bane. If a product helps the user form a habit, then the person can act on autopilot. The product team, and the user, can move on to tackling harder problems—just like the "cheating" strategy discussed earlier. But "bad" habits work on autopilot just as much as "good" ones. The next two sections talk about how to form (hopefully "good" habits) and clever ways to attack existing "bad" ones.

How to Build Them

Chapter 1 described the two basic types of habits: habits created out of simple repetition (cue-routine, cue-routine, etc.), and habits that have the added feature of a reward at the end (cue-routine-reward) that drives the person to repeat the behavior. Your product's users could form habits by simple repetition, but then the burden of work and willpower is all on their side. When designing for behavior change, add a reward at the end to help bring people back while the habit is forming.

The cue-routine-reward process is depicted in Figure 3-2. Charles Duhigg popularized the process in the *Power of Habit* (Random House, 2012), building on an old tradition in applied behavioral analysis.[57]

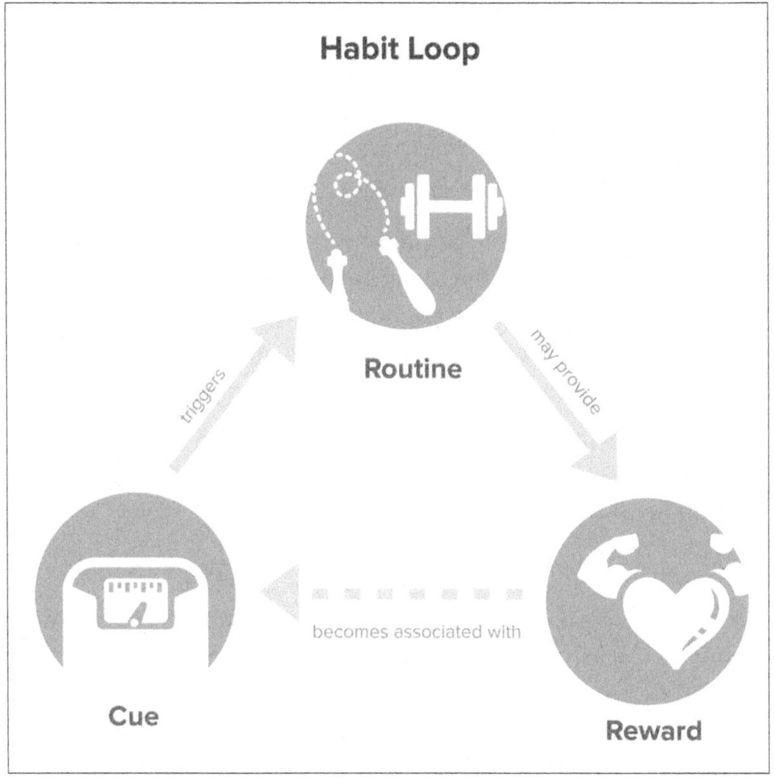

FIGURE 3-2.
The cue-routine-reward process described by Duhigg (2012). For example, seeing the scale in the morning triggers the exercise routine. The immediate reward is a pleasant muscle burn.

To build habits with a product, here is a straightforward recipe:

1. Identify a routine that should be repeated dozens of times, without significant variation or thought each time.
2. Identify a reward that is meaningful and valuable for the user.

3. Identify a clear, unambiguous, and single-purpose cue in a person's daily life or in the product itself (an email, an alert, etc.).
4. Make sure the user knows about the cue, routine, and especially, the reward.[58]
5. Make sure the user wants to and can undertake the routine (i.e., the user needs to make the conscious choice to act).
6. Deploy the cue.
7. Either facilitate the routine or, at least, seamlessly and immediately track whether the routine has actually occurred.
8. Have the product *immediately* reward the user once the routine has occurred. That allows dopamine in the brain to reinforce neurons associated with the cue and routine before the memory fades.
9. Repeat steps 6–8, tracking completion times and rates, and adapting the process until it's right.

There's a lot of nuance there, of course.

First, the *cue* really needs to be single-purpose and unambiguous (i.e., after the habit is formed, the cue is linked to the specific routine and nothing else), because you want to avoid the mind having to think about what to do when the cue occurs. Fogg and Hreha (2010) argue that the triggers (i.e., cues) can be:

- Directly tied to another event (e.g., looking at the bathroom mirror first thing in the morning is connected to picking up your toothbrush)
- At a specific time of day every day or every week

The trigger/cue can be "internal" (boredom or hunger) or "external" (seeing the clock first thing in the morning, or getting an angry email). Internal triggers are great, since they are inherent in the human condition; however, lots of other things in one's life compete for the same triggers (which makes them not single-purpose and thus ambiguous). External triggers can be just as effective, if wisely constructed.

Second, while the *routine* must be structured so that it can occur effectively without thought, it need not be "stupid" or "simple." Good driving, for most people, is a (complex, impressive) habit. Remember how hard it was to learn to drive? Remember all of the thought that was required just to start the car and get it going? Yet, after learning, we avoid getting too close to other cars while on the road, we coordinate what our eyes see with what our hands do to steer, and so on. The reason is that driving uses a set of hierarchical habits—large, complex habits built out of thousands of small, routinized behaviors that are cued from the environment and linked to one another in succession. Each piece is structured so that it can be consistently executed after the cue without conscious thought.

Routines that can be made into a habit often will have a strong and clear feedback loop (i.e., after the action is taken, the reward is immediate and unambiguously tied to the success). Habit formation is not a conscious event, though we can consciously put ourselves in situations where we'll learn them.

Third, the *reward* need not be offered every time, as long as it is still clearly tied to the routine. Random rewards are quite powerful in some circumstances. In the operant conditioning literature, habits with random reinforcement take the longest to *form* but also take the longest time to *extinguish* once the reward is no longer given. Gambling provides the ultimate random reward—and once you have the bug, it's difficult as all heck to get rid of. One reason that random reinforcement is so powerful is that our brains don't really believe in randomness. We look for patterns everywhere. So, part of the desire driving a random reward is our brains trying to find a pattern (ever talk to a gambler who has "a system"?).[59]

And finally, a key part of using products to build habits is experimentation and fine-tuning. Your product is probably going to get it wrong the first time—the cue won't be clear or won't grab the user's attention, the user may stop caring about the reward, or the context for the routine might change, and conscious thought is required.[60]

Changing Existing Habits

This book is about helping users take action. Sometimes, though, that may require intentionally stopping a habit, instead of just adding new behaviors. For example, at some point, improving fitness through exercise means not just exercising more, but also sitting less. And that means overcoming an existing habit.

Unfortunately, it can be extraordinarily difficult to stop habits head-on. Brain damage, surgery, even Alzheimer's disease and dementia sometimes fail to stop habits, even as other cognitive functions are severely impaired (Eldridge et al. 2002). BJ Fogg, for example, argues that stopping existing habits is the hardest behavioral change task to undertake (2009b).

Why are habits so difficult to change? First, it's because habits are automatic and not conscious. Our conscious minds, the part that would seek to remove them, are only vaguely aware of their execution (see Dean 2013); we often don't notice them when they occur, and we don't remember doing them afterward. Across dozens of studies on behavior change interventions, researchers have found that the conscious mind's sincere, concerted intention to change behavior *has little relationship to actual change in behavior* (Webb and Sheeran 2006).

Second, it's because habits never truly go away—once a habit is formed (i.e., the brain is rewired to associate the stimulus and response), it doesn't normally un-form. It can remain latent or unused, but under the right circumstances, that circuitry in the brain can be activated and cause the habitual behavior to reappear.[61]

Another way of thinking of habit cessation is this: if stopping bad habits were easy, we wouldn't need so many darned books on everything from stopping smoking to dieting.[62] Nevertheless, one can draw lessons from the literature on habit formation and change—which can save product teams needless pain and suffering. There are five main options that product teams can take to handle an existing habit:

1. Avoid the cue.
2. Replace the routine.
3. Cleverly use consciousness to interfere.
4. Use mindfulness to avoid acting on the cue.
5. Crowd out the old habit with new behavior.

In each case, the person doesn't engage in a direct confrontation to simply suppress the habit. That takes constant willpower, which is finite and unsustainable in most cases.

OPTION 1: HELP THE PERSON AVOID THE CUE

The cue signals the brain to engage in the problematic behavior; one way to stop a habit is to avoid the cue (Wood et al. 2005). For example, in addiction counseling, counselors advise addicts to change their environment so that they don't encounter the things that remind them to act. If you always stop for a drink when you see the bar on the way home, then change your route home so you don't see the bar anymore.[63]

Designing a *product* to help people avoid cues is especially tricky. First of all, most cues for bad habits are, by definition, outside of the behavior change product. People use the product in order to change the habit—the product didn't cause the bad habit. So, the product must help the person avoid the cues themselves: the product must provide guidance and instruction. And the individual must first know what the cues are—and be able to successfully avoid them.

Second, because the routine is outside of the product, the application usually won't know if the person has engaged in the behavior. It's up to the user to report falling off the wagon—which is doubly difficult. External monitoring systems are required—like the breathalyzers that alcoholics install in their cars to stop them from driving drunk. Much more is required in the case of chemical addictions like alcoholism, but we can learn from these efforts as we design products to stop less intractable habits.

While this route is clearly challenging, there are products that have successfully done it. One example is Covenant Eyes[64]—software that helps people who are struggling with sexual addiction or want to avoid the temptation before a habit is formed (see Figure 3-3). It helps users avoid cues (by filtering out sites with explicit content) and/or automatically monitors web usage to inform accountability partners of when the person does access pornography.

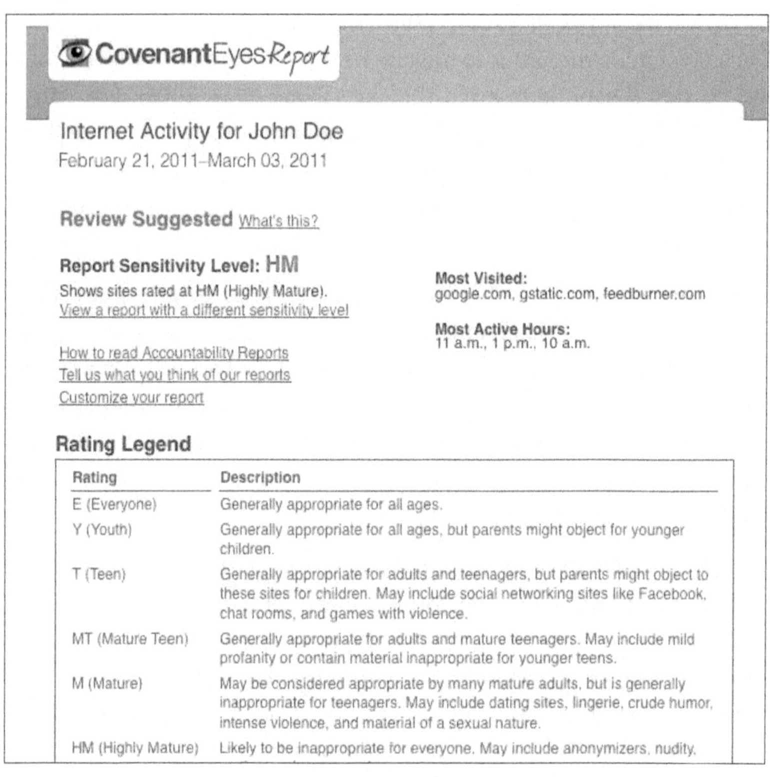
CovenantEyes Report

Internet Activity for John Doe
February 21, 2011–March 03, 2011

Review Suggested What's this?

Report Sensitivity Level: HM
Shows sites rated at HM (Highly Mature).
View a report with a different sensitivity level

Most Visited:
google.com, gstatic.com, feedburner.com

Most Active Hours:
11 a.m., 1 p.m., 10 a.m.

How to read Accountability Reports
Tell us what you think of our reports
Customize your report

Rating Legend

Rating	Description
E (Everyone)	Generally appropriate for all ages.
Y (Youth)	Generally appropriate for all ages, but parents might object for younger children.
T (Teen)	Generally appropriate for adults and teenagers, but parents might object to these sites for children. May include social networking sites like Facebook, chat rooms, and games with violence.
MT (Mature Teen)	Generally appropriate for adults and mature teenagers. May include mild profanity or contain material inappropriate for younger teens.
M (Mature)	May be considered appropriate by many mature adults, but is generally inappropriate for teenagers. May include dating sites, lingerie, crude humor, intense violence, and material of a sexual nature.
HM (Highly Mature)	Likely to be inappropriate for everyone. May include anonymizers, nudity,

FIGURE 3-3. Covenant Eyes, an application to stop the habit of viewing sexual material online, via filtering and automatic monitoring

OPTION 2: CHANGE THE HABIT INTO SOMETHING ELSE

The other strategy that products can use to change a bad habit is to transition an existing cue and reward to a different (more beneficial) behavior. In *The Power of Habit* (Random House, 2012), Duhigg describes two elements that are needed: routine replacement and a real belief that the habit can change.

Routine replacement works by hijacking the cue and the reward, and inserting a different routine between them. He uses the example of taking a snack break when you're not really hungry. The cue may be that you're having a down moment at work or watching a commercial on TV. The reward would be the relief of (momentary) boredom and the pleasant crunching sensation of the snack. To hijack this process, one needs to:

1. Identify the trigger, and the reward (if appropriate).
2. When the trigger occurs, consciously engage in a different routine that provides a similar reward (like doing a crossword puzzle when bored during commercials).

3. Continue that conscious switching of routines until the new habit is instilled.

The process of consciously replacing routines is also known as "competing response training." It is used in the treatment of people with Tourette's syndrome (involuntary tics), and has shown dramatic results in experimental testing (Piacentini et al. 2010; Dean 2013).

For especially difficult habits, like smoking and drinking, swapping in a new routine isn't enough, though. The new reward is never quite like the old one. Swapping can handle everyday behavior, but when times are tough, people can be immensely tempted to "fall off the wagon." Something else is needed to get through those dark times and back to the day-to-day humdrum that they *can* handle. That something else can be faith that the hard times will pass. It can be a religious faith, a personal faith in themselves, or a faith in others that pulls them through. Either way, it's an internal narrative that things will get better.

How does routine replacement work in practice? One of two ways. First, you can ensure that the product itself is present at the moment when the cue normally occurs. At that moment, it would remind or entice the user to do the new routine instead of the old one. After the routine is done, it would reward the user—or encourage him to reward himself.

The other route is trickier and is needed when the product *isn't* present when the user encounters the cue. As with avoiding the cue (described in the previous section), the product must advise and prepare the individual for the moment of temptation, and find some way of tracking what action the person took. ChangeTech.no has an intensive program of support and tracking that accomplishes this, with over 400 points of contact with individuals during their smoking cession program. And, its method has shown positive results in randomized control trials (Brendryen and Kraft 2008).[65]

An example of in-the-moment hijacking of habits that we're all familiar with is shopping in brick and mortar stores with a smartphone:

- *Cue.* See a camera, computer, or something else you like.
- *Old routine.* Pick it up, go to the cash register, buy it.
- *New routine.* Look it up on the phone, compare price (usually lower), and buy it.

- *Reward.* Feel great about saving money, imagine yourself using the cool camera, receive item, and so on.

This habit hijack is killing brick and mortar stores. It's not a "beneficial behavior change," but it's the same underlying process.

OPTION 3: USE CONSCIOUS INTERFERENCE

Our big brains are really good at blocking our own autopilot; properly deployed, they can interfere with habits in progress *without requiring direct willpower to overcome the action*. Thinking = bad, for a habit at least. In sports, masters of their game sometimes "choke" because they consciously cut into a process that normally runs on autopilot, and this happens in any field of mastery (Baumeister 1984; Gallwey 1997). To interfere with a habit: think about it. Look especially for what triggers it. Then closely examine the routine that's normally automatic—just by thinking about it (consciously), we can interfere with its smooth execution.

Products that do this should be present at the time of action and can grab the user's conscious attention to his or her behavior. The Prius is well known for functioning this way. The car's consumption monitor provides ongoing, immediate feedback about the car's gasoline consumption. This in-the-moment feedback can break people out of their existing driving habits by making them consciously aware of what's going on, causing them to use less gasoline, aka "the Prius Effect."

In order for this approach to work, like all habit intervention (and habit formation) approaches, it must be voluntary. If someone doesn't care about mileage or finds the car's consumption monitor annoying, he won't listen to it. It starts with the conscious choice to act.

OPTION 4: USE MINDFULNESS

Another, subtle way to overcome bad habits is by employing mindfulness. Mindfulness is a concept used in Buddhism to refer to awareness of the present moment and its experiences, without judging or trying to control them. It's a mental state of openness and acceptance of events and sensations as they occur. Mindfulness-based therapies are increasingly popular in the treatment of mental conditions, such as acute stress, anxiety, and depression (Hofman et al. 2010). Similar to mindfulness meditation in Buddhism, these therapies entail an intentional focus on the present moment without interference or judgment (Shapiro et al. 2006).

By bringing the cues that trigger habitual behavior into conscious awareness, it's possible for one to be aware of the trigger without acting on it. For example, mindfulness has been shown to limit undesired, but habitual, binge drinking (Chatzisarantis and Hagger 2007). A number of apps, such as Headspace,[66] support mindfulness to reduce stress or increase focus, though do not target habit change in particular.

OPTION 5: CROWDING OUT OLD HABITS

Another way of approaching habit change is to crowd out the old habit with new behaviors—a method that combines option 1 and 2 (and sometimes 3). In this method, you *focus on doing more of what you want instead of less of what you don't want.*

For example, think about someone who is in bad shape, spends lots of time watching TV, and has bad eating habits. The person starts to go to the gym to exercise more (creating a new habit). As the person goes to the gym, he meets new people, and enrolls in exercise and cooking classes with them. Slowly, the amount of time available to watch TV decreases. The person simply isn't at home as much, which leads him to avoid the old cues to watch TV. Also, because of the cooking class, and new ways of eating and cooking, there simply isn't the hunger and opportunity to use his old eating habits; they are slowly being replaced.

Naturally there are multiple forces at work in his life, such as changing self-identity, and changing social norms. However, as the structure of his daily life changes, the old habits fade away—not through a direct assault, but because other things are taking up his time and satisfying his hunger pangs. This only works if he gets far enough down the path of habit change—and doesn't quit going to the gym soon after signing up, as so many other people do. The initial choice to push ahead, before the habit is formed, is a conscious one.

Strategy 3: Support the Conscious Action

You probably noticed that both of the previous two strategies involved removing user work and simplifying the problem. But the simplified problem still requires a conscious choice to act. That's unavoidable, and it's even a good thing. The conscious mind must be engaged at some point. Ideally, that interaction entails informed consent—and the product automates or defaults the rest. Or the conscious choice can be to start down the path of habit formation or habit change.

The explicit strategy of making a conscious choice over each part of the action should generally be avoided because it requires additional effort on the part of the user. All else being equal, more effort means less chance of acting. But sometimes, a head-on approach is used (or required). That means passing through all five stages of the Action Funnel (cue-reaction-evaluation-ability-timing), in order to execute the action itself.

The conscious choice to act is a primary focus of this book, and Chapters 6–8 cover it in great detail. They describe how to support users to take conscious action—whether the action is the original behavior that the company sought to address, or a restructured action like giving consent to an automatic action taken on their behalf.

A Recap of the Three Strategies

This chapter discusses the three primary strategies for behavior change. In each case, there is a choice that individuals make, but the nature and subject of that choice changes. Here's a quick recap of when to use each one, and how they fit into the larger picture of behavior change:

Cheat

- *What it is.* Help the user avoid the work of the action altogether by making the outcome occur by default when the user interacts with the software or when the user takes a *different* action, or fully automating a repeated behavior after consent is given.
- *What is consciously chosen.* Whether or not to give consent to the action occurring on the user's behalf.
- *Examples.* 401(k) auto-enrollment; substituting healthier ingredients into the food people already eat.
- *Use this strategy.* When you can replace a hard action with informed consent. This is not appropriate for overcoming ingrained habits, nor is it appropriate for cases in which the user needs to personalize the action to specific needs—that requires conscious, active involvement.

Make (or change) habits

- *What it is.* Help the user avoid conscious effort and thought by making the desired action an automatic response to a trigger. Or when changing habits, cleverly attack the habit's structure to hinder it from occurring.
- *What is consciously chosen.* Whether or not to set up the conditions for a habit to form (or be broken).
- *Examples.* At the supermarket, go down the produce aisle before the canned foods aisle; walk once a day.
- *Use this strategy.* Whenever the user wants to undertake a behavior that is done multiple times, in a consistent context. Also use this when trying to overcome existing habits, with the tricks described as part of the strategy, rather than using brute force to consciously override habits.

Support the conscious action

- *What it is.* Help the user think about the action, and take the necessary steps (consciously) to make it happen.
- *What is consciously chosen.* Whether or not to take the target action.
- *Examples.* Educating people to get a good mortgage; encouraging people to sign up for (and attend) a yoga class for the first time.
- *Use this strategy.* Whenever the first two strategies aren't feasible, especially when the action is complex, novel, and requires the user to make numerous small choices that can't be defaulted.

On a Napkin

- Look for technical solutions to remove user work wherever possible; it's often much more effective to engineer a solution than it is to change behavior.
- Three technical solutions are automating the action behind the scenes, using intelligent defaults, and making the behavior a side effect of something else the user is doing.
- Habits are immensely powerful ways to lock in repeated behaviors. They require an unambiguous cue, unvarying routine, and a meaningful, immediate reward.

- When possible, avoid trying to stop an existing behavior. The product should build new ones instead.
- If stopping a habit is required, help users avoid cues, replace the routine, crowd it out, or draw conscious attention to the trigger and routine via mindfulness.
- No matter what, some type of conscious choice is required for voluntary behavior change—the strategies presented here are all means to simplify the choice and the work required of the user.

[*Part II*]

Discovering the Right Outcome, Action, and Actor

Here's the scenario: your company has a vision, something that it wants to build and a population it wants to serve. The new product or feature is intended to help users do something, like stopping asthma attacks. It's done market research and identified the existing user need that the product will solve. But how exactly it'll help users change their behavior isn't clear.

Part II takes that vision and makes it specific and real. We'll start by identifying the measurable, real-world outcomes that the product is supposed to drive (like fewer asthma hospitalizations or deaths). We'll identify *who* the product is supposed to help (like adult asthmatics between the ages of 25 and 55 in the Central Valley of California, where the air quality is terrible). And we'll identify what action we think will help them achieve their goals (using an automated asthma tracker like Propeller Health).[67]

In making things concrete, we have a few goals. First, we want to generate clear guidance on what should be built, so that we can inform the product team. Second, we want to draw out and test our implicit assumptions about our users and how human behavior works. Third, we want to pull failures from the future into the present—we want to fail fast—so that we don't waste time building the wrong product. That's similar to a lean startup approach.

In the Preface, I mentioned that companies can apply the principles of designing for behavior change to their existing process for product development (all product processes have some form of "discovery," for example). For those who weren't sure where to start though, I offered a simple iterative product development cycle as an example; that cycle is redisplayed in Figure Part II-1 and shows how the chapters in this part fit into that product development cycle.

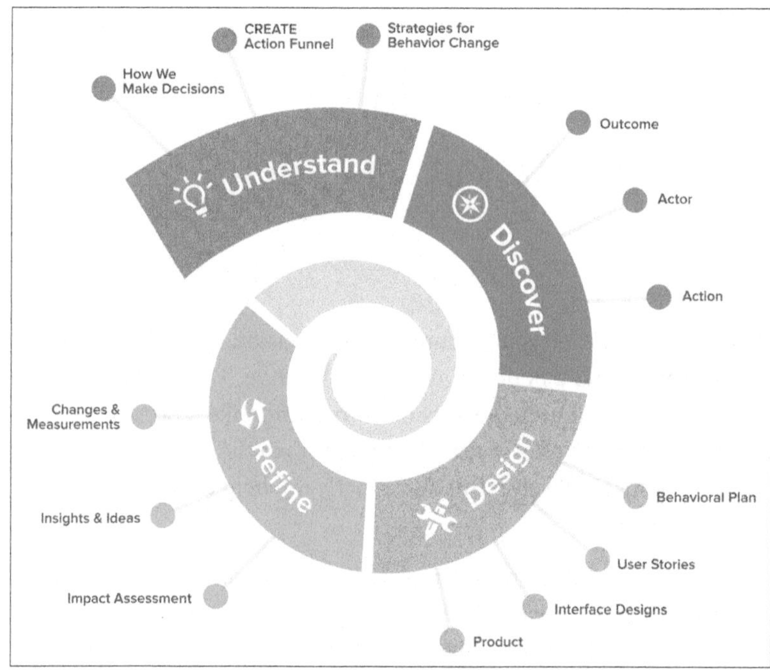

FIGURE PART II-1. Designing for behavior change using an iterative product development process; Part II covers the *outcome*, *actor*, and *action*

Chapter 4 introduces the discovery process and shows you how to document the product's target *outcome* and the target audience (the *actor*) and how to start generating ideas for the potential actions that the actors will take. Chapter 5 evaluates those actions in terms of their cost-effectiveness at changing behavior and how well they fit the company's goals and culture, to select the final *action* that the new product (or new feature) will support.

Chapter 5 also pares down the potential behaviors to their Minimum Viable Action—the simplest, smallest action that people could take to achieve the outcome. Focusing on the Minimum Viable Action will allow us to simplify the design process, more quickly get real feedback on the psychology of the product from users, and start refining and improving the product sooner.

[4]

Figuring Out What You Want to Accomplish

If you wanted to develop a new product to help people lose weight, what would you do?

How about something that helps people track how many calories they're eating, like MyFitnesPal?[68] Or a diet plan that says what we should eat and what we should avoid, like the Paleo Diet?[69] How about a diet pill that reduces appetite, like the once highly popular (but unfortunately fatal) fen-phen?[70] Or, of course, an exercise app, like the many other such apps already out there?

These are all things that jump to mind because they're familiar, and relate to seemingly obvious actions that people can take to lose weight. Brian Wansink has a different approach. He's studied how we eat food for decades. He directs Cornell's Food and Brand Lab and has authored over a hundred academic articles and numerous books about eating.[71] He's also really funny (he used to be a stand-up comic).

Wansink has studied what happens when you give people free but really, really stale popcorn before a movie (they eat it anyway), and what happens when you secretly refill people's soup bowls while they are eating so they can't reach the bottom (they don't notice and just keep eating; see Figure 4-1). He's coined the term "mindless eating" for how our eating behavior is often on autopilot (Wansink 2010). And Brian has a new weight-loss product for us—it's called a smaller dinner plate.

He's started the "Small Plate Movement," encouraging people to use smaller dinner plates, which in turn decreases how much food they eat *without making people feel hungry*. His research has shown that we usually have no idea how many calories are in the food we eat, and we don't even know if we've eaten enough to be satisfied. Instead, our minds use cues in our environments to tell us how much to eat and whether or not we're done eating. One of the most common cues we use is seeing that we've eaten everything on our plate.[72] Shrinking the plate in turn shrinks how much we eat.

FIGURE 4-1. A cartoon from Brian Wansink, illustrating that the larger the serving container, the more we eat[73]

First of all, that's amazing. Second, that's a powerful example of how important it is to carefully think about alternative approaches and evaluate potential changes in behavior *before you build the product*. In other words, we should think about product discovery explicitly—to determine what's the right thing to build—rather than jumping to an "obvious" solution, like an exercise app. Part of that discovery process also means finding the right match between the behavior, the users, and the company—to find out what is both interesting for your users and cost-effective for the company.

By the end of the discovery process, we'll clarify three things:

The target outcome
: *What* is the product supposed to accomplish? What will be different about the real world when the product is successful? For example, overweight people should lose 10 pounds because of this product.

The target actor
: *Who* do we envision using the product? Who will do something differently in their lives, and thus accomplish the target outcome? For example, normal, everyday people who eat dinner at home or at a restaurant.

The target action
: *How* will the actor do it? What behavior will the person actually undertake? For example, users should serve food on a smaller dinner plate.

Throughout the book, we'll use those three terms to describe the outputs of the discovery process: the outcome, the actor, and the action. Along the way, we'll elicit, evaluate, and refine these three ideas, until the key stakeholders are all on the same page, and potential problems have been identified early and have been resolved. Here are the five stages of behavior discovery:

1. Clarify the overall behavioral vision of the product.
2. Identify the user outcomes sought.
3. Generate a list of possible actions.
4. Get to know your users and what is feasible and interesting for them.
5. Evaluate the list of possible actions and select the best one.

This chapter covers steps 1–3, and Chapter 5 covers steps 4 and 5.

Your company may have already have completed some of the initial stages of the behavior discovery process, though. You should feel free to jump ahead to the part that's relevant; however, you may also find it useful to quickly scan the earlier parts to see if there's anything you missed.

Start with the Product Vision

Let's say a company has an overarching vision for its new product and its impact on its users, the company itself, and on society. The vision for the *product* may come directly from the company's mission statement. For example, the Sunlight Foundation, a nonprofit that works toward government transparency, gives its mission statement on its website:[74]

OUR MISSION

The Sunlight Foundation is a nonprofit, nonpartisan organization that uses the power of the Internet to catalyze greater government openness and transparency, and provides new tools and resources for media and citizens, alike.

The vision for each of its products clearly follows from this organizational mission. For example, it has a tool, Poligraft, which "allows anyone to uncover levels of influence in federal and state-level politics and the news coverage of it."

For a company developing a wearable computing device (e.g., the Nike+ FuelBand or Fitbit One), its product vision might be "helps people exercise more."

Let's start the discovery process off by simply getting the product vision down on paper. The vision can be general and somewhat vague—that's fine. It allows us to start the conversation about the more specific, concrete impacts that the product should have—the target outcome.

Nail Down the Target Outcome

After you have a general sense of the vision for the product, you should ask the following: what should be different about the world when the product is successful? What's the specific, concrete change that should occur because of the product? What could a third party see, hear, or touch?

The answer to that question is the product's desired *outcome*. Another way of thinking about it is the tangible thing that the company *seeks to accomplish* with the product (remember, I use "company" as shorthand for corporation, nonprofit, or government agency). The outcome is the company's concrete and measurable goal that it hopes to accomplish with the product. I like the word "outcome" rather than "goal" because it feels more concrete—it focuses attention on something changing in the world.

Write down an initial statement of the product's desired outcome (or outcomes).

Clarify the Outcome

Next, let's refine your target outcome with some probing questions.

Which type?
: Does the product ultimately seek to change something about the environment (e.g., clean water) or about people (e.g., healthier bodies)?

Where?
: What is the geographic scope of the impact (e.g., Chesapeake Bay)?

What?
: What is the actual change to the environment or person (e.g., decrease nitrogen pollution)?

When?
: At what point should the product have an impact? We're looking for the order of magnitude. Unlike the others, this doesn't need to be precise at this point—"in a few months" or "in five years" is fine.

Write down the answers to these questions with a simple, clear statement that summarizes them. For example, "This product should cause a decrease in nitrogen levels, an environmental pollutant, in the Chesapeake Bay over the next five years."

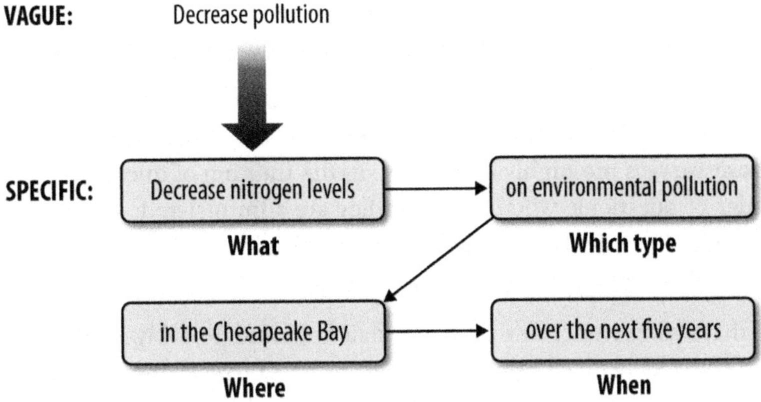

Based on that statement of the desired outcome, define a metric that you can use to gauge whether the product is successful or not—nitrogen levels in the water or body mass index (BMI) of school children, for example. You don't need to settle on the exact measurement yet—but if you can't define one at all, then the outcome isn't concrete enough.

Here's an example of clear outcomes that are readily measurable, and ones that aren't:

Clear, measureable outcomes

Californians will have an average BMI of 24. Employees at Company X won't smoke.

Unclear, difficult to measure outcomes

Users will gain experience with exercise. Users will understand the dangers of smoking.

Having a clear outcome in mind doesn't mean that you're omniscient, or that you're locking your company into a strict path for the next few years. Instead, it's a solid point of reference. As problems arise, you can settle disagreements of fact (does this design work or not?) by measuring against the outcome. And, you can settle disagreements of vision (is this the right goal for the product or not?) by redefining the target outcome when needed—*as long as the new outcome is also clearly defined.*

AVOID STATES OF MIND

A common problem that many companies face as they define the product's target outcome is that they want to talk about something within their user's heads. Education. Confidence. Even skill at doing something. There are two reasons why states of mind are problematic.

Firstly, they are difficult to measure in a consistent and unambiguous way. States of mind can be measured with surveys, but the results of those surveys are highly dependent on the framing of questions, the order of questions, when and how they are administered, and more. "Highly dependent" = open to debate, misunderstanding, and argument. That's exactly what we're trying to avoid.

Perhaps more importantly though, states of mind probably *aren't what the company actually wants.* Consider an NGO that trains women to be entrepreneurs: do they want the women to know what it takes to be an entrepreneur, or do they actually want the women to start new, successful businesses? If the clients knew how to be entrepreneurs, but never actually started businesses, would the NGO consider the program a success? Probably not.

Instead, we want the outcome to be something observable, outside of the individual's head, absolutely unambiguous (to avoid arguments within the company about whether something is successful or not), and easy to measure (so you can gauge success quickly). *The target outcome should define the success (or failure) of the product.*

Being Effective Sometimes Means Being Controversial

Often, we focus on states of mind because they are noncontroversial. Everyone can support education; far fewer people are comfortable talking about what the education is supposed to do: change people's behavior, which then changes something in the real world.

Remember, we're not trying to be noncontroversial. We're trying to be *effective* at actually changing behavior. That takes a measure of self-reflection and honesty—what is your real goal?

OTHER WAYS TO ARRIVE AT A DEFINITION OF OUTCOMES

If you're stuck thinking of what the specific outcomes of your product should be, then here are some questions to spur thought before you answer "which, where, what, and when":

- What happens next? If you have an outcome that feels right but isn't measureable, ask yourself: what happens after that outcome? What can someone see, hear, or touch that occurs next? How do people use the new knowledge/pride/etc. they have? For example, "people learn to dance" becomes "people go dancing once a month."
- What would a stranger see? Imagine someone visited the place where the product is used (including the Internet, if that's where it's used), before the product was deployed, and after. That person knows nothing about the product itself, and *can't talk to anyone.* What would be different? For example, "users build tighter families" becomes "users exchange more emails and phone calls with estranged family members."

- What's the impact of the product? Why would someone pay for this product? For example, "users feel in control of their email" becomes "users have zero messages in their inbox at the end of each day."

PRIORITIZE AND COMBINE

If you're stuck with more than one outcome, that's OK. They need to be organized. If there's a clear, top-priority outcome, excellent. If not, get the stakeholders together and see if there is a majority opinion on what's most important. Or, take the list of desired outcomes and ask for each one: would the product still be "successful" if this did not occur? Drop them, one by one.

If winnowing down the list isn't feasible, there is another, more challenging route. Create an aggregate outcome that combines the contenders for top-priority. To do this, you need to get very specific and define a formula that combines them in a way that everyone can get on the same page. This formula is a formal definition of success for the product.

For example, say the two "highest priority" outcomes are "the product will cause decreased blood pressure" and "the product will cause decreased BMI." A definition of success that combines them both would be "the success of the product is defined as 1 point for every decrease in average blood pressure across the target population and 2 points for every decrease in average BMI."

Unfortunately, most companies just don't have enough information to understand the complex impacts of the product across related but nonidentical behaviors before the product has actually been built. Personally, I'd avoid making up a formula that combines multiple outcomes and settle on a prioritization that identifies one outcome as the top priority.

AVOID STATING HOW THE PRODUCT (MIGHT) DO IT

You may have noticed that there are two key questions I didn't suggest asking at this point:

How?

For now, try to avoid delving into how the product works its magic (i.e., what action it encourages users to take to make the outcome happen). We'll get to that shortly, after we're armed with additional information.

How much?

We don't need to define a specific level of change caused by the product at this stage. (If you have one in mind, great, but it's just not required). Often, companies just don't have enough information to set a realistic target at this point.

WHY GO THROUGH THE TROUBLE?

Why do we need to define the desired outcomes so carefully and clearly? We want to pull problems into the present and resolve them. If the team has a mess of conflicting objectives, or something that can't be measured, then there are problems lurking in the future. The team is likely to argue over what the product should look like as each member tries to meet conflicting, unstated objectives. The head of the company may think the product isn't successful, but the engineers do. The grant funding agency (for NGOs) might cut off funding because it had implicit assumptions about what the product would do that aren't being met.

A clear statement of measureable outcomes that key stakeholders can sign on to at the beginning of the project can resolve many of these problems early. And, just as with any product development process, finding and resolving problems early on is much cheaper than trying to fix things later.

In addition, a clear outcome statement is essential for revising the product to improve its impact. It forms the basis for measuring the product's success, finding problem areas, and gauging whether proposed changes to the product are worth their salt.

WHAT IF NO ONE CAN AGREE ON THE PRODUCT'S INTENDED OUTCOME?

One possible result of trying to state the desired outcome of the product is that there isn't one. Either the stakeholders fundamentally don't agree, or the product was poorly conceived and doesn't have real-world outcomes. In that case, the product shouldn't proceed in its current form. In the spirit of failing fast, that's a really good outcome—and should be embraced, painful as it is.

That doesn't mean the team needs to have *consensus* about what the ideal product should do; few companies operate that way. But everyone should know what to expect and sign on to the goal once the decision has been made about the product's intended outcomes. If there are still deep divisions in the team, then problems lie ahead. The team should move on to other interesting products, or change its membership, rather than arguing for months over a product that's ultimately doomed.

Working with Company-Centric Goals

Thus far, we've talked about a product development process that's focused primarily on the user and what the product can do for him or her. But I've found that companies sometimes take two very different approaches to behavior change. They can:

- Focus on how the product will *benefit the user*, which in turn helps the company's bottom line; or
- Focus on how the product will *benefit the company*, by way of providing value to the user.

This difference is in how companies think about the *value* of changing behavior; it isn't related to the behavior itself. The target behavior could be inside the product or outside the product, socially important or trivial; that doesn't matter as much.[75]

In the first case, a company might have a vision of improving financial wellness (like HelloWallet does) and need to figure out what actions users can reasonably take that will best make that happen. In the second case, a company might have a purely self-interested goal, like increasing customer renewals, but needs to provide real value to the user in order for that to succeed. The second approach includes red-blooded capitalists as well as NGOs that need to make their case to their funders. There's nothing wrong with that approach—as long as the companies build products that people like. But it does mean that the process of behavior discovery is different.

In the user-centric approach, the discovery process develops these concepts in turn:

Product Vision → User Outcome → Action → Actor

In the company-centric approach, the discovery process adds another step:

Product Vision → Company Objectives → User Outcome → Action → Actor

The product vision is *why the product is being developed*, at a high level; and the company objectives are *what the company seeks to achieve*, for itself, by building the product.

Since the previous section highlighted examples of the user-centric approach, let's now walk through the company-centric process (you can safely skip this is you're using a user-centric approach).

STATE THE VISION

As before, the discovery process starts by writing down the high-level vision the company has for the product. That vision, however, should answer how the product will generally benefit the company. For example:

- This product should expand the company's appeal into new markets.
- This product should increase revenue.
- The product should demonstrate the expertise and capacity of the organization to take on new projects, to support new grant funding.
- The product should increase public awareness and interest (or brand prestige) of the organization.

STATE THE COMPANY'S OBJECTIVES

With the company's vision for the product in mind, translate that vision into one or more specific, measurable objectives that benefit the company. For example, ask:

- How will the product be judged a success or failure at fulfilling the company's vision? How will success be measured?
- What would a third party observe about the company that's different, because of the product? Increased retention of customers? Increased upsell? More referrals of new customers?

The company's objective might be to win 35% of the market for exercise bands among 21 to 35-year-old women. Or, it might be to win at least $1 million of additional grant funding for the next year. Write down that initial company objective.

Based on that initial statement of the company's objectives, fine-tune it by asking who, what, when, and where the outcome occurs (similar to what we did in the last section):

Who?

Which customers are affected? New ones? Existing ones?

What?

What is the actual change to the company (revenue, brand value, etc.)?

Where?

What region or division should be affected?

When?

How long, very roughly, should it take? If the product doubles sales, but requires 10 years to do so, is that a success or failure?

Write down the answers, and develop a single clear statement that the product development team and company leaders can rally around. You should have enough information to define how the product's success or failure will be measured (e.g., customer renewal). We don't necessarily need to define the precise expected value (1.5 increase in sales), nor do we need to define how the product will accomplish this magic, yet.

DEFINE THE USER OUTCOMES

Building your business or establishing your expertise to funders is great, but your users probably don't care. Sorry. You need to deliver something of value to them. Without that value, you can't meet your business objectives.

So, putting aside the financial (or other self-interested) goals of the product for a moment, what does the product mean for users? We want to define the measurable changes in the world that are caused by the product *that the user would care about.* Here are some questions to help draw out those outcomes:

- What does the product deliver? What's its core value proposition, as the user would see it and measure it?
- After users have used the product, what's different about the world?
- What tangible thing would a user look at (or hear or see), sometime after using the product, and say, "Hey, I want to use that product again"? (The product itself doesn't count, sorry.)

- How would you know that your users have gained the maximum value from your product?
- What do the users *do* because of the company's increased brand awareness?

For example, consider the company objective of winning 35% of the market for exercise bands among 21 to 35-year-old women. A specific user outcome might be: the product helps the user lose 25 pounds over six months. Or the product helps the user drop two waist sizes.

In the previous section, we discussed a set of rules and tips for clarifying target outcomes. All of them apply here: avoid states of mind, make sure the outcome is measurable, find disagreements early, and don't obsess about *how* the product will achieve these outcomes yet.

Identify Additional Constraints

Every product team has constraints. Constraints turn the unmanageable task of "building something" into a real concept that the team can actually design and engineer. We've already talked about some of those constraints—the vision of the product, the product's target outcome, and the company's business objectives. Now, we want to identify additional constraints that will shape how the product will interact with and affect its users.

Many of these questions are normally answered as part of a project brief for a design consultancy or a marketing requirements document. They may be part of a company's standard set of operating assumptions. Either way, make sure they are clear. The goal is to avoid dead-ends further down the line.

Here are constraints that are especially relevant for this process:

Channel
: If the product must be a mobile app (for whatever business reason), you need to know that up front.

Time frame
: How much time does the product team have to work? This will be essential when we evaluate particular behaviors that the team needs to design into the product.

Resources
: What resources will be devoted to the team, if known up front?

Tone

Some companies need a serious application that fits their internal culture and outward identity.

Scope or target audience

Does the product absolutely need to impact a particular portion of the target audience for political or business considerations?

Be careful about what "constraint" means, though. It's only a constraint if there is a mandate. If it's an assumption about how the product *should* function in order to deliver its behavioral impact, put it aside for now. We're looking for hard constraints.

Generate a List of Possible Actions for Users to Take

After identifying the top-priority outcome that the company seeks to accomplish with the product, the next step is to translate it into actions—a list of specific behaviors that a user might take to make that goal a reality.

Let's say the top-level outcome is to help users have more money for savings—something near and dear to our hearts here at HelloWallet. There are numerous actions a user could take to make this happen—like finding a higher paying job, selling unused assets, getting a lower mortgage rate, or spending less money on daily purchases.

For most companies, especially those with existing products on the shelf, the universe of possible user actions is tightly constrained by the company's business model, product strategy, and internal culture; that's why we drew out these constraints in the previous section. At HelloWallet, for example, we looked for actions that would be appropriate for a wide range of users and weren't being well covered by existing products. So, job-hunting tools were out, as were mortgage finders.

The goal is to generate a list of potential actions: at least five actions that are very different from one another but still fit within the realm of possibility for the company. For each action, we want to define:

- Who is doing the action?
- What, specifically and physically, is the person doing?
- How does it cause the target outcome?

Usually the "who" is simple—it's the users of the product. But not always: the user may influence another person, who then does the real work.[76]

Naturally, we want to make sure the proposed action has some chance of being successful. So, dig into the question, how does it cause the target outcome? The proposed action should directly and clearly cause the outcome that the company is seeking. If the current action doesn't actually cause the target outcome, then ask, is there another, subsequent, physical action that is required to cause the outcome? If there is a clear subsequent action, focus on that one instead. We want the behavior that directly supports the outcome.

For example, going to a seminar about the importance of community engagement is one possible action that people can take to get involved in their communities. But the direct link between the action (go to seminar) and outcome (more members in community organizations) is a bit tenuous. What if the person doesn't pay attention? What if he has been forced by his spouse to attend lots of "get more engaged" events in the past? A better, more immediate action is "volunteer at local soup kitchen." That's the real point of the seminar (we assume) and has a direct link to the outcome we care about.

Clarify Each Action

As we did for the company's target outcome, we're looking for a concrete, specific definition. Physical, measurable actions the users will take. Avoid actions that just affect the user's mental states (reading educational material) and dig deeper into what the user does with his new education that causes him to *do* something differently, and achieve the outcome.

For example:

- Outcome sought: people don't get lung disease.
- Vague action: users avoid cigarettes. (Does that mean they cut down on smoking? Go cold turkey?)
- Action that's too far removed from the outcome: users attend a seminar about the dangers of smoking (OK, but do we care if they attend? Or that they actually stop smoking?).
- Clear action: users don't buy cigarettes at all.

You'll notice that the action doesn't specify how exactly the product will help the user not buy cigarettes. It could be by helping him avoid stores where cigarettes are sold. Or by decreasing the desire to smoke with nicotine patches. That's coming up soon.

Like the target outcome, the target action isn't written in stone. It should be clearly defined so that it can be built into the product and clearly measured. The definition, and measurement, will help with fine tuning the product. They'll also help with revisiting and revising the target action itself, if the need arises.

Techniques for Generating Ideas

How can you figure out the actions that people could take? What actions could your product cause, which would make the target outcome happen?

There are lots of brainstorming and creative thinking techniques out there. I cut my teeth reading Edward de Bono, who provides fascinating discussions of lateral thinking (de Bono 1973). But use whatever works for you. Don't stop until you have at least five different actions.

If you don't know where to start, here are some approaches that can help:

- What does someone do right before the outcome occurs?
- What's unique about the company? What user actions are easier to facilitate because of those unique aspects of the company (specialized skills, a special relationship with the users, etc.)?
- What do users already do that's similar?
- Why aren't people making the outcome happen?
- Why would users want to make the outcome happen? What action is most natural for them to take, if they are motivated?
- Observe your users in practice. People find creative ways to change their own behavior all the time. Watch them for inspiration on what the product can do.
- Draw from a list of random words (yes, I really mean random—this is a technique from Edward de Bono). How is the word related to the outcome? How would a person act based on that word, in support of the outcome?

If possible, start small: go with the small, easy things that the person could do to accomplish the outcome. That will make it faster to test and can be expanded upon later if needed. Look for the existing skills and habits of the users wherever possible, and build on them. Try some crazy ideas. At this stage, don't self-censor and limit actions that seem impossible.

Some companies will be tempted to skip this step because there is an "obvious" action for their users to take, given the target outcome. Bear with me for a second and give it a shot anyway. It's sometimes difficult to mentally separate the target outcome from the "best" action for users to take. For example, let's say you have a clearly defined target outcome: helping users put more money into savings. The "obvious" answer is to set a budget and spend less on something. The problem is that that's also a really hard action for most users to undertake (at least, head-on). Other, less "obvious" actions may work better (e.g., automatically deducting the money from your paycheck, so it's never in your checking account to tempt you).

The action doesn't need to be something that the user would do while using the product itself—dieting is a great example. People don't (usually) eat while they are logged in to a dieting app on their computer or phone. Dieting occurs when people make choices about what to eat and how much. Many dieting applications are designed to help inform and prepare individuals so that when they *are* making food and eating choices, they avoid temptation and make better choices for themselves. There's a danger there, though—the further removed the product is from the action itself, the less likely it will be that it causes people to take action.

As you think of actions, there's necessarily a leap that occurs between the action and the outcome—the assumption that the action will actually work and produce the outcome the user and company seeks. We'll draw out that assumption and judge how risky it is a bit later. For now, I suggest focusing on coming up with some cool new ideas, even if some of them are uncertain.

Look for the Minimum Viable Action in Each Case

The Minimum Viable Action is the shortest, simplest version of the target action that users absolutely must take to so that you can test whether your product idea (and its assumed impact on behavior) works.

It builds on the lean startup concept of the Minimum Viable Product: the smallest set of features that allows the product to be deployed and tested in the field.

You can think about the Minimum Viable Action (MVA) like this. You've mapped out what you'd *like* users to do. Excellent. Along the way, you've made some core assumptions about how the user will feel, react to, and interact with the product. The problem is: no one really knows how people will respond, and the more intractable the behavior, the less certainty we have that a product will be able to change it. As I mentioned at the beginning of the book, there aren't any behavioral magic wands, and we should expect to be wrong about some things. For that reason, I strongly believe in testing ideas out in the field. And, in *testing as early as possible* to adapt and learn as you go along.[77]

How do you find the Minimum Viable Action? Look over the list of potential actions you've generated. I think of the Minimum Viable Action as something that you arrive at by cutting back on what naturally came to mind the first time. Cut back from the obvious until only the necessary remains.

- If you have a repeated action, can you start by building the product to support a one-time action? One-time actions are easier for users to perform and engineering teams to build than repeated ones, all else being equal. And they still provide valuable insight into whether the software works at supporting the behavior. For example, if you want to help people lose weight by using smaller plates, see if they will use a smaller plate *at all* before trying to change their dining habits at home.
- Even if the target outcome won't be achieved initially, can you cut the action down into something smaller and shorter but still fundamentally the same basic task? The goal is to test the core premise, as with a Minimum Viable Product (i.e., instead of asking people to replace all of their plates, can they just start with one small plate?).
- Can you identify the high-risk, most uncertain, aspects of the action (i.e., having people eliminate other plate options from their house) and either remove them altogether from the target action (e.g., it's OK if they keep the old plates, as long as they are hidden) or test them before developing the lower-risk aspects (having the person eat dessert on a saucer plate)?

- Will the target outcome be achieved if the user takes a shorter, simpler action?

I waited to introduce the concept of a Minimum Viable Action because I find that people don't naturally think about the smallest possible action to change behavior. We like to think big. That's fine. It's useful, good, and most natural (i.e., easiest) to express that big vision first. That provides a blueprint that the team can go back to and draw upon as the product develops.

However, once those big behavior change thoughts are up on a board, and we see all of the pain we're thinking of putting our downtrodden users through, then reality should hit—the more work that users have to do, the less they are likely to do it (with some important exceptions I'll cover later). Hence, the Minimum Viable Action.

Here are some examples of actions that the team might think up in order to help users learn Spanish:

- Complete an online training course.
- Visit Spain for a few weeks to be forced to speak Spanish.
- Label each item in the household with their Spanish names.

And here are some simpler MVAs to test the core assumptions of the approach and its impact more quickly:

- Complete a single module of an online training program.
- Get a Spanish-language conversation partner who is committed to only speaking Spanish with the user.
- Label a few items in daily use with their Spanish names.

OK. Now that we have a rough set of potential actions that "the users" can take, the next chapter will dig deeper into exactly who the users are so we can evaluate what action will be most effective for them to take.[78]

Examples from Various Domains

Talking about desired outcomes and target actions can be a bit abstract, especially given the tremendous range of possible products that this approach can be applied to. So, let's looks at some concrete examples (Tables 4-2 and 4-3). Since the approach is somewhat different for user-centric versus company-centric products, I've broken them up into two different tables. To make the comparison clearer, I've started both tables off with a single product—an exercise tracker—to show how the analysis would proceed from each perspective.

TABLE 4-2. User-centric examples

	EXAMPLE 1	EXAMPLE 2	EXAMPLE 3
Product	Exercise tracker and app (e.g., Fitbit)	Financial wellness app (HelloWallet)	Government transparency app (e.g., Sunlight Foundation)
Vision	Improve fitness of young city dwellers	Democratize access to financial guidance	Inform public about corrosive power of money in politics
Outcome	Decrease BMI	Americans have sufficient emergency savings	Decrease in vote buying
Action	Users should walk 10,000 steps a day	Users automatically transfer money to savings account each month	Users research lobbying money in their congressional district

TABLE 4-3. Company-centric examples

	EXAMPLE 1	EXAMPLE 2	EXAMPLE 3
Product	Exercise tracker and app	Grocery store website	Conference calling app/website (e.g., Speek)
Vision	Build new customer base among young city dwellers	Expansion of business into upscale grocery shoppers	Build business around premier features of new conference call system
Company objectives	Double number of urban customers	Double number of upscale buyers	Increased usage of free Speek app among users
User outcome/user need	Desire to be healthier	Learn how to cook healthy meals	Easy conference calls
Action	Users should walk 10,000 steps a day	Users take free cooking classes on grocery website	Users distribute their free Speek URL to conference call participants

There are a few things to point out here:

- Despite our best efforts, there may be a big leap between the outcome and the action. Does user awareness of congressional lobbying decrease vote buying? That's a tough question to ask.

The purpose of this chapter was to provide a clear direction for the product development process, uncover hidden assumptions, and, sometimes, determine that a pivot is needed, and a different approach or behavior should be targeted.

- Sometimes the outcome that's really important is an action that the user takes. The first example could easily have had "users walk" as the outcome, as well as the action. This occurs when the action itself has an unambiguous, real-world outcome (like walking). However, I argue that companies should avoid equating the two in most cases. It's an easy way to hide assumptions about why the action is important, and thus to potentially choose the wrong action.

On a Napkin

Here's what you need to do

- Define the real-world outcome that the product should have. Avoid states of mind—focus on measurable outcomes that define the success or failure of the product.
- Translate company-specific goals (e.g., increased profit) into real-world outcomes that the user actually cares about.
- Brainstorm actions that people might make the product's intended outcome a reality.
- Trim each action down to its Minimum Viable Action.

How you'll know there's trouble

- The company can't agree on the intended outcome of the product.
- The company knows what it wants but doesn't offer something that users care about.

Deliverables

- A clearly defined outcome and a list of possible actors and actions they would take

[5]

Selecting the Right Target Action

Each of us has different routines, different experiences, and different ways that we respond to the world. To design for behavior change, you need to discover the right action for your users based on this complex terrain of routines, experiences, and responses. The action must be effective at helping them achieve their goals. And, at the same time, you must balance user needs against the needs of the company building the product—to generate revenue and to cost-effectively deploy design and engineering resources.

In Chapter 4, we clarified what the company sought to accomplish with the product (the *target outcome*, like people losing weight) and generated a list of potential actions that users *could* take in order to make that happen (like using smaller plates, exercising more, or going on a diet). That initial list of target actions was initially developed in a vacuum, without a lot of discussion about the users themselves—to avoid stereotyped actions that we think people are "likely" to take.

Now it's time to confront that list of potential actions with real users. We'll refine the list and then evaluate it according to company and user needs. Along the way, we'll also gather vital information we need about the target users for designing the product itself.

Research Your Target Users

In order to help users change their behavior, the team must understand where the users are starting from and what behaviors are realistic and worthwhile to change. This process focuses on three distinct questions:

- Who are the users who will be interacting with the product?
- How do these (potential) users think and act in their everyday lives?
- How do these users interact with and behave within the existing application (if any)?

Who Are the Target Users?

Usually the company's business objectives and market research specify who the product is supposed to serve. For a private company, the target audience consists of those people that the company believes will buy the product. For NGOs and government agencies that don't "sell" anything, the target audience would be the people who they are tasked with helping, and who they believe will use the product.

Write down who the target users are, as specifically as possible: age, gender, location, number of people, and so on. It can also help to write down who is *not* being targeted: for example, people without smartphones, people who are wealthy, or expats. The target users may vary across the list of potential actions you identified in Chapter 4. That's fine. Next to each potential action, write down the target users.

In all likelihood, some of the target users really aren't a good fit for the product, and you would waste your time trying to target them. That will be part of the user research and discover process; for now, we want to know the *potential* users that you should investigate further. You may end up targeting only a subset of them.

If the company has no idea who it is trying to serve, then it's back to the basics. A behavioral product, like any product, must serve a user need. It can only help people change their behavior to the extent that they care about the product at all. To get a handle on the unmet user need, you need a traditional market research or (nonbehavioral) product discovery process. That's beyond the scope of this book though; from here on, I'll assume you have a general sense of the target user already.

How Do the People Behave in Daily Life?

By the end of this process, the product team will have built a brand new experience. That new experience has to make sense for its users, given their existing habits and beliefs, their existing terminology, and their existing desires and needs. To do that well, the team needs to learn about their users up front.

To make this discussion concrete, I'll use an example from my past life as a microtargeter (someone who analyzes data about large numbers of individuals in order to identify people who are likely to take action, and what will appeal to them). One of my company's clients was an advocacy organization, which I'll call ActMore so they don't feel obliged to sue me. ActMore is an environmental NGO, and wanted to help its constituents become more involved in their community of like-minded environmentalists. They had a large number of people who had signed up for their email mailing list and newsletter, and had said they wanted to do more, but hadn't yet really gotten involved. First, ActMore needed the basics—information about age, location, income level, race, gender, political interests, and so on. My company used data that the organization already had to fill in most of the basics. We could use that to target the appeal and provide guidance on the website.

That type of analysis is all standard stuff and is well covered in any book on product development or assessing market opportunities (as well as in political advocacy books, in ActMore's case). We then started on the more interesting part, though, focused on behavior. We wanted to understand how strong the members' interest would be in a specific event the organization was putting together—a rally on Earth Day. We were looking specifically for divisions within the member base: groups of people that would respond differently to appeals to join the rally. Each group would get its own personalized appeal that made sense given its background and level of experience. The product that we were shaping was an outreach campaign and associated website (and, as I remember, there was a phone-calling component as well). So, we started digging into the data available about the members to understand what different types of members the product would need to serve.

With ActMore, and with other companies and organizations I've worked with, here are questions that I've found are most relevant to ask about the user base, from a behavior-changing perspective:

Prior experience with the action

Do these users have experience taking the target actions? (For ActMore—have they been to other, similar rallies?) How do they think about the action? Are there strong emotional associations, or is this fresh ground? It's much easier to increase an action than to start a new one. Existing *habits* around the goals are especially important.

Prior experience with similar products and channels

If the product employs email and a website, do some users have regular access to computer (and know how to use it) and others don't?

Relationship with the company or organization

To put it bluntly: do users trust you? You'll have a harder time making your case, and need a different set of appeals, for the people who don't trust you versus those that already know you and love you.

Existing motivation

Why would users want to achieve the outcome, completely separate from what the product offers them? In other words, what can the company build upon, so it doesn't need to do all of the work itself? One especially powerful aspect of motivation is social motivation (positive or negative). What will users' friends and family think if/when they take each of the actions on the list? Will they face a community of support, ridicule, or simple apathy?

Physical, psychological, or economic impediments to action

This isn't as common, but sometimes arises. Are there groups of users for whom the action is especially difficult? For example, users that are homebound or don't have the money to travel to the rally (we faced this with ActMore, in fact).

These five things make up the behavioral profile of the users. To gather this information, you can use the standard tools of market research and product development—look for existing quantitative data on user demographics, deploy field surveys, and conduct qualitative research with users in focus groups and one-on-one interviews.[79] *If at all possible, include some direct observation in the field—see how people actually act (and not just what they say they do).* If you're just exploring the idea for a product informally, or if no direct contact is possible with the user base (if business or privacy restrictions make it infeasible), then talk to people who have had contact with the target users, and glean what you can from them.

This approach obviously builds on existing tools and techniques. The innovation here is in adding questions directly focused on the target action: not how people feel about the product or their "user needs" per se, but their actual experiences, motivations, and problems vis-à-vis the company's target outcome and target action.

As you observe your users, you may witness or think up completely new ideas about what behaviors to change. For example, for your weight loss app, you may have thought about having users exercise or go on a diet, but after observing them, you realize that changing behavior to shop at a different grocery could be much more effective. Add that idea to the list and evaluate it along with the others. You may also realize that one (or more!) of the ideas just doesn't make sense. Later on in this chapter, there's a formal evaluation process. But if you know at this point without a doubt that one of your early ideas isn't feasible, save yourself time and cross it off the list.

Along the way, the team might also identify particular terms and concepts that resonate with the users; that's not the focus now, but it's still useful—put them aside to inform the UX design later on.

How Do the People Behave in the Application?

If your company or organization already has an existing application or product, great—it can be used to understand the diverse groups of users you have and how they will respond to the new product or feature being considered. If you don't already have a product serving these users, you can safely skip this step.

In my personal example, we couldn't work with ActMore's prior products to learn about users. So, I'll stretch my example a bit. Assume that ActMore already had a mobile and web platform for facilitating political action—called ActMore Now! In studying an existing product like ActMore Now!, start with standard questions from the user testing arena: how do users feel about the application, what features are they lacking, what different types of people use the product, who is most active in the system and why, etc. Then, add new questions focused on behavior:

Prior experience with the action

What features of the existing application are similar to the targeted action? Have the users built up existing habits that can be leveraged for the new targeted action?

Prior experience with the product

Which features were unsuccessful? What did those failures reveal about the characteristics of the users (particularly low attention space, impatience, or lack of background knowledge about a topic)?

Relationship with the company or organization

Are they showing that they trust you with their current usage of the application?

Existing motivation

What motivations or interests are underlying the most successful features of the application? How does using the current application interact with users' daily lives, and especially their social lives? Are there communities built around using the application?

As you can see, the questions are very similar to those used when analyzing users outside the context of the product: motivation, prior experience, and trust. But the answers are all the more valuable as a guide because they relate to user behavior in the context of the product itself.

Practically, this process means watching, interviewing, and/or surveying existing users to understand their views of the application, their frustrations, and their joys. Make sure to include some direct observation of people as they go about their lives and use the application.[80] It also means analyzing existing usage patterns within the application to see what parts of the application have been successful at catching users' attention. Especially important is measuring the behaviors of users on tasks related to the application's top-level goal and analyzing how the population has responded to existing interventions.

Generate Personas

Next, you can use the information you've gathered to identify broad groups of (potential) users within your target population. I know the term is a bit loaded, but I like to generate formal user personas—short descriptions of archetypal users, with a simple background statement about a sample user's life. (You can accomplish the same thing, in your own way, without the life-stories part, as long as you get a clear idea of the groups of users within the population). Since designing for behavior change entails changing nitty-gritty details of peoples' lives, it's valuable to keep in mind vivid, realistic, specific personas—and not an amorphous vague concept of "our users."

Unlike traditional user personas, these personas are all about behavior: groups of users who are likely to interact with the application differently and *who are likely to respond differently to behavioral interventions*. Each persona should have information about the topics discussed; Table 5-1 gives one way to organize them. The examples are inspired by my work at HelloWallet, and the target action is saving money for emergencies among a population that hasn't used online savings tools before.

TABLE 5-1. Two sample personas about saving money for emergencies

	FRUGALS	SPENDTHRIFTS
Experience with similar actions	Always keeps emergency savings	No real experience saving for emergencies
Experience with similar products	Hasn't needed to use online products—saves by default	Only passing familiarity with online saving tools, and they seemed boring
Relationship to the company	None	None
Existing motivations around emergency saving	Saving for emergencies is clearly important, and something this group already does. So why listen to advice? Key motivations and uncertainties include: are they saving enough? What else and when should they save for other things?	Saving for the future is far away and not a motivation on its own. However, this group wants to be able to continue to live a fun lifestyle. Saving for future *fun* (especially when short on cash and they don't want to look boring) is a possible motivation.
Hard barriers to action	N/A	Doesn't have excess money to save currently
Sample bio	Jane is 33, married, and fears falling into poverty like her parents did when her father lost his job at the auto factory.	John is 28, single, lives with friends, and spends everything he's got on good food and good times.

REPEAT THE PROCESS FOR EACH POTENTIAL ACTION

These behavioral personas are *relative to a particular target action*, since the goal is to create a set of personas that are likely to respond differently to the product's attempts to change behavior. In other words, quickly look over each of the five questions (experience with similar actions, experience with similar products, etc.) and generate additional personas as needed for each of the potential user actions. Often, the resulting personas may be the same across various actions, but be prepared for them to be different. Next to each target action, list the personas that are relevant for it. We'll simplify down to a few personas once we've chosen the target action for the product.

TWO TECHNIQUES FOR GENERATING THEM

Here are two approaches to synthesizing the personas themselves. First, you can use the five questions (experience with similar actions, experience with similar products, etc.) to spur ideas for personas in an open-ended way. For example: is there a group of users that is clearly more experienced taking this action than others? What are they like? Who would be an archetypal example of that group?

Second, you can use the questions in a more formal way to selected from a fixed set of possible characteristics. For example, there are five questions, and, at their simplest, each of them is a binary yes-no. Look at each possible combination of answers to those questions. On a first pass, you can eliminate most of them as not relevant to your population (e.g., physical impediments may not be relevant to your product; that cuts the options down in half immediately). After that quick pass through the options, you can ask whether you really have any users that fit those criteria, and what they are like as a group. Each remaining option gives you a persona.

One reason that I like the second method, odd as it may appear, is that is completely covers the range of possible users. It makes you think about each "type" and decide whether or not it's relevant. Ideally, your personas should be *exhaustive and mutually exclusive*: every person in the target population *best* fits into one, and only one, persona. You can do this in a less structured way than the previous example by drawing a simple box that represents your entire user population (Figure 5-1).

For each persona you think of, mark it off as a portion of the box, with a rough estimate of the group's size. If personas overlap—or one is part of another—that's OK. Look at each overlapping piece as a separate group of people. As you're running out of ideas, ask, *who isn't in one of these groups?* What are they like? Label each group, see if some of them are redundant from a behavioral perspective (i.e., you expect them to respond to the product's appeal to change behavior in the same way). Then, use those informal groups to come up with more detailed personas.

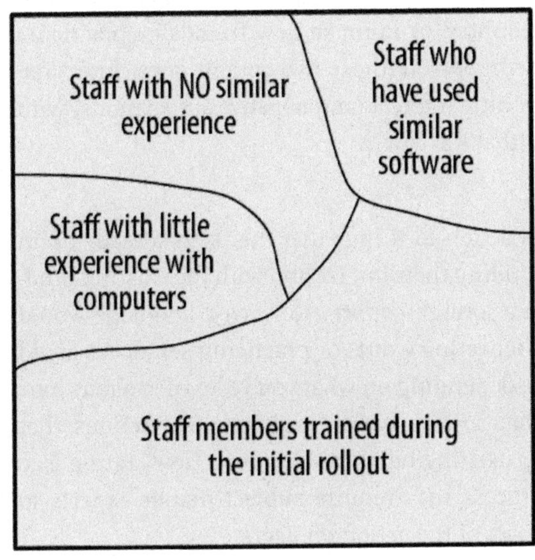

FIGURE 5-1.
A sample population breakdown to generate personas. This is from a startup I spoke with about encouraging employees at an office to utilize a package their employer had purchased for them.

Select the Ideal Target Action

By this point, the company has a list of potential actions that users can take, and a set of user personas (with their motivations, prior experience, and impediments to action). Now it's time to combine them, and narrow down the list.

Before getting too fancy, remove actions that are directly blocked by known impediments, especially if similar actions were tried but weren't successful in a previous version of the product. Next, take each action and score it along the following criteria, ranking it *low*, *middle*, or *high*. To make the process more concrete, imagine that the target outcome is to help users learn a new language:[81]

Impact (on outcome)
: How effectively would it achieve the outcome? In other words, assume that every user does the action, without reservation—how much would it help? When learning a new language, the action of repeating one word is not very effective and gets a "low"; practicing some sentences might be "middle"; immersing oneself in a foreign country gets "high."

Motivation (for user)

What motivation do users have to perform the action? Draw upon the data about the users' existing motivations and their social interactions around the product. Users may be really excited to travel to a foreign country, or to make new friends by practicing their language skills in person (those two options get a "high" rating). They may have little interest (and negative associations) with rote memorization (that's a "low").

Ease (for user)

How similar is this action to things that the users already do in their daily lives (including their interaction with the existing product)? Immersion in a foreign country to learn a language would (usually) be "low." Repeating words or practicing sentences could be medium or high, depending on what you've learned about your users. Existing habits always get a "high" rating. Actions that require users to *stop* existing habits always get a "low" rating (see Chapter 3). This process may require subject matter experts to gauge the likely impact of the action on users.

Cost (for company)

How easy would it be for the company to implement a solution around the action? True language immersion would be "low" for online products. Live conversation with native speakers could be a "medium," depending on the existing resources and capabilities of the company. Providing scripts for users to repeat would be easy. This rating may require a lead engineer to assess potential resource costs.

With these ratings in hand, look for obvious outliers. If there's a standout winner, great. If not, remove any hands-down losers. If this doesn't narrow down the list enough, make a judgment call about what's most important and feasible for the company, given their business strategy. If resources are tight, then the cost of implementation naturally becomes rather important!

Behavioral economics can be useful here—certain behaviors and ways of thinking are inherently more difficult for (most) users. We covered many of the high-level lessons from this literature in Chapter 1. For example, behaviors that require extensive mental calculations are difficult and often avoided. Actions that focus on long-term gains over short-term losses are also contrary to much of our cognitive machinery (losses are more painful than gains are good, short-term gains are valued more highly than long-term ones).

Beyond that, there's not more guidance to give here, unfortunately. Keep narrowing down the list until one top choice remains, or two neck-and-neck options that can be tested in practice.

After you've decided your target outcome, actor, and action, and have a set of behaviorally informed user personas, then what? Let's fine-tune the target population a bit.

Define Success and Failure

You now have all the things you need to determine what success and failure would mean for your product *before you build it*. You know who the product is supposed to serve. You know what action you're trying to drive. And, you know what real-world outcome that action is supposed to cause. You don't have all of the details, of course, but that's OK. At this stage, you have the rough outlines you need.

Write down in a sentence that says what the product is supposed to be doing, and for whom. For example:

> *This product will help active people (actor) track their exercise (action), and maintain their ideal weight (outcome).*

From your user research about what's feasible for users to accomplish, and from your market research about what will differentiate and sell the product, you should be able to add in additional specifics about the proposed product and its impact on your business. For example:

> *This product will help 25 to 35-year-old active people in urban areas (actor) track their daily exercise routine (action), to build muscle tone and lose five pounds more per year than they otherwise would (outcome). When successful, it should double our current revenue (company objective).*

In this statement, the team is saying: if this happens, the product will be a success; if not, it will be a (complete or partial) failure. In a lean startup environment, you would then generate specific hypotheses around each of these elements, and test your assumptions in the field. Later on, in Chapter 12, this statement will also drive the metrics we use to measure whether the product actually succeeded or failed at its goals.

Our goal isn't to create a false sense of security by thinking we can forecast the future and how the product will actually play out. There are lots of assumptions built into this definition of outcome, actor, and action. We want to draw out those assumptions, to get something that can be explicitly tested and then revised as lessons are learned. And, perhaps most importantly, it helps us fail fast—to make sure that the key stakeholders in the company are on the same page before building the product. If they aren't, now's the time to fix it.

How to Handle Very Diverse Populations

While you were generating behavioral user personas, or evaluating how effective your target action would be for each them, you undoubtedly found some differences across the population. One lesson I've often found is that, *for most behaviors, a one-size-fits-all product won't work*. We are all just too different. An exercise program that recommends that couch potatoes and Olympic athletes run a mile a week is going to fail them both—too difficult for one, and too easy for the other.

If you have a homogenous user base, cool. Not a problem. But if you have very different groups of users, especially with widely varying levels of prior experience, then the product team needs to make some tough choices.

You may confront this problem as you're initially researching your target user population, because you already have a general sense of what you'll ask them to do and see trouble coming. Or, it may come out only as you are trying to identify the ideal action for your users and recognize that there really isn't *one* ideal action that covers all of them. Whenever it occurs, here are two approaches you can take:

- Plan to adapt or personalize the app to diverse groups.
- Narrow down the target audience, and accept that the product won't work (as) well for some people.

In each case, if a single (nonadaptive) product can't serve all of the intended audience, it's best to identify that now rather than after months of wrangling with the product to do impossible things.

Planning for Adaptation or Personalization

Faced with a diverse population, the company can plan to adapt the product to serve its needs. Here are ways that adaptation can work, with an example of a mobile app that encourages daily exercise:

- *The application learns about the user* and provides guidance and support relevant for the user's needs. For example, by swapping in and out relevant actions (run versus walk), or by customizing each action (run for 10 minutes versus run for 5 hours).
  - *Benefits.* Greatest degree of personalization.
  - *Challenges.* If the application guesses wrong, it can anger and lose the trust of the user.
- *The application allows the user to self-select* what is most relevant for her. For example, "How much would you like to run today?" or "Click here for beginner suggestions or here for advanced ones."
  - *Benefits.* No guesswork on the part of the application.
  - *Challenges.* The user may not know the right level for her. This is especially true for people just starting out with a new behavior.
- *The application has multiple versions.* The company then segments the audience and markets/delivers the version of the application that is most appropriate for that audience.
  - *Benefits.* Clear branding and expectations on the part of users. Can be combined with other techniques like user-level personalization.
  - *Challenges.* Very costly in terms of resources and team focus.

Narrowing Down the Target Audience

If the proposed product simply can't be adapted to meet the diverse needs of the target population, then some people are going to be left with a suboptimal experience. If the company tries to create a single (nonadaptive) version of the product that appeals to everyone, then the lowest common denominator is unlikely to please anyone. Instead, the company should intentionally target subsets of the audience and make them the main focus of the product.

There may be clear business reasons to focus on some users over others. For example, maybe parents with children will pay more than single people for a service that promotes healthy eating at home. For NGOs and government agencies, there may be a clear mandate to serve certain populations (like helping subsistence farmers in arid climates to use crop insurance, before working with other farmers).

Adapting Dynamically to Each Person

You've probably noticed that after you've searched for a product online, you start seeing ads for it everywhere you go. Advertisers can dynamically adjust which ads you see on the Web based on your unique online history—it's called behavioral targeting (Deschene 2008; Drell 2011). They collect data across numerous websites and social networking services to build a live profile of what you're interested in (and what they can make money from), and then deploy ads accordingly.

Similar adaptive techniques are now being explicitly used for persuasion and for behavior change. For example, researchers Kaptein and Eckles developed a method to dynamically create *persuasion profiles* of individuals as they interacted with an online bookstore; the profiles assessed the types of recommendations that were most effective at convincing each person (Kaptein and Eckles 2010; Pariser 2011). This method has been used for positive behavior change as well; for example, researchers provided a series of dynamically targeted reminders to users of an exercise tracker (Kaptein and van Halteren 2012).

Adaptive, individualized content is not widespread yet in the behavior change space. However, over time, I expect that will change.

If you aren't sure, a simple strategy is this: focus on the people you think you can actually help. Build a product that works for some people and for whom there's a market. Then expand or adjust it to work for others, if needed. That's much easier, and more rewarding for the team, than trying to take on the hardest population to serve first, and struggling to get any traction at all.

For example, if you're developing an exercise tracker *that is eventually intended to reach a general audience*, it makes natural sense to focus initially on people who are already fit and active.[82] Trying to build an exercise tracker that appeals to clinically obese and sedentary people is a much harder problem, and one that you can work up to over time as you build on prior successes. It might take a completely new product to reach that audience, or significant changes to your current product; either way, you'll at least have some experience under your belt as you tackle the challenge.

No matter what choice you make, make the choice early. Be clear on who exactly you need to serve, before you build the product.

On a Napkin

This chapter is all about getting your ducks in a row so you're ready to tackle the design.

Here's what you need to do

- Research and document the characteristics of your users, especially around prior experience with the action, prior experience with the product, existing motivations to act, their relationship with the company (trust), and barriers to action.
- Generate behavioral personas—groups of users that you expect will respond differently to your product's attempts to change behavior.
- Rate the actions on your list of potential action for users to take (from Chapter 4) in terms of their effectiveness, cost, motivation, and feasibility for the user.
- Select the ideal target action, based on these criteria.

How you'll know there's trouble

- It looks like all of the users are alike—they usually aren't. You probably haven't dug deeply enough into their existing experiences and behaviors.
- When rating potential actions, all of the actions are rated similarly, or all of them are too expensive to the company or infeasible for the user to be realistic (sorry, go back and think up more user actions).

Deliverables

- Detailed observations about your users
- A set of user personas, indicating the main groups of users of our application (or potential users) and their characteristics
- A clear statement of the target outcome, actor, and action

[*Part III*]

Developing the Conceptual Design

The task of designing a product around a specific behavior might seem daunting—there are hundreds of cognitive mechanisms at work, a wide diversity of personalities and needs among potential users, and countless small choices that need to be made about how the product itself looks and acts.

We can make that process manageable by breaking it down into small chunks. In Chapter 2, we talked about the mind's five processes that are preconditions for action—a *cue*, an intuitive *reaction*, a deliberative *evaluation*, the *ability* to act, and the right *timing*. But how do these preconditions come together at the same time?

Each decision to act (or not) occurs within a particular context: made up of the *user*, the *environment*, and the potential *action*. The decision is shaped by users' backgrounds—their prior history, personality, knowledge, and other traits. The decision is also shaped by the characteristics of their *environment*—what the product does, the person's physical surroundings beyond the product, their friends and colleagues, and the external rewards (or punishments) they'll receive if they take the action. Finally, the decision is shaped by the *action* itself—whether it is difficult for them to take, how it is structured, and what subtasks are required, if any.

That context (action, environment, and user) will either enable the user to pass all five stages of the Create Action Funnel, or it will block them. In order words, the Create Action Funnel indicates *what* needs to be in place for action to occur; the context indicates *whether* those preconditions actually come together (or not).

The purpose of the design process is to create a context that drives action. Products can shape each aspect of that context by:[83]

- *Structuring the action* to make it feasible and inviting for the user;
- *Constructing the environment* to support the action; and
- *Preparing the user* to take the action.

To make this concrete, think about what it would take to help someone build a building (see Figure Part III-1). First, you can design the building itself in a way that is feasible for the user to build, and document it with a blueprint. That's *structuring the action*. Second, you can provide products (a building planning application, wood and other materials, a paycheck for doing the work) that give the person the motivation and resources needed to act. That's *constructing the environment*. Finally, you can *prepare the user* with the necessary education, skills, and confidence to make it happen.

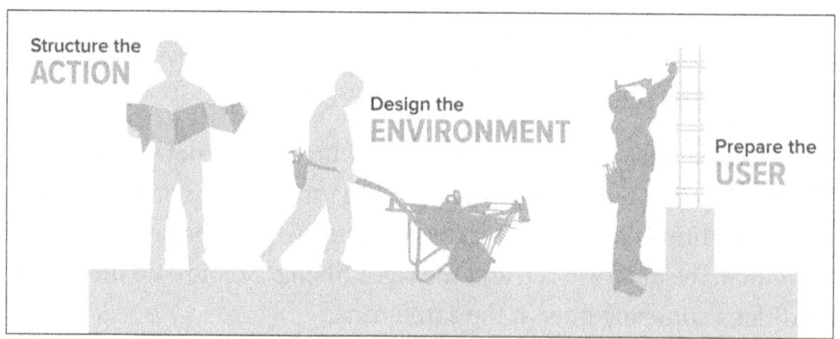

FIGURE PART III-1. The three targets of design: the action, the environment, and the user

In each case, we are setting up the preconditions for action to occur. But we focus our attention in different areas (action, environment, and user) in order to make the process manageable and to make sure we don't miss key opportunities to support the behavior.

The next three chapters undertake each of these steps—structuring the action, constructing the environment, and preparing the user—one at a time. We'll begin by developing the *conceptual design* of the product, which provides the team with the product's core concepts and *functional* goals.

[6]

Structuring the Action

Barack Obama was in the midst of the struggle over the Affordable Care Act (aka "Obamacare"). His team wanted to mobilize supporters to call into radio programs in support of the legislation. In the last election cycle and beyond, they had built an impressive set of online tools to onboard potential supporters and get them involved in the campaign—from calling potential voters to making campaign contributions themselves.

But calling into a radio show? That was a particularly nasty challenge, and something that most American's aren't familiar with doing, especially about a piece of new, complex legislation.[84]

How did the campaign do it? Figure 6-1 gives a screenshot from the campaign's online mobilization platform, circa February 2010. They intelligently structured the action into something volunteers could reasonably do. They broke the action down into three manageable chunks. They automated parts of the process, such as figuring out what number to call. They simplified and provided "defaults" for other parts of the process, with a script of discussion points to mention during the call. They gave clear instructions. They provided positive encouragement.

That's what this chapter is about—structuring an action so people can actually do it. We'll start by breaking down the action into its component parts, and then simplifying them and tailoring them to what we know about our users. In doing so, we'll develop a start-to-finish *behavioral plan* showing how we envision people using our product to change their behavior.

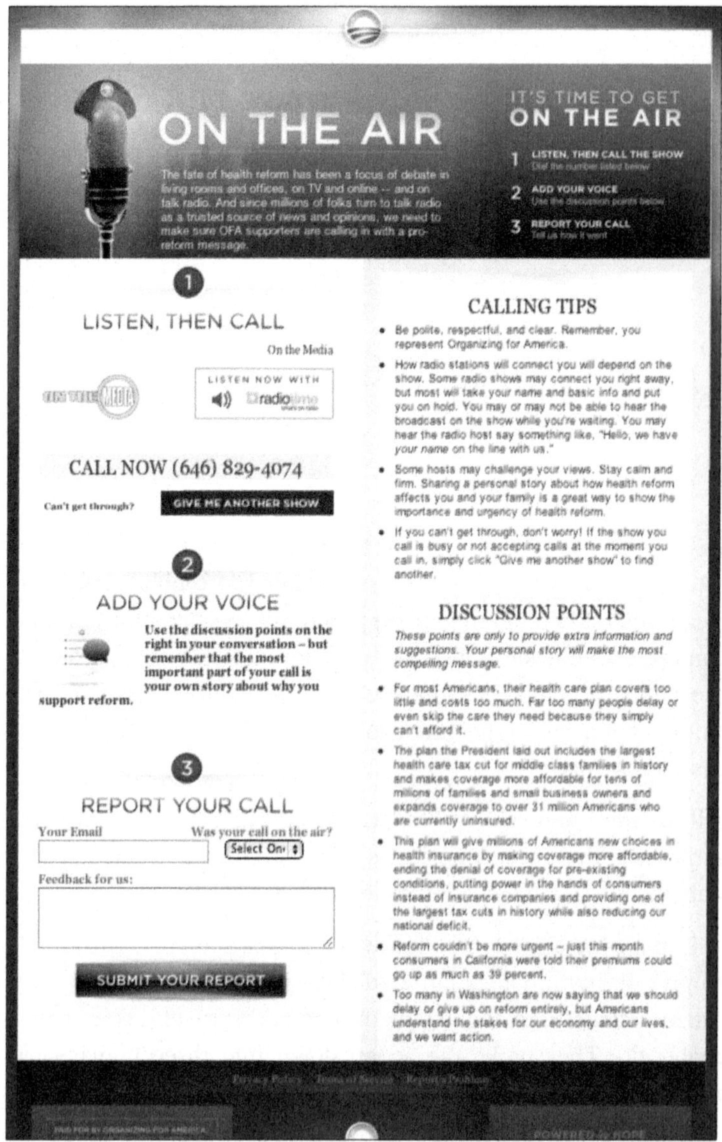

FIGURE 6-1. Image from *barackobama.com* as of February 2010; snapshot taken by *http://www.thepoliticalguide.com/*

Start the Behavioral Plan

You know what you want to do—help volunteers call a radio show on behalf of your cause. You know something about your users—they are interested volunteers, but most have never called a radio program as part of an advocacy campaign. Now what?

Well, in order to call into a radio program, the volunteer will need to:

1. Find a quiet time and place with a radio and a phone.
2. Identify the radio program.
3. Listen to the radio program for an appropriate time to call.
4. Get the number to call.
5. Work up the gumption to actually call.
6. Call the program.
7. Convince the person screening calls that the volunteer has something interesting (and not crazy) to say.
8. Say something intelligible on the radio show itself.
9. Tell the volunteer HQ that the call was made, so other volunteers can spread out their efforts to other shows.

That's a heck of a lot to do. Imagine if your product simply told users to "find a radio program and call them about this issue." Each person would have to plan out the long list of things required, find the confidence to try this new strange thing, and not get distracted by other concerns along the way. They would also need to do some serious prior planning—planning ahead to find the program, find time in the day to call with having access to a radio, thinking about what to say, and so on.

Good luck. In fact, only a fraction of Americans have *ever* called into a talk show, and an even smaller subset has called in this premeditated, advocacy-oriented way.[85]

To use another example, for someone to take up running as exercise, there's a lot more that's required than simply walking out the front door and starting to run. Some of the prior steps include (a) getting running shoes, (b) identifying a route and "reasonable" distance, (c) finding the time to do it, (d) remembering to do it, (e) making sure you haven't eaten heavily beforehand, and more. Again, a heck of a lot to do.

That's why we have products that can help people take action and make unwieldy tasks like these feasible. The process starts by writing out the obvious steps a user would normally take to complete the action. Make it detailed. List each physical and mental piece of work that's required, like the radio program example.

Now that you have a basic list of steps, let's flesh it out into a full behavioral plan.

Write or Draw It Out, and Add Behavioral Detail

The behavioral plan is a depiction of the individual steps users should take from whatever they are doing now, all the way through using the product and completing the target action. Some of those steps will occur inside of the product, and some require behavior that is completely outside of it. The plan examines, at each step of the way, what's going on with users and *why* they would continue to the next step.

For those in the UX world, this should sound familiar, and intentionally so. You can express the behavioral plan with a variety of design tools. I'm partial to customer experience maps, like the one depicted in Figure 6-2. They can not only include the stages of the individual experience, but they can also draw out the "customer types" (similar to our personas), areas of frustration and delight, and user emotions along the way. Related tools include a touch-point inventory and map, empathy maps, and journey maps (Kolko 2011).[86]

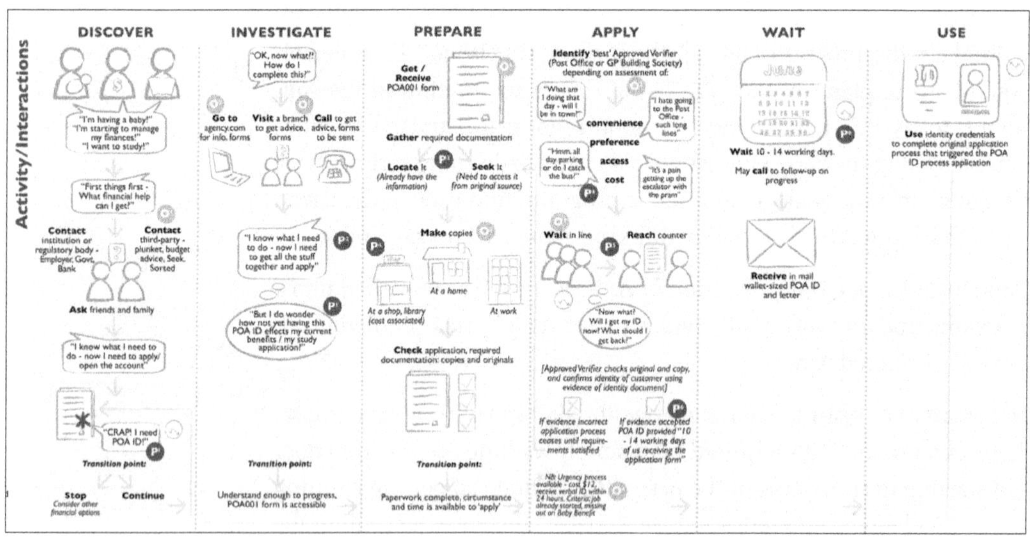

FIGURE 6-2.
Part of a customer experience map from Mel Edwards, *desonance.wordpress.com*

Personally, I don't have a graphic design background, so I've used much simpler tools to accomplish the same thing:

- The humble flowchart, with notes in a sidebar
- A written narrative, describing the user's experience and mental state at each step

- A hierarchical outline, where each top-level point is a step in the user journey and under each point is a description of what's happening with the user during that step

No matter which tool you use to express it, developing the initial behavioral plan is a bit different than a normal customer experience map process (if you're familiar with that process; if not, don't worry). Namely, make sure you cover the following points:

1. Write/draw out the rough sequence of steps in the real world—not just in your product—that a user must take to complete the action. (That's what we did in the previous section, listing the nine steps that person would have to take to call into a radio program.)
    a. The reason I start with the real world is that for many behaviors—controlling finances, exercising, getting politically active, decreasing energy usage—the product only interacts with part of the story, but all of it determine whether users will actually change their behavior or not.
    b. To be successful, you'll usually need to plan for how the product indirectly affects those other steps.
2. Label each of the steps as:
    a. Something that the user must do *within the product*;
    b. *Something the product should do* in response to the user; and
    c. *All of the other things that need to be accomplished* "in the real world" (outside of the product) on the behavioral plan.
3. *Look for missing steps, especially for new users.* Take the perspective of a completely new user—one who has never interacted with your product. Are there additional steps required in the beginning (e.g., registration)?
4. *Look for one-time steps.* Take the perspective of an experienced user—one that has often interacted with your product. Are there steps that can be skipped for experienced folks?

For example, in the case of the Obama campaign, with volunteers calling in to radio programs, some of the steps clearly had to occur outside of the product—such as 1, "Find a quiet time and place with a radio and a phone" and 3, "Listen to the radio program for an appropriate time to call." Most of the rest could be done within the app. For repeat-callers, they might need to do 2 or 4 ("Identify the radio program" and "Get the number to call").

That's the initial behavioral plan. Nothing too fancy. Now it's time to refine it and add some more behavioral magic.

Tailor It

With a simple sequence of steps in hand, now it's time to apply what you learned about your users in Chapter 5. This is the same basic process that we went through in that chapter, but now we repeat it for each of the individual steps in the behavioral plan.

1. Take each of the main personas developed in Chapter 5, and *walk through the process from their perspective*, as if you've never thought about the product before:
    a. Is this familiar or unfamiliar? What are you thinking? What're your motivations? Would *you* continue to use the app?
    b. The responses to these questions can be expressed with a set of simple comments on sticky notes.
    c. Jot down or attach the personas to the behavioral plan to help keep them in mind.
2. See if the steps can build on existing skills the users already have.
3. Note particular obstacles users face, and see if the steps can be changed to avoid those actions.

You have the most control over steps that occur within the product itself, of course. But you can also use the product to *reach out of screen and touch the user's daily life*. For example, guidelines given within the product, and even the marketing materials that surround the product, define the action for the user. They shape how the users think about the action, and what it is they try to accomplish, in their daily lives outside of the product. The basic definition of what behavior is being changed (and how) can and should be tailored to fit the user base.

Back to the Obama example: two of the personas that designers had to contend with were completely inexperienced, first-time volunteers and very experienced and efficient "just get it done" folks, who wouldn't want to be slowed down by a lot of handholding. Major obstacles for the first-time volunteers would be step 5 ("Work up the gumption to actually call"), and step 8 ("Say something intelligible on the radio show itself"). Clear instructions on the screen, with a sample script, could help inexperienced people get past that hurdle, without unduly interfering with experienced callers.

Simplify It

Pare It Down to the Minimum Viable Action

Remember that the Minimum Viable Action is the shortest, simplest version of the target action that the users absolutely must take to test the idea. As you've thought through the target action, and broken it down into a sequence of steps, you might have realized that there are extraneous parts. Or that you can think about the action differently and make it simpler. Or you might have started with a MVA, but were tempted to add on bells and whistles as you sketched out the sequence of steps. Well, now it's time to tighten up that MVA. Cut back until only the necessary remains:

- *Cut repeated actions down to the first action.* One-time actions are easier for users to perform and engineering teams to build than repeated ones, all else being equal. And they still provide valuable insight into whether the software works at supporting the behavior.
- *Cut big actions down to simpler ones.* Will the target outcome be achieved if the user takes a shorter, simpler action? The goal is to test the core premise, as with a Minimum Viable Product (i.e., instead of asking people to call all of their local radio stations, can they just call one?).
- *Drop steps in the sequence altogether that are just nice to have.* For example, allow the user to take notes on how the call went.
- *Focus on the high-risk, uncertain, parts of the sequence and flesh them out* (i.e., getting the person comfortable making a call at all) before developing the lower-risk parts (having the person customize the script to use during the call).

Cheat If You Can

Now that the action itself is back down to the Minimum Viable Action, let's see how we can shift the burden for the remaining work from the user to the product—i.e., use the "cheating" strategy overall, or within each of the individual steps the user has to take.

Look over the behavioral plan again. It is possible to automate away the whole action? If not the whole action, is it possible to cheat at any of the individual steps along the way?

With the Obama call-in radio program, it was impossible to automate the whole thing. But certain parts of it could easily be automated and defaulted. For example, the advocacy platform could:

- Automatically match the user up with a call-in radio program and provide the necessary phone number to call, saving the user the need to research relevant radio shows.
- Make finding a radio unnecessary (incidental to using the software), by streaming the call-in program through the app itself.
- Provide intelligent defaults for what to say while on the air (e.g., a simple script that the user can edit and personalize as needed).

Obama's call-in campaign for the Affordable Care Act, shown in Figure 6-1, did all three of these. That's where it really shined.

By simplifying the process, automating, defaulting, or making steps incidental, you remove unnecessary work for the user. In terms of the Create Action Funnel from Chapter 2, that means decreasing the costs of action (part of the mind's conscious evaluation) and increasing the basic physical ability to take action. This simplification process allows you to focus attention on more intractable behaviors or more exciting (to the user) parts of the application. Another way to accomplish this is to find potential habits.

Identify Potential Habits

Look over the behavioral plan again. Are there steps that are frequently repeated without much variation? For example, maybe your behavioral plan includes "run each morning for 30 minutes." Those are candidates for habits. Following the discussion in Chapter 3, is there a clear cue that either already exists or can be added to the product that will tell the user "it's time to act"? Is there an immediate, meaningful reward at the end of the step? If so, then you can simplify the problem of "help the user do X 1,000 times" to "help the user build a habit around X."

Make It "Easy"

In addition to simplifying the action itself, you can help make it "easy" for the user to do, in two ways:

- Easy for the user to understand, and thus for the application to convey to the user
- Feasible to accomplish, from the user's perspective

The first one is relatively straightforward. Look at the behavioral plan, and specifically the parts that the application instructs the user to do something. Write down how those parts would be described to a prospective user in at most two sentences.

For each step, ask whether each of the user personas identified in Chapter 5 would understand that description. As needed, run it by some sample users (I'll talk about formal user testing later, though).

Another way of thinking about understandability is *cognitive overhead*, or "how many logical connections or jumps your brain has to make in order to understand or contextualize the thing you're looking at" (Demaree 2011). Figuring out what to do shouldn't be guesswork for the user. That may mean making the action slightly more *difficult* to undertake, in order for it to be easy to understand (Lieb 2013).

The second part is all about appearances, from the user's perspective. We briefly discussed this in Chapter 2 under the ability stage of the Create Action Funnel: if you think you aren't going to be able to do something, you're less likely to even try. The underlying research comes from Bandura's concept of self-efficacy: the belief that you yourself can be effective at the task (Bandura 1977a).

Combine Where Possible

Each step in the sequence should represent the *largest* possible chunk of the work that is still understandable and feasible. Look for ways to combine multiple steps into one. *Largest?* Yes. There is a tension between breaking the action into steps to make each one more manageable and having so many steps that it overwhelms the user. There's no hard-and-fast rule, but keep this in mind especially when you see any sequence that's more than a dozen individual steps!

Avoid Common Mistakes

Here are two of the common mistakes I've seen at this stage.

IT IS EASY!

The first common mistake is to be satisfied when it's easy for *you* to do. Too often, especially in my prior political advocacy work, I've seen campaigns that expected people to come to a night-long vigil, write a letter to their representatives from scratch about an issue the author knew little about, or organize a local group of activists on their own. These are each daunting, complex tasks to someone who has never done them before—though relatively straightforward to those who have already built up the expertise.

It's quite difficult to step outside of your own experience (if only because once you think of the action, your System 1 immediately activates the relevant prior experiences, and it really does *feel* easy on an intuitive level). If there's any doubt though, run the proposal by someone who has never taken the action before.

HARD WORK BUILDS COMMITMENT

Another common mistake is to believe that work makes commitment, and to allow the user's tasks to be difficult *on purpose*. This view is half-right, half-wrong. Effort can build commitment to a product, and a commitment to continue what you've started. People that complete difficult tasks (successfully, and without undue grief) are more committed to continuing further. In psychology, and economics, there's the well-known mental blip called the "sunk cost effect": the more work you put into something, the less willing you are to let go of it—even when it is not in your economic interest.

If users see the target action as a difficult, substantial task—great. *After* the action is completed, they will be committed. The product's job is to get as many people as possible across the finish line. The "make 'em work hard" approach leads to very committed people who finish—but those committed people are only a small subset of the people that could have completed the task; that creates the illusion of effectiveness—because everyone else has already been filtered out!

So, building commitment doesn't mean that each step needs to be a pain in the butt, or that we should *design* an application to be difficult. For any "hard" behavior (exercising, learning a language, etc.), there will be things that the product can make easier, and things that it can't. Make the things that can be made easier easy—and then build up the excitement on the remaining tasks that are hard. Provide users with a sense of accomplishment for the tasks that are truly difficult—and not just badly designed.[87]

Provide "Small Wins"

In addition to being *easy*, each step should be *meaningful* enough that the user can feel a sense of accomplishment afterward. It's up to the product to help users feel that accomplishment (often by presenting it as progress toward the target action), but the step itself needs to support it. In the research literature, this is called "small wins"—if after each small step, people feel they've done something, and they're closer to finishing their goal. They are then more likely to continue.

For example, in my work at HelloWallet, we had a tricky problem when we designed our guidance—how much should you encourage people to commit to save each month? Authors such as Jean Chatzky (2009) tell their readers to save about $10 a day. That is simple and clean, but either way too easy or too hard for many users. We have users that struggle to put aside $10 each week, let alone each day; we also have users to whom $10 is a rounding error, and a laughable goal. So, we constructed a meaningful step on the path to greater savings that provided small wins, regardless of their financial means—we calculated the target amount as a percentage of income (and then rounded to the nearest clean, simple number that people would remember).

In order for an action to provide a "small win," it needs another characteristic—it must be clear to the user that the step has actually been completed. In other words, there must be a clear definition of success or failure. Weight loss applications are a great example—they set a specific, unambiguous weight target. An example of an unclear target would be a step that tells users to "cut down" on smoking. It doesn't allow users to know if they are succeeding: if users have to wonder whether they've done it right or not, they are distracted, and you lose them.

On a Napkin

Here's what you need to do

- Break the target action into discrete steps that the user needs to complete. These pieces should be:
  - Simple and straightforward (easy to understand)
  - Easy to complete (both appearing easy to the user and being easy in practice to execute)
  - "Small" (so that the user sees clear progress after each step)
  - Meaningful enough to reward after completion
  - Straightforward to see when they are complete (so they the user will clearly know if the action was successful or not, immediately after making an attempt)

How you'll know there's trouble

- When team members can't clearly and simply convey what the user is supposed to do
- When no one outside the company has been asked how difficult the action is

Deliverables

- The behavioral plan: the specific sequence of steps users should take

[7]

Constructing the Environment

My wife has a Fitbit One—a small exercise tracker that hooks onto clothing, displays progress on a screen, and sends over detailed information to a computer or smartphone.

The Fitbit One does many things right to help encourage exercise. It automates two very annoying (and therefore action-inhibiting) parts of the exercise process: it automates the process of tracking how much exercise the person has had, and it automates uploading that information onto a computer or phone. Those are examples of structuring the action—by shifting the burden of work from the user to the product (aka "cheating").

The device also does a number of things, beyond changing the action itself, to help users *take* the action of exercising. For example:

- *It reminds people to exercise.* For example, it gives random "Chatter" messages on the screen; I still smile as I remember when I first saw the message, "Walk Me."
- *It provides immediate and meaningful feedback.* Shortly after my wife got it, I remember her looking at the screen and seeing she'd walked something like 9,945 steps. She just started running around the room, to break the 10,000-steps threshold.

These tactics are two examples of how a product can construct the user's decision-making environment to help them take action. That's the topic of this chapter.

Tactics You Can Use

Thus far, you should have a clear sequence of steps that the user will take in order to complete the target action. You've found the Minimum Viable Action, automated parts of it, and made parts of the process shorter, less taxing, and more familiar to the user.

Now, let's assume the action itself is set in stone. Users need to do X, Y, and Z to succeed. How can you help users take that action? One way is to structure the environment to encourage the action.

By environment, I mean two things:

The product itself
: For software applications, the primary "environment" enveloping the user is the product—particularly, the web pages where the user takes action, or the tiny progress screen on the Fitbit One tracker.

The rest of the user's local environment
: While using your application, the user is also embedded in a physical environment (trying to use your application while on the subway, with a spotty Internet connection), and a social environment outside of the application (a set of expectations from friends on the "right" behaviors).

Clearly, you have the most control over the first part of the environment: the product, including the app and related hardware like the Fitbit One tracker. However, with good user research, you can leverage the rest of the individual's environment to increase the impact of the application.

Remember that the design process occurs at two levels. You start with the conceptual level, where you develop a behavioral plan that describes steps the user takes within and outside of the product. Then you proceed to the interface design level, when you develop and review individual screens of the product and the interactions that occur on them. Thus far, we're working at the conceptual level with a behavioral plan (expressed as a journey map or narrative, for example); we'll stay at that level for now. In a later chapter, we'll come back to the interface design level, but the design considerations and process are very similar.

There are five main ways that products can construct the users' environment (the product software itself, and, sometimes the surrounding environment) to help them take action:

1. Increase motivation.
2. Cue the user to act.
3. Generate a feedback loop.
4. Remove competition.
5. Remove obstacles.

Let's look at each of these, in turn. To keep things concrete, I'll use the example of exercising throughout this chapter. I'll draw examples from the Fitbit (what my wife has and loves) and a similar product, which was much less effective and shall remain nameless (I had one of them, before I returned it for reasons I'll explain later).

Increase Motivation

How can the product motivate people to act? There are myriad ways, and you can think about them along four dimensions:

New versus existing
: A product can add new motivation or highlight a user's existing motivation to act. *Ideally, you want to leverage existing motivations first.*

Rewards versus punishment
: A product can reward people for taking an action or punish them for not taking it. *You should avoid punishing your users.*

Type of motivator
: A product can pay people to act, increase their esteem among friends, help them feel a sense of mastery and accomplishment, or provide a variety of rewards via other motivators. *There are no "best motivators"—find the right motivators for your particular users.*

Current versus future motivation
: The benefit of changing behavior may be far in the future; for example, one benefit of getting in shape is living longer. The problem is, the future just isn't real. *Translate future motivations into something meaningful in the present.*

The following sections provide a bit more detail on each of these topics.

Leverage Existing Motivations Before Adding New Ones

Does your product need to add a new motivation for users to act, highlight existing ones, or both? First, understand what currently motivates users to act. Use the information you learned about your users in Chapters 4 and 5, about why they want to take the action. Maybe their doctor has told them to exercise more; maybe they really enjoy running but can't seem to fit it into their schedule. Since we're often distracted and thinking about other things, simply reminding people of their existing motivation at the moment of action can be powerful. And, *it's really cheap to remind people of what they already care about; it's much more costly to add a new motivation.*

If you're not sure what currently motivates your users, you can do some simple field tests—check how important particular motivations are versus other things in the person's life. A good way to gather that information is to present a series of trade-offs—ask which of two things the person wants more (e.g., as motivations for exercise: "living five years longer" versus "going on a date next month"). It's less ideal to simply ask people, "How important is this to you?" because we often don't have a real baseline against which to answer that question, and it engages a different part of our minds than usually makes the actual decision to act.

Another reason the existing motivations are important has to do with extrinsic versus intrinsic motivation (Deci and Ryan 1985; Ryan and Deci 2000). *Intrinsic motivation* comes from the inherent enjoyment of the activity itself, without considering any external pressure or reward. *Extrinsic motivation* is the desire to achieve a particular outcome, such as receiving a reward for it (like money or winning a competition).

Your users can have preexisting intrinsic *and* extrinsic motivations, and your product can leverage both to drive behavior. But when the product *adds* a new motivation to act, the source of that motivation is almost always, by definition, outside of the user and outcome-oriented, or extrinsic. For example, people using the FitBit One often have both a preexisting intrinsic motivation and a new extrinsic motivation: an inherent enjoyment from exercising and using one's muscles, and the desire to reach a particular goal and be congratulated for it by the product.

Intrinsic motivations can keep people going when the product isn't directly involved in their lives. New extrinsic motivations, provided by the product, can't do that. They are only effective when the product is directly involved: when they stop, so do the users. If your product adds extrinsic motivations, it can also "crowd out" people's existing intrinsic motivations—meaning they lose the joy of doing something for its own sake if they start being paid to do it (Deci et al. 1999).[88]

However, that doesn't mean new extrinsic motivations are always a bad thing; they just have to be used judiciously:

- *When the person doesn't have a strong existing motivation for a particular step in the sequence of actions.* For example, someone really wants to get healthy, but doesn't see how regular blood pressure checks are important. A little boost can help.
- *For one-time actions where crowding out intrinsic motivation is irrelevant.* For example, someone really wants to exercise but has no motivation to go buy gym clothes. An incentive can get them past that barrier, and closer to their goal.
- *To help users transition from extrinsic to intrinsic motivation—to get people started as they find the joy of the activity itself.* For example, conversation clubs can use a small incentive (free dinner) to get together people who are learning a new language for the first time. While they are there, they experience the intrinsic joys of being immersed in the language, which pulls them forward for future learning.[89]

Avoid Punishing Your Users

There's great debate on whether rewards or punishments are more effective at motivating people in general. However, in the context of products that design for behavior change, the choice should be clear: *avoid punishing your users.* If you give people a consistently bad experience, in most cases, they will stop using your product and do something else with their time. If you could hypothetically force people to endure your punishment, that might be effective. But you can't, and the user has the option to ignore or avoid you.

Not punishing your users doesn't mean completely avoiding the *threat* of properly selected punishments. One powerful type of threat is a commitment contract: in which people pre-commit to taking an action, and they forfeit something they care about if they fail to follow through.[90] For example, Stickk.com employs commitment contracts to generate creative, personal punishments, like automatically donating money to an NGO you hate if you fail to lose weight. Importantly, their punishments are self-imposed and self-calibrated; people choose their own punishment. We react much more negatively to externally imposed punishments than we do to self-imposed ones.

Overall, the trick is to carefully use the threat of punishment (and ideally, a self-imposed one) to motivate action without actually punishing people and driving them away.

Test Out Different Types of Motivators

As humans, we don't lack for things that could motivate us. Money. Food. Control. Esteem. Researchers have tried to make sense of our various motivations for decades,[91] from Maslow's hierarchy of needs (we address deficiencies in a successive set of needs, from basic comfort to self-actualization), to von Neumann and Morgenstern's expected utility theory (we should do what provides us the most benefit). I won't try to argue which motivations are most important for all of humanity, but rather will make an observation. The most important form of motivation is the one *that's actually compelling for your users, given their life circumstances.* Identifying that motivation is part of getting to know your users, and what resonates with them.[92] It may also entail experimentation—trying out a cash payment, or public acclaim, or providing a sense of mastery. Three big areas you can explore with your product are:

1. Monetary rewards, like cash
2. Social motivations, like status or esteem of peers
3. Intrinsic benefits like exploring something new (the product can accent the intrinsic rewards that users already receive)

Also, try varying the motivation over time—we become satiated in any single area, at least in the short term, and start looking for new rewards. That's obvious with food (if you're no longer hungry, more food just isn't that motivating), but it also applies to other forms of reward (if you've won a competition against your friends 10 times in a row, winning again isn't that interesting).

Pull Future Motivations into the Present

We like stuff now, rather than later. We're far more motivated by current goods and experiences than in future ones, even after accounting for inflation, uncertainty, and so on. This "temporal myopia" (focusing on the present even to our own detriment) is deeply ingrained, and something that too many behavioral change programs forget.

For most people, most of the time, "a few years from now" doesn't exist. It's not real, and whatever happens *then* isn't motivating *now*.

And that presents a serious problem. Let's say we sincerely want to slim down our weight to avoid heart disease, or we may really think that saving for retirement is important. But if the threat of heart disease, or the need for retirement money, is still many years off, it just isn't real to us.[93] Daniel Goldstein refers to this as the struggle between the present and future self (2011). We have noble long-term goals but are tempted to do other things in the present.

How can we make that future motivation affect our near-term behavior? We can use moments of strength (when we are actually thinking about the future) to lock in that motivation. Commitment contracts—described in an earlier section—are one option. An extreme version of them, called the Ulysses contract, was described in Homer's *Odyssey*: Ulysses had the crew members on his ship tie him to the mast so that he was physically unable to respond to the alluring call of the mythical (and deadly) sirens. In a Ulysses contract, people make binding commitments that restrict what they can do in the future.

Another method is to try to bring the future into our current awareness. For example, researchers have used photo imaging techniques to help people visualize what they will look like in the future, and act according to their future self's motivations (Hershfield et al. 2011).

Dan Ariely (2011) tells a personal story about how he turned a long-term motivation into something meaningful and useful in the present with "reward substitution." He needed to take a highly unpleasant, painful medication for over a year that had a long-term benefit (beating a disease). But that long-term benefit wasn't enough to overcome the temptation to stop taking the medication. So, he linked taking the medication to something that he enjoyed in the near-term—in this case watching movies. He'd only watch movies right before taking the medication, effectively substituting one motivation (beating the disease) for another one (enjoying the movie).

If these don't work, we can forget about the long-term motivation altogether and simply look for a completely different motivator that isn't far off in the future. For example, instead of talking about the long-term health benefits of getting in shape, highlight the immediate benefits it will have on someone's love life.

Each of these is a technique to make the action motivating now, when it otherwise would be far in the future. Just remember: when we ask people to just think about what a wonderful retirement they'll have in 20 years or all the things they'll be able to do after they lose 300 pounds, we're asking them to do something that's deeply foreign to how our brains are wired (Laibson 1997; Kirby 1997).

Don't Forget the Other Preconditions for Action

The reason I mentioned motivation as the first tactic is that it's the one that most of us jump to when asked how we can encourage people to do X. The problem is, it's often not what's really needed, or at least, not on its own.

Here's an example: the monetary rewards to investing in a retirement plan when your employer contributes money (i.e., a "matching" contribution) are tremendous. We're talking about free money that grows for decades, tax free, with the magic of compound interest. The users need to personally contribute some of their own money to get the match; but that's something they know they need to do anyway—in order to enjoy their retirement (and not live in their kids' basement when they're 70). But up to 50% of people won't do it unless something more is done to change their behavior (Nessmith et al. 2007)—like automating the process (automatic enrollment) or forcing people to make a choice (a strong trigger to act).

To make this point another way, think about this: what is the most effective way to earn gads of money? That is: how can you receive the most monetary rewards? For most of us, we simply have *no idea*, and we don't waste our time looking for that "optimal-money-producing" answer. We've picked the best career path among those presented to us—through a mix of what we're aware of, what seems feasible, the diverse set of motivations and options that fit our personal stories and prior experiences. Money, as with any other type of motivation, is only part of the story.

Here are some challenges that arise when focusing too much on motivation:

- When a product is helping a person take an action he or she already wants to do, the person by definition already has some motivation. For most "good" behaviors, like exercising, everyone has already told that person how important it is—another voice in the choir isn't going to add much. (Though sometimes the motivation is too far in the future, as mentioned earlier.)
- There are *always* competing motivations to do other things. Understanding which exact action we take, why, and when, is the kicker. The answer is often not "the most motivating one."

This isn't to say that making people more motivated isn't important—it is. It's just not enough. Tactics to increase motivation (like highlighting the user's existing reasons to act, or experimenting to find the right motivator for your users) work best when carefully executed along with other parts of the Create Action Funnel from Chapter 2. More motivation improves the chances that a person will successfully pass the intuitive reaction and conscious evaluation components of the funnel. But don't forget that there's other work to be done as well!

Let's say you offer a badge of recognition when users complete an action, which is a tactic to increase motivation. That's useful, but needs to be combined with the rest of the Create Action Funnel. For example, in order for the users to benefit from that extra motivation, and to eventually take action, they first need to be aware of the reward. In other words, they need to be *cued* to think about it. The target action must also *out-compete* (be relatively more motivating, more urgent, etc.) other potential actions the user could take. Those two tactics—cueing and blocking the competition—are coming next.

Cue the User to Act

The sight of the overgrown grass prompts you to mow the lawn. A TV commercial for steak reminds you that you're hungry. For many behaviors, the motivation is often present, but it's in the background. Something needs to cue you to think about it *now* rather than later: that cue is the first step in the Create Action Funnel we talked about in Chapter 2.

Cues, wisely placed, are essential for changes in behavior. This is true for nonconscious habits—a cue in the environment starts a habitual routine—and for conscious decisions to act.

One simple way to cue people to act is just to ask them. If you do it nicely, and don't ask too often, it rarely leads to less action than not asking. Asking for action within a software product has three distinct effects:

Cueing (attention)
: Not only are people busy, but their attention is extraordinarily limited. Dean Karlan (among others) shows that increasing mere attention to an issue is a key factor in driving behavior—especially if the person already has the motivation to act (Karlan et al. 2011).

Obligation
: It's uncomfortable to tell people "no" to a reasonable request. If the company (and especially, a particular *person* that the product personifies) can be seen as a friendly, anthropomorphized presence, then this can help spur action.

Immediacy/urgency
: Most "good" actions, like saving money, exercising more, or smoking less are things that a person can do at any time, and therefore can be put off. Asking people to do it *now* (with some reason for the urgency) helps people get over the "I'll do it later" hump.

It doesn't take much to ask users to act. Emails. Text messages. Big honkin' "Act Now" buttons on websites (Figure 7-1). These are obvious and effective ways to trigger action.[94] Don't waste time on complex psychological approaches to help people to act if you haven't already tried the obvious ones.

FIGURE 7-1. The first place to start: just ask people to act

Another way to cue action is to help users reinterpret an existing feature of their environment as a cue. Let them specify something that they see or hear normally in their lives—like the morning show on their favorite radio station. Then, have them make a plan to act once they see or hear that thing (e.g., "Once the morning show finishes, go running" or, "On Thursday, when I exit from the metro, I'll go buy my running shoes").

Simple mnemonics like this have been used for thousands of years—and your product can help people use them by building an association between something they'll see, and something they want to do. More recently, researchers have experimentally established the impact of "implementation intentions" (Gollwitzer 1999), in which people make specific plans for action in the future. Implementation intentions are a way to tell the mind to do X whenever Y happens. They pull the burden of thinking from the future to the present, allowing the person to invest time in setting up the plan to act now, and simply executing it automatically when the environment cues action in the future.

Here's a nice, clean example of how setting up a concrete plan establishes a cue to act in the future. It's from *http://twords.2lch.com/*, a simple online program to encourage writers to write regularly. Figure 7-2 shows what I filled out when I first signed up.

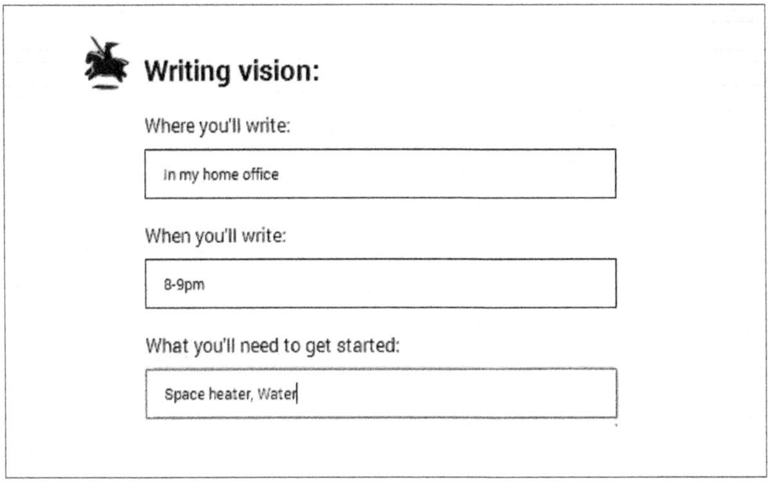

Writing vision:

Where you'll write:

In my home office

When you'll write:

8-9pm

What you'll need to get started:

Space heater, Water

FIGURE 7-2.
My plan to write each night, from *twords.2lch.com*

Generate a Feedback Loop

The current crop of wearable computing products, like Jawbone Up, LarkLife, Fitbit One, and BodyMedia Fit CORE, are built around providing feedback to users about their exercise and sleep habits. For example, my wife's Fitbit One provides constant feedback on how much exercise she's gotten. When she makes an adjustment in her routine, it's quickly reflected in the tracker, and she can see how she's doing. That feedback loop allows her to adjust her behavior throughout the day to meet her goals.[95]

For feedback to be effective at actually helping people change their behavior, it should be:

Timely
: Ideally, the feedback should occur while the action is being undertaken so the user can make live adjustments and see the impact.

Clear
: The user must understand what the information means.

Actionable
: The user must know how to act on the information.

In addition, and this may seem obvious, the user must *care* enough about the feedback to change behavior. Being intrigued and entertained by feedback is not enough. The user must want to, and be able to make the adjustments necessary to, improve performance. The user must also be paying attention. In this combination of motivation, attention, and the ability to act, we find many of the same issues we've already discussed about designing for behavior change.

Knock Out the Competition

There's a flip side to encouraging a behavior, which hasn't received nearly as much attention in the behavior change world. Namely, each distinct type of behavior is in competition with (almost) every other type[96]—competing to be the most motivating, to grab the user's very limited attention (i.e., competing triggers), and to claim the user's time (i.e., competing to be easier and faster). One can draw out these competing or blocking factors with a series of questions:

1. What in the environment *demotivates* the individual, or, more subtly, *motivates the individual to do other things* and thus crowds out the target action?
2. What in the environment already has the user's attention, and thus *crowds out awareness of your action*?
3. Similarly, is the environment crowded with other actions that are already *easy or simple* to take?

When faced with serious competition, here are three strategies to counteract it.

First, if the competing factors are within the application, the product team needs to make hard choices and potentially decrease the motivation/attention/ease provided for other behaviors. Often you really don't need to change all of them—just focus on pulling the users' attention to one thing at a time. If you have their attention at the time they are doing what they need to do, it doesn't matter (as much) that the application motivates them to do other things at other times. One straightforward way to minimize competing attention-getters is to simplify: remove other calls to action, remove distracting text, and take out anything else that isn't essential from the page. Put those other actions in another part of the application that is clearly, conceptually different from the current one.

Second, you can use competing factors to your advantage. If the user is really engaged in something else, look for a clever way to connect it to your target action. Wherever the user's attention already is, that's the best place to be. That's why many applications are built for Facebook—that's where users are already putting their attention.

Third, there's the brute force approach—shout louder for attention, be more motivating, and make using the product easier than breathing. I don't recommend this. If the user is doing something (else) there's (a) probably a good reason, and (b) it takes more than a slightly better behavior to overcome an entrenched one. There are real costs to switching behaviors; for example, we've already discussed the challenges of changing habits. However, if you can't directly dampen the other actions, or find a clever way to use them to your advantage, this may be your only option. Over time, you can build up competing habits and experiences within the application that crowd out those other actions. Or, you can go back to the drawing board and find a different target action that doesn't compete so strongly with other existing behaviors.

Remove or Avoid Obstacles

This tactic is a bit of a catch-all, to remember to review the obstacles identified in the user research process (Chapters 4 and 5). Look over the behavioral plan, and see if the obstacles identified previously will stop users from acting.

If some of the users have serious physical handicaps (can't walk long distances) or are strongly resource constrained (don't have the money for special running gear), for example, is there anything the company or product can do to assist them? Some obstacles have obvious solutions. If some users aren't comfortable with or don't have smartphones, ensure that there's a desktop or web version of the software (the Fitbit One does this). Others are trickier—like physical handicaps—and there just aren't any universal solutions; the team will need to think them through and look for particular solutions for their product.

This tactic is also a reminder to use standard practices in interaction design and product development to remove friction for users in all of the tasks they do within the application (Krug 2006).

Update the Behavioral Plan

Each of the five tactics just discussed can make action more likely, both independently and when working together. So, look over the behavioral plan you created previously. For each step, jot down the following:

- What is the user's motivation to complete this step? How does the user's software environment contribute to that motivation? Are external (physical or social) motivations already in place that can be highlighted?
- How will the user be cued to take the action *now*?
- Will the user get clear feedback on performance, and can the user act on that feedback to improve it?
- What else is distracting the user?
- What is blocking the user?

You should have a clear answer for each one (even if it is "we've done all we can here"). Tweak the behavioral plan accordingly.

As you review the plan, you'll probably come up with lots of ideas about how the product itself should look (i.e., you'll naturally move from the conceptual level to designing individual pages). Jot these ideas down, but try to keep them separate from the behavioral plan itself—so you'll have a list of requirements on what the product does (the plan), and suggestions on how the plan can do it (the product itself; discussed in Chapters 9–11).

On A Napkin

Here's what you need to do

- Ensure users are motivated to act, and that motivation is at the front of their minds. Either accent their own existing motivation (best), or motivate them with money, approval, social status, or other goods.
- Ensure they are cued to act *now*. Easy version: ask them.
- Ensure they know they are succeeding or failing—give them actionable feedback.
- Avoid or coopt other behaviors that are competing for their attention. Ideally, piggyback onto something they are already doing.

How you'll know there's trouble

- There don't appear to be any actions competing for the users' attention and time.
- Your product is trying to shout over the competition.

Deliverables

- A more detailed, refined, behavioral plan that describes the decision-making environment
- A separate list of ideas for how that functionality might look in the product

[8]

Preparing the User

One of the best studies I've ever seen on behavior change was run by Tim Wilson, a social psychologist at the University of Virginia. He took a group of first-year college students who were struggling—they weren't doing well in school and were worried about their future—and randomly assigned the students into one of two groups: one group received a short, 30-minute intervention; the other received nothing special.[97]

Wilson was concerned that the students saw themselves as failures. His intervention entailed giving the students information about potential *interpretations* of their bad performance in school:

> *We gave them some facts and some testimonials from other students that suggested that their problems might have a different cause...namely, that it's hard to learn the ropes in college at first, but that people do better as the college years go on, when they learn to adjust and to study differently than they did in high school... (Gilbert and Wilson* 2011*)*

The randomly selected group that reinterpreted their bad grades got better grades in the future. They got better grades *all the way to their final year in college*; they also were less likely to drop out of college. While the study did not track their full academic performance over time, we can posit that the effects were not immediate. Rather, it appears that students would have slowly changed how they saw themselves and gradually changed the amount of effort they put into their studying, after this initial push.

A 30-minute intervention that changed performance for years? Impressive.

Wilson is a leading proponent of the idea of "story-editing": like the students in his experiment, we can reinterpret what's happened to us in the past by changing the story we tell ourselves about it—our self-narratives (Wilson 2011). That reinterpretation then affects our future behavior. When we change our behavior, we also change the experiences we'll have in the future, making them marginally more likely to support our self-narratives. And with each new experience, our internal story of who we are changes a bit more, spurring a new cycle of behavior change.

For the students, it would have worked like this: Wilson helped half of them interpret their performance differently. Those who saw themselves as going through a temporary tough spot (and not as failures) would be slightly more likely to work harder and perform better on the next test. They would then look back at that (improved) performance and reinforce their understanding of themselves as students who *could* study and could overcome the challenges of first-year life. They would then work even harder on the next test, perform better, and so forth. With time, the internal stories, or self-narratives, of the two groups diverged, thanks to a small push from the initial intervention.

We interpret and reinterpret our experiences every day of our lives, and thus shape our self-narratives and our future behavior. These cycles of interpretation and behavior can clearly support beneficial changes, like studying more. They can also lead to negative ones, like when someone feels like a failure and doesn't put in effort to try to change that. It depends on how we use our past experiences and whether we see ourselves in control of the outcomes of our lives.

Tactics You Can Use

Tim Wilson's story-editing technique is an example of preparing the user to take action in the future. By changing the students' perceptions of the past, they were more likely to succeed in the future. This chapter is about techniques to prepare users for action. In each case, the intervention helps the user think about things differently, and that shapes how they act. Here are the three tactics:

Narrate
: Change how users see themselves.

Associate
: Change how users see the action.

Educate
: Change how users see the world.

I'll focus on the preparation that occurs *before* the action itself; in Chapter 7, we covered how the user can be "prepared" to act via increasing motivation at the time of action. This approach is different—it's about changing some part of the individual that carries over into the future, often for a lasting and sustainable impact. Let's start with the self-narrative.

Narrate the Past to Support Future Action

Our self-narrative, as you saw in Wilson's experiment, is how we label ourselves, and how we describe our behavior in the past. Products can help people see themselves differently. The goal, from a behavior change perspective, is to *help people see themselves as someone for whom the action is a natural, normal extension of who they are.*

In other words, if you want to help people begin exercising (like the Moves app does),[98] help them see themselves as people who have already been exercising in small ways,[99] and just need to do more (e.g., first-time Moves users may be surprised to find out how far they normally walk each day). An easy way to support this process is by merely asking people about things they've done in the past that are related. And congratulate them for the work they've already accomplished. Where their past experiences have been negative, as they were with Wilson's first-year college students, help them see those experiences as surmountable challenges and not inherent character defects.

Essential to a supportive self-narrative is the belief that one can actually succeed in the action (i.e., users need to feel that the action is under their control and that they have the skills and resources to—potentially—make it happen). That's the sense of self-efficacy (Bandura 1977a) discussed in Chapter 2 under the ability to act. Reminding people about their prior successes at related tasks can help build that sense of self-efficacy; so can the "small wins" and positive feedback described in the last two chapters.[100]

Stepping back a bit, there is another very subtle influence that one's self-narrative, or overall mindset, has on behavior: it can change how our body responds to activity. In another famous study, researchers analyzed the fact that hotel maids often do a lot of physical work in their daily lives—but don't see themselves as exercising. Ellen Langer offered one set of maids information about how many calories they burned in their daily lives, and others received no information. The maids with exercise information became significantly more fit. But they didn't necessarily exercise *more:* their bodies apparently burned more calories due to how the mind interpreted the exercise in the maid's normal routines (Crum and Langer 2007). The effect was a placebo, as NPR's Alix Spiegel put it: "If you believe you are exercising, your body may respond as if it is" (2008). Our beliefs not only affect our behavior directly; they also affect our bodies.

Associate with the Positive and the Familiar

Chapters 1 and 2 talked about how, for many of our choices in life, we intuitively know whether taking an action feels right or not to us. A big part of that is our prior *associations*—our learned experience that buying a fancy pair of shoes is going to make us feel great when we walk out of the store with them, at least for a few days.

Products can build these associations to help a person change behavior. In Chapter 6, we talked about changing the *action* itself so that it leverages prior experiences. Here, the *product* can be changed so that it helps users make the mental connection between the action they want to take and their prior experiences. I call this a *behavioral bridge,* because it helps the user cross from one type of behavior to another by making it less "new" and difficult. The bridge connects past experience with future actions.

Here's an example: Speek is a conference-calling application that allows people to switch from using a dial-in number and long PIN code to using a simple link in a URL (Figure 8-1). Dial-in numbers and PINs are frequently misplaced and annoying to enter. When a user clicks on the URL, Speek calls them and patches them into the conference line. The challenge is that using a URL is new and strange. In the product, the company highlights the new and unique aspects (ease of use, etc.) but is also careful to leave a behavioral bridge in place—a comforting bit of information about how users can treat it like a normal conference call if they need to, since the underlying technology is a conference line with a dial-in number and access code.

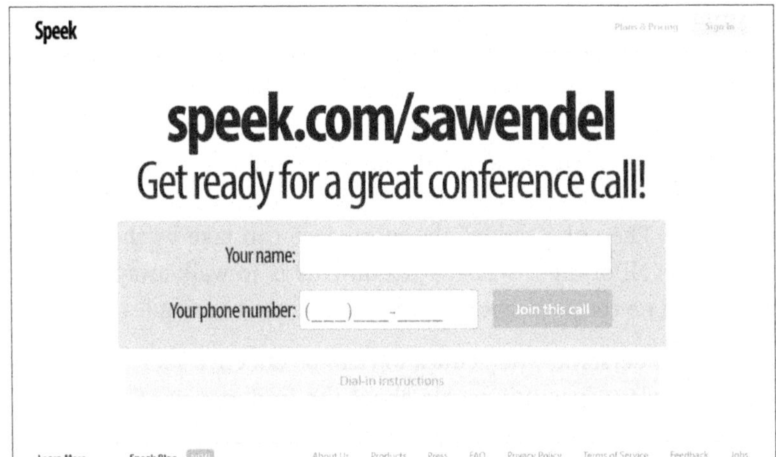

FIGURE 8-1.
Speek does something new: URL-based conference calls.
It also provides a behavioral bridge to associate it with a more familiar action—using a standard dial-in conference call (in gray under the main box).

Educate Your Users

Education is all about giving people the information they need, and then hoping that when the time comes to act, they will make an informed choice to act.

Focusing on information is a noncontroversial and common approach to behavior change. We think that everyone would believe like we do if only they had access to the same information and training. This has been an approach taken by many of my otherwise favorite NGOs and government agencies.

Unfortunately, information doesn't equalize us and doesn't make us behave the same. As we saw in Chapter 1, conscious information may have nothing to do with action at all—the action may be habitual or based on intuitive reactions. Or, when it does have an impact, it is filtered through all of the rest of our experiences and information.

Providing users with information can be immensely powerful. But one should be thoughtful about how and when it's applied. Education efforts falter when:

- The action that people will take isn't consciously thought through at all—it's habitual or otherwise automatic.
- People are overwhelmed with too much information.
- The information comes too long before (or after) the decision needs to be made. We rapidly forget unconnected, unused facts.

An example of an education-only approach that clearly didn't work is mortgage disclosures in the United States. Mortgage lenders are required to provide reams of documentation on everything from how the loan works to the fact that most older homes have lead paint in them. This is all important information—and rarely read. It's too much to take in, not structured to demand attention, and isn't clearly actionable. The only "action" the mortgagee can take by the time he or she gets all of the disclosure documents is to walk away, with no house, and no certainty about where the escrow money goes.

To better understand when education can be effective, let's use a common example: educating people about the importance of saving for retirement with financial literacy seminars. In the 1990s, there was a significant increase in the use of retirement planning seminars, as employers have shifted from pension plans to 401(k) plans that individuals directly contributed to and managed (Bayer et al. 2009). These seminars, and other financial literacy programs in high schools and beyond (Mandell and Klein 2009), have been the subject of quite a lot of controversy, with numerous researchers questioning their impact (Lyons et al. 2006).

Consider three different approaches that a retirement education product could take. It could educate people about *why* an action is important, *how* the action works and the raw data needed for a good decision, or *what to do* to take the action:

Why

> By and large, we already know that saving for retirement is important. No one wants to die in poverty. However, for other beneficial actions, users of the product may not honestly know the importance of the action; for example, I didn't know that skin cancer screening was important for (relatively) young people until recently.

How

> We don't understanding the inner workings of 401(k) plans and score poorly on financial literacy questions about basic topics like compound interest (Lusardi and Mitchell 2007). And, there's evidence that this knowledge helps us make good financial choices (Hilgert et al. 2003). But if the information is delivered too far in advance from a moment of decision, as many financial literacy programs are, we simply forget it.

What to do

We don't know what to do when confronted with dozens of 401(k) options—in fact, we often take a naïve strategy of putting an equal amount into each fund we're faced with. A simple heuristic for easy diversification—use a stock market index fund or a target date fund—can simplify and shape that decision to users' benefit.

Which type(s) of education is best depends on the particular situation. With voluntary behavior change, we assume that the user already has some motivation to act. Information about *how* a system works can be fascinating for those already in the know, but overwhelming and too removed from the actual decision for those who aren't. Logistical information (*what* to do) can provide clear actionable guidance and increase the user's ability to act immediately, a key component in the Create Action Funnel.

How Training Your Users Fits In

You can effectively provide users with information—educate them—at the moment they start interacting with your product, and thus prepare them for the tasks ahead. But you can't suddenly change their *skills* once they start; that takes time. You can, however, use their early interactions with the product to boost skills that are important for later interactions.

In Chapter 6, we already broke down the task into small steps that provided small wins and built toward the final goal. The early steps should already provide the structure you need to train the user for later interactions. For example, in Chapter 6, we talked about an application that encouraged people to run regularly. Some of the early steps included buying running shoes, planning out a path for the first run, and placing the running shoes by the door to remind the person. Here's a quick way to check that the necessary skills are being developed, using that running app as an example:

1. Look over the sequence of actions the user is taking. For example, getting running shoes, planning out a course, and so on.

2. *Starting from the end*, identify the most challenging parts where the user is most likely to fail. What skills are required for the person to take that action? For example, your users might need the skill of adapting to bad weather and maintaining their routine, or they'll get out of the groove.

3. Given what you know about the user, and the previous actions in the list, would the user have those skills already?
4. If not, are there ways to build in similar, but smaller, challenges earlier in the process?

Building in a series of incrementally harder challenges is, of course, related to a standard technique in game design: game designers look at ways to build a succession of challenges that grow progressively harder as the gamer gains experience with the system. Similarly, it's a standard technique in education. We learn addition before algebra, and algebra before calculus. Sometimes we forget these lessons in designing our product, because we ourselves already have the skills required to act. This is just a brief reminder to look at the process from the perspective of the skills your *users* have, now that you're almost fully done with your behavioral plan.

In some cases, you can add in skill-building exercises within the app; in others, it may require a previous training program. For example, I remember that I had to take an intensive math training over the summer (aka a "catch-up class") before I was *allowed* to even apply for a particular program in school. If your company has a suite of related products, they can be explicitly designed to build on one another: like Rosetta Stone's language-learning programs.

Update the Behavioral Plan

Use the tactics from this chapter to review and update the behavioral plan. Specifically:

- With respect to the action, how do users think of themselves? Do they see themselves as people who can (generally) be successful? Yes, it's kitschy, but it's true—if people don't believe in themselves, good luck getting them to take action. Story editing can help turn a negative self-perception around.
- What positive, similar experiences can the product hook into? How can it build a behavioral bridge between those experiences and the action the user needs to take?
- Is there any information that the user absolutely needs to know before embarking on the journey? I say *absolutely*, because overloading users with less-than-necessary information can distract and slow them down.

- Are there skill-building exercises or experiences that should be added early in the process to prepare users for harder, later steps?

Once you've updated the behavioral plan, let's take a look back at how these techniques relate to what we learned about the mind's decision-making process in Chapter 1.

How Behavior Change Techniques Relate to the Thought the Behavior Requires

Remember in Chapter 1, where there was a spectrum showing the different ways that the mind makes decisions, from those that required very little thought to those that required lots of conscious thought and attention? Now that we've gone over the major techniques you can use to create a supportive context for action, let's revisit that spectrum.

Each of the techniques discussed thus far maps onto the spectrum—each is appropriate for particular types of behaviors and their level of thought:

- Building habits is important for often-repeated, familiar situations (go to refrigerator, get snack), where we're not really making any "choice" to act at all. Techniques to *change* habits are similarly relevant where there's an existing habit in place; and most conscious efforts simply won't do much.
- Automation and "cheating" are even more extreme, requiring no thought at all except for the initial step of getting consent. They are appropriate in cases where the user's involvement isn't required to adapt and personalize the solution; and it's acceptable (and possible) just for the person to sign off on the action occurring on their behalf.
- Building associations with prior experiences and changing one's self-narrative are important for semi-familiar situations where we make a conscious choice, but still use our intuitions.
- Structuring the action into a sequence of small, easy steps decreases the amount of work a user needs to do at a time. That's most appropriate when there *is* a lot of work to do—when there's some conscious thought required.
- Educating your users, as part of a broader array of tactics, is especially important for unfamiliar situations where the most work is done—and you consciously weigh the pros and cons of a behavior.

Revisiting the graphic from Chapter 1, now with ways to *change* behavior, we have a set of inventions (on the bottom) and the scenarios for which they are appropriate (on top); see Figure 8-2.

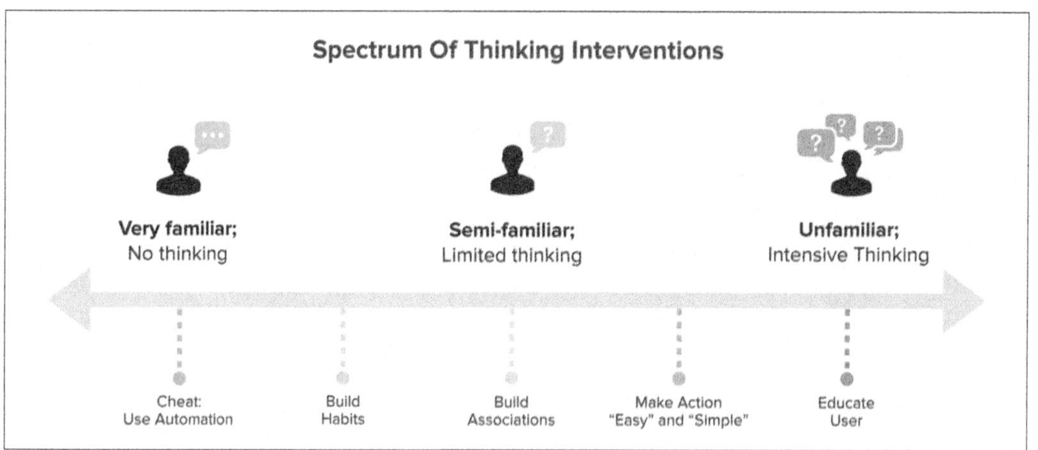

FIGURE 8-2. In familiar situations or where little thinking is required, products can employ habits or automation to shift the burden away from conscious user attention

This graphic can help you choose the right intervention for a given behavior. Misunderstanding the behavior and using the wrong intervention can have serious consequences. For example, there are countless well-meaning programs that try to educate people about the dangers of smoking to get them to stop. But by the time someone is a smoker, smoking is already a habit—people don't think about it much. In fact, some great research with brain scans shows that attempts to provide information to smokers about the dangers of smoking just triggers the habit—they want to smoke more, right then (Lindstrom 2008)!

So far, this book has been designed to help you carefully plan out the application to make it effective and avoid such errors. By combining knowledge of how the mind works with specific strategies and tactics to change behavior, you can understand the type of behavior change problem you face, and develop a conceptual plan for the product. Next up: how to apply the same understanding, strategies, and tactics to developing wireframes and mockups of the application.

On a Napkin

Here's what you need to do

- Help users see themselves as people who would naturally take the action.
- Help users build strong associations between things they are already familiar with and enjoy and the new action.
- Provide users with clear instruction on what they need to do and any other *essential* information to act.

How you'll know there's trouble

- You're providing users with reams and reams of information or trying to get them to *think exactly like you do* about the action.

Deliverables

- The updated behavioral plan, which describes how the user moves from inaction to action, including how the product prepares them for that action

[*Part IV*]

Designing the Interface and Implementing It

In the following chapters, we take the conceptual plan for the product and turn it into something real and tangible that people can see and react to. We'll go through a very similar design process as we did in Chapters 6–8, when we first developed the conceptual plan (Figure Part IV-1):

1. *Structuring the action* to make it feasible and inviting for the user,
2. *Constructing the environment* to support the action, and
3. *Preparing the user* to take the action.

But instead of designing the high-level functionality, we'll use these techniques on the interface designs and on the implementation of the product itself. In terms of the iterative product development process first introduced in the Preface, we're in the middle of the third stage.

Chapter 9 describes how to extract *user stories* (in an agile development environment) or *formal specs* (in sequential product development), and how to generate the initial *interface designs* based on them.

Chapter 10 discusses the ins and outs of tuning the *interface designs* for their behavioral impact. And, finally, Chapter 11 talks about how the team actually builds the *product* itself.

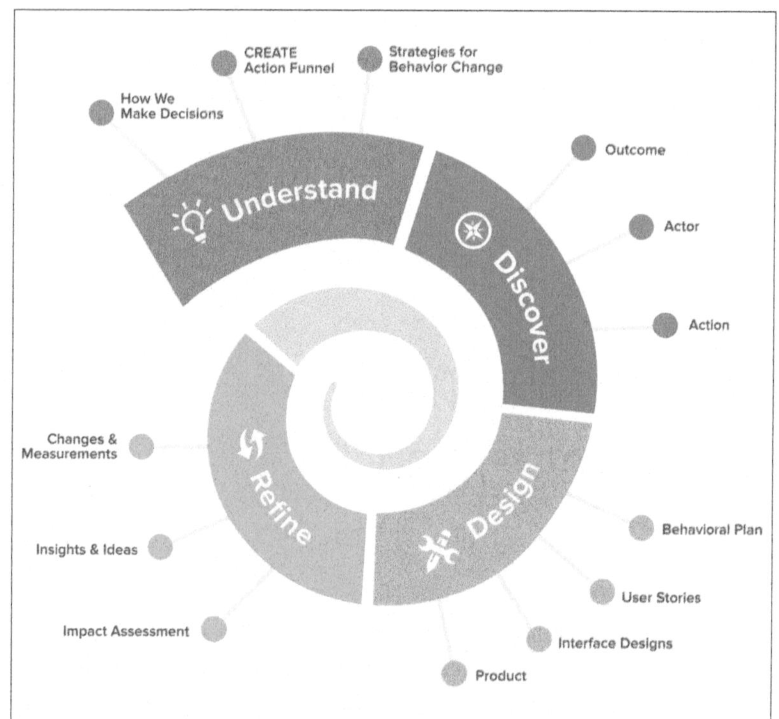

FIGURE PART IV-1. Part IV covers the user stories, interface designs, and building the actual product

[9]

Moving from Conceptual Designs to Interface Designs

Take Stock

We now have a behavioral plan that says what the product needs to do. We've found the Minimum Viable Action, tailored it based on users' prior experiences, automated parts of it, and made the rest understandable and easier where possible. We've thought about how the environment (the product and the user's real-world context) builds conscious and emotional motivations, provides cues, generates feedback, and side-steps competing behaviors. And, finally, we've thought about the information and preparation the user needs to succeed.

What we have is an essential, vital, unavoidably important to-do list for the user and for the product. The design team must now transform the sequence of steps from a dull to-do list into something that people want to interact with. I've seen too many apps take their to-do list of user behaviors and string them together into a "product." Unfortunately, most people just don't get very excited about a to-do list.

Instead, the final result may look nothing like a sequence of steps. For example, those actions can be carefully embedded in a game, in self-serve modules, or in a simple mobile app with a single screen that evolves over time. There's nothing wrong with a sequence of steps, but that's not the only form that a behavior change application can take. Let's explore how to move from the list of steps to an engaging product.

Extract the Stories or Specs

To move from the conceptual level to interface designs, we need to chop up the behavioral plan into pieces that the product folks and interface designers can use. Those pieces provide the raw material for the team to then flesh out exactly how the product will be structured and how it will do its job. Every product development methodology and every product team has its own way of doing this (Cagan 2008). For example, some product people absolutely hate written specs. Others live and die by them.

I'll take two archetypal product development methodologies as examples:

- An agile+lean product world, where development is broken up into short periods of time (aka "sprints"). The various functional roles within a team work in parallel, and there's an assumption of rapid iteration of the product across development cycles.
- A sequential development world, also derisively called "the waterfall method," where development occurs in distinct sequential phases over longer periods of time. Each team hands off work products to the next stage of development (design, engineering, testing, etc.) in a predefined order.

These are two common methodologies in the field, and the two that I know the best. Since I can't possibly cover all of the variations out there, you'll probably need to tweak these examples to your particular needs and team. For each example, though, I'll walk through the process of chopping up the behavioral design and developing the interface designs accordingly.

Agile+Lean

In the agile+lean development world (where I live now), user stories convey product ideas in outline form (Cohn 2010; Rubin 2012). The development team is free to elaborate upon and innovate within those outlines. They are short, plain-English statements of what the user wants to do. Ideally, they also include *why* the user wants to do it. For example:

> *As a user, I want to quickly sync my exercise tracker with my phone, so I can see how I did today.*

User stories can come straight from the behavioral plan. Each step in the sequence of actions the user takes building up to the target action gets a user story. For example:

- If the product should trigger the user to act, like sending out text messages to remind her to run, that's a user story: "As a user, I want to be reminded when it's time to run so I don't procrastinate."
- If the product should help users develop a particular self-narrative, like thinking about previous times they've gone running, that's a user story: "As a user, I want to think about the previous times I've succeeded at running so this new challenge doesn't seem so scary."
- If a tutorial is required, like how to sync up the tracker, that's a user story: "As a user, I want to know how to update my logs online so my friends can react."

Each step in the sequence should already be annotated with user motivations—that becomes the "why" part of each user story. Get the idea?

The user stories indicate what the user needs to do to get a particular job done. They are immensely helpful, in part, because they force the product team to think about the specific actions that the user takes *from the user's perspective*, and not from a top-down analysis of what the company thinks the user should be doing. As the team extracts the user stories, they will naturally add, remove, or change some of them as they think about the process in a new light. However, if they are unsure of the *spirit* of the stories and what the stories are trying to convey, they can refer back to the behavioral plan.

Sequential Development

In a sequential development world,[101] formal specs convey product needs to the development team. Each division of the company may have its own template for those requirements. But in general, they encourage specificity, and provide much less flexibility (and room for confusion) than user stories do in an agile development environment. For example:

> *The application will allow users to sign up for text messages that alert them about their commitment to go running.*

The specs tell the team what the product needs to do to get the job done. They usually are written from the product/company perspective, rather than from a user perspective.

At this point in a sequential process, we just want to create the *outline* of the specs—the parts that come directly from the behavioral plan. *We don't want to develop fully detailed specs yet.* Why? Usually, specifications are much more detailed than user stories; they tell the team not only what's needed but also how to deliver it. We don't know the "how" part yet; the behavioral plan only provides the "what." We'll flesh out the "how" part shortly.

There Are Many Sources for Specs and Stories

The behavioral plan provides one of the sources for user stories/specs. There will be many others—from business considerations to meet customer needs, to technical needs for the data infrastructure. These various stories/specs need to be prioritized according to business goals, staffing, and engineering constraints. I'll talk about ways to balance between behavioral and other concerns in the next chapter. For now, and for the sake of simplicity, I'll focus on just the stories/specs derived from the behavioral plan.

Don't Specify the Interface Just Yet

As the user stories/spec outlines are extracted from the behavioral plan, there's a natural tendency to overspecify, and indicate how the product should look and not just what it should do. Resist that temptation for now!

There's a tension between structured planning and creativity. Thus far, we've used a rather planning-heavy process—thinking through what the user should do, what the environment does, and how the user should be prepared. It's just too tempting to think that the *things we want* users to do, and the *way we want* them to behave is how they'll *actually* behave.

When, in reality, there's a lot more required. Users have to want to change their behavior. When there's a product helping them change, that means they have to want to use the product. The product must not turn them away: no product can be effective at changing behavior if people never use it. The desire to change won't pull most people through an ugly, uninteresting product. Developing a product that people enjoy using takes more than a top-down behavioral plan—it takes creativity, and it takes the team's product development and interaction design expertise.

So, how can you integrate planning and creativity? Part of the solution is development philosophy: think of the planning for behavior change we've done so far as specifying desired product functionality, and not specifying how the product will accomplish it. Another, more subtle, part of the solution is to avoid a strong reference point by intentionally separating the behavioral plan from the interface design process. The goal is to avoid using the plan as an implicit, unintentional starting point for what it should look like that strongly shapes what the final interface design looks like.

How can you open up the design process and avoid getting a cookie-cutter product? Don't try to push an interface design into the user stories/spec outlines. Keep them focused on the what, and not the how. Then, let the design team (or members of the product team who are fleshing out the requirements) put aside the behavioral plan for a bit, and work only from the user stories/spec outlines and the previously developed personas. Brainstorm ideas on how the product might look; sketch them out. Prototype them. That process is a special type of magic.

Provide Structure for Magic to Occur

With user stories or an outline for formal specifications in hand, it's time for the team to specify the exact form that the product features will take, and the content on each screen.

There are no strict rules here, and there are already many books on how to lay out an application's information architecture and do the user experience and interaction design (Cooper et al. 2007; Saffer 2010). Since this isn't a book of interaction design or user experience design, I'll leave that to others.

Instead, think of the interface design process as a form of structured magic. Creative thought conjures up interesting, usable content and interaction, within well-defined constraints. The constraints, if not too restrictive, make it *possible* for the creative process to occur; otherwise the range of possible options would be overwhelming.

Designing for behavior change provides three types of constraints that shape the magic within:

- Functional constraints
- A model of how the mind makes decisions
- Product design patterns: templates for how the product *might* look

"Mix together some functional constraints, a model of decision-making, and a product design pattern or two. Excellent!"

Functional constraints indicate what the product should accomplish. We've developed them already—first in the behavioral plan, and then in the user stories or specification outlines created earlier in this chapter. In Chapters 1–3, we developed an understanding of how the mind makes decisions (keep things simple, don't assume continual conscious attention, leverage the user's prior associations, etc.), and what that means for behavior change (the Create Action Funnel and three strategies to pass through it). Product patterns, however, need a bit of explanation.

Product Design Patterns for Behavior Change

One question you may be asking yourself as you start to design the structure of the application is this: what *type* of application is best for behavior change? Is it a game? A serious-minded tutorial? I'm a firm believer that there is no "best" way to structure a product for behavior change. Instead, it's the psychology that matters, and many different types of products can work. If you don't know where to start though, there are a variety of templates you can draw from.

Software products, like physical products, usually fall into well-defined categories. People involved in the product development space know what a new social media app is basically going to look like and do, even before the first line of code has been written. We know what an edutainment app for kids is basically going to do. We know what a shoot-'em-up game looks like or what a note-taking app looks like for example.

These categories, or product genres, provide us with an overall set of expectations for the product. Each new product innovates at the margins. Only the rare product actually creates a new genre *and* gets traction with users; usually it's in hindsight that we recognize a new genre out of things that have already been built.

In the behavior change space, a variety of templates have already been established that can be used for mobile and online applications. Often a given product employs more than one of these templates in different parts of the application. In that sense, you can think of the templates not just as genres for entire products, but as *reusable design patterns for behavior change* that you can deploy within your app where needed (Gamma et al. 1994; Alexander et al. 1977).[102] Each pattern provides guidelines for promoting behavior change in a particular context, and a template for the look and feel of that part of the application. Dan Lockton's Design with Intent Toolkit (2010) and Stephen Anderson's Mental Notes Deck (2013) each provide examples of these behavior change templates.[103]

One set of patterns for behavior change can be applied to high-touch, functionality-rich online or mobile applications, especially where there are major decisions to be made or frequently repeated behaviors. They offer many opportunities to interact with users and reshape the context of the decision and action to best suit the individual user. A different set of patterns can be applied to limited, low-touch interventions—like sending an email or text message. Here are examples of both high-touch and low-touch design patterns.

HIGH-TOUCH APPROACHES

Decision-making support

A user is planning for his kid's education, and the application helps him evaluate the options to save up for it. The app could analyze and present the information, automate part of the process, and make the user aware of other priorities and challenges. HelloWallet is one such product.[104]

Behavior change games

Users are in a classroom setting and are learning about cooperation. Two people play a game together that requires cooperation and communication, learning as they experience it. *Way* is one such game.[105] Under the banner of behavior-change games (and serious games and games with a purpose, etc.),[106] designers have developed games with explicit social or behavioral "lessons." Users may play the games as part of a job requirement (as in military simulations or job training games), physical or mental therapy, or in a school context.

Gamification

A user wants to get healthy by eating better and exercising more. As the user does the tasks, he forms teams and competes against others for status in a shared scoring system. Keas is one such product.[107] Whereas behavior change games deploy full-fledged games, gamification employs aspects of game design in nongame contexts—often social rewards and elements of competition around a set of target actions (see Deterding 2011 and Zichermann and Cunningham 2012 for two perspectives on gamification).

Planners

Users want to eat healthier and plant a vegetable garden toward that end. They decide to make a specific plan for what should go into their garden, when to plant it, and how to design the garden for optimal growth and beauty. *Mother Earth News* has a vegetable garden planner, for example.[108]

Reminders

A user wants to organize his day, and the application reaches out to remind him when and where to go grocery shopping, what time to pick up the kids, etc. To-do list and self-organization apps like Omnifocus and Nozbe are examples.[109]

Social sharing

A user hopes to go running each morning. He shares that goal with friends via their mobile running app, and their support and their ability to hold him accountable keeps him on target. RunKeeper is one such product.[110]

Goal trackers

A user wants to exercise and needs a product in which to set a goal and track progress toward it. Tracking the behavior (either manually or automatically), provides feedback so the individual can adjust his behavior. Fitbit One and Jawbone Up are two such products.[111] Trackers are a mainstay of the Quantified Self Movement.[112]

Tutorials

Going back to the vegetable garden example, let's say users want to learn how to build a raised bed, and the site provides how-to videos. There are countless such tutorials out there; master gardener Ed Bruske has a sample collection up on MonkeySee.com.[113]

LOW-TOUCH BEHAVIOR CHANGE

High-touch interactions aren't always feasible—you may only have a single shot at interacting with the user, may be limited to a passive medium (like one-way email or print), or know that the opportunity for user attention is fleeting. Here are some patterns that are more appropriate in a low-touch environment (a single email, a few text messages, a single web page or print ad):

An appeal to "think differently"

Users spend a lot of money on electricity and would prefer to spend less. They see a comparison of their spending to their neighbors—making them think differently about how much they should and can spend. Opower does this (successfully)—with a simple physical letter.[114]

Call to action

A user is concerned about a major political issue, like the Keystone XL Pipeline (either for or against it). He receives an email with a link to quickly send a letter or donate to the cause. The user can take the action in a few seconds and move on. There's nothing more to the email or landing page. Lots of advocacy organizations do this, such as the Sierra Club.[115]

How-to tips

A woman is about to have her first child and is uncertain about what she needs to do to prepare. Through here mobile phone, she receives simple, short tips each week on what to do. Text4Baby does this.[116]

Simple reminders and planning prompts

Employees of a company don't want to get sick with the flu (or get their families sick). They receive simple mailers reminding them when and where to get vaccinated, and a prompt to plan for when they'll go themselves. Milkman et al. (2011) did this, with up to an 8% boost in vaccination rates.

Status reports

The user is new to the city and wants to get to know people. He receives regular notices on upcoming events in his areas of interest. Meetup.com[117] does this, as do many organizations that host in-person activities.

I don't know of any rigorous studies comparing these high-touch and low-touch approaches, but my intuition and personal experience says that you have more freedom to innovate and have greater impact with high-touch approaches.

HOW TO USE DESIGN PATTERNS

If you need a template to start with, how do you select one? First and foremost, find something that makes sense with the company and its products. Some companies aren't comfortable with a gamified experience, and won't build one. That's perfectly fine. Pick something that fits the culture.

A design pattern can fail to fit the corporate culture even if the underlying *psychology* could work. For example, love it or hate it, the National Rifle Association is a stalwart advocate for individual ownership of firearms. When they want to encourage their members to act, a serious call to action design pattern fits their image. It would be very strange if they asked members to buy a slick protest-planning armband that encouraged them to set an "individual protest goal" and support them with small daily affirmations (think: an NRA Fitbit). The NRA could certainly use the *psychology* of providing goals and support as part of their campaign; but the product template, *the expected look and feel*, of a geek-chic NRA armband tracker would be rather odd.[118]

Second, identify what's familiar—familiar to the target population (not necessarily familiar to the "market"). In other words, if the product seeks to help people exercise more, and the user base is familiar and comfortable with pedometers, then a souped-up pedometer will have an easier time integrating into the users' lives than something completely new and different. A good dose of user research early on can help: keeping the discussion user-centric and focused on the real experiences and expertise of the target audience.

You also don't need to, and shouldn't feel obligated to, follow one of these templates at all. If you can, build something entirely new and different. Take something as mundane as employee hygiene at a restaurant (good for the employee and for the customers!). You can build a social game to encourage hygiene that will be really successful, as long as it addresses the core psychology, the Create Action Funnel. You can also build a personal reminder app, again, as long as it addresses the psychology. Or you can do something that no one has ever seen before.[119] It's the psychology underlying the product that matters, as long as the look and feel of the product doesn't turn people off.

Draw It Out

While designing the interactions and the look and feel of the product, the product team will develop wireframes (or mockups, or prototypes, as fits their style) of what the user actually sees and interacts with.[120] While developing those wireframes, the team should focus on the core value and usability of product. They'll need to answer the following questions:

- Does the user experience actually make sense (especially given the user research)?
- What's a clear way to express the content to the user that fits her prior experience?
- What's an engaging, interesting way to interact with the user?

The person adding a behavioral perspective to the product team (whether a dedicated behavioral social scientist, an interaction designer, product manager, or whomever) should serve as a resource as these ideas are being put on paper. She can answer questions about behavior and the desired product functionality (similar to a product owner role in a Scrum environment).[121] She can provide behavioral feedback as the UX expert and product manager identify how to best translate the behavioral strategies into attractive, sensible features for the user. Beyond this feedback, though, remember to let the creative process work, to build a good, clean product.

Human behavior and emotions are complex and hard enough to decipher, let alone to change them. I've found that it takes all of one's energy to focus on behavioral change; designing a sensible, beautiful product is just too much to do at the same time. If the behavioral expert is a separate person within the product team, then it's time to leave it to the nonbehavioral, product experts. If the behavioral expert wears many hats and is also a product manager or user experience expert, take off the behavior change hat. Go look at beautiful products for a while to clear your head. Then design one. There's time to return to behavioral considerations later.

A Cautionary Tale: My 2012 Exercise Band

In 2012, a new wearable computing band hit the market. The product combined exercise and sleep tracking, with a band you wear at night and one you wear during the day. It sounded great, and I preordered mine—I received it right before Christmas. The product turned out to be an excellent example of what happens when a company makes something that is strongly focused on behavior change, but forgets to build a good product. (I won't mention their name, since the company is continuing to revise and improve its products, and it isn't the only company to build an exercise band that had problems in the early stages!)

My wife and I made the product into a twofer gift: I would use the exercise band, and my wife would use the sleep tracker. So, on Christmas day, I installed the app and started trying out the exercise band.

The product did a lot of things right, from a behavioral perspective. It automatically tracked sleep and exercise, which are difficult to do by hand. It had a simple, clean user interface. It helped me set reasonable goals to start with, and then provided constant feedback and nice rewards (little icons on the screen) as progress was made.

The next day I went into the office. After a long day of sitting on my duff, I checked how much exercise I'd had. I saw the screen shown in Figure 9-1.

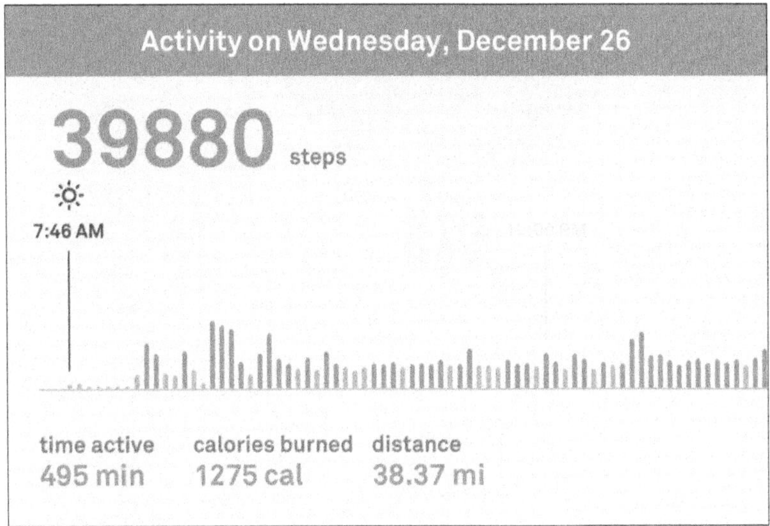

FIGURE 9-1.
My daily exercise—while sitting at the computer

Believe it or not, I didn't walk 38 miles that day, while sitting at my desk. I wish I had. Disappointment number one: clearly a bug in the tracking system.

As I got ready to go home, I put on my jacket. The wristband came off. The small magnetic clasp that held it together wasn't strong enough. (It would accidentally fall off multiple times over the following days; I'm lucky I didn't lose it.) Disappointment number two: industrial design problem.

The next day, I forgot it on the counter of my desk. Shortly after lunch, I saw the screen shown in Figure 9-2.

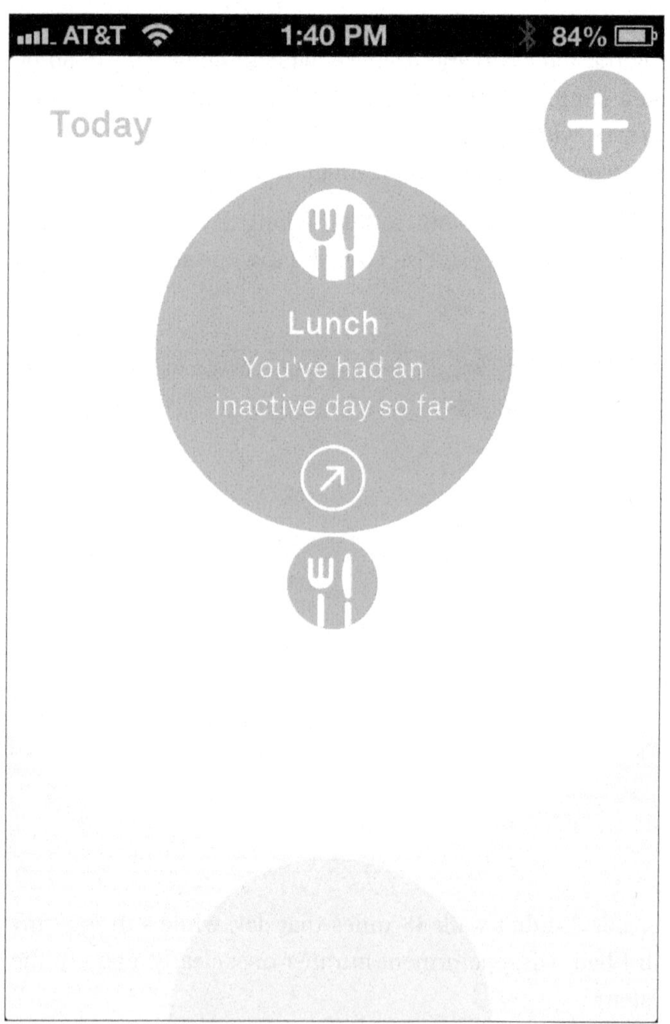

FIGURE 9-2. A little judgmental aren't we?

Not the best experience. If the product had been absolutely correct and I had been inactive, maybe I would have taken the message better. But from its lack of knowledge about me, it inferred that zero data meant a problem in my behavior, rather than in its knowledge. A good interaction designer should have caught this.

Ah well. I returned it quickly. I'm still really excited about the concept and look forward to the next version. But for now, this is a cautionary tale about what happens when you focus exclusively on behavior change, and not enough on building a good product first. *Remember that behaviorally effective products must also be interesting and usable.*

On a Napkin

Here's what you'll need to do

- Chop up the behavioral plan into the raw material for designing the product. In an agile world, that's user stories. In a sequential development world, that's an outline for the full product requirements.
- Initially, try to avoid specifying the interface design based on the behavioral plan. Focus on *what* the product needs to do, and not on *how* the product should do it.
- Let the creative team do its magic—coming up with a compelling experience for the product.
- You can use design patterns for behavior change that are familiar to users, such as trackers or reminders.
- Develop the wireframes (or mockups).

How you'll know there's trouble

- When the product team is too focused on building a product that addresses behavior that it forgets the fundamentals of product design—usability, feasibility, etc.

Deliverables

- Wireframes of the user experience

[10]

Reviewing and Fleshing Out the Interface Designs

Once there is something real and tangible that the product team can look at—wireframes or mockups that convey the interface design—you can review them from a behavioral perspective and give feedback. Two different types of review should occur:

- Looking for gaps in the overall user experience across the product
- Looking for opportunities to apply specific tactics

Look for Big Gaps

The product design process is necessarily one of translation—converting concepts and intent into designs of something users can actually interact with. Along the way, the core aspects of the behavioral plan—the behavior change strategies used, the sequence of steps, the structuring of the environment and preparation of the individual—may change. Those changes can be highly beneficial from a behavioral perspective, if the designers were inspired to come up with new ways to meet the same ends. They can also be detrimental and miss key aspects of the application's intended psychology.

Think of the interface design as a new behavioral plan, one that should be evaluated on its own merits and run through the design wringer we employed in Chapters 6–8. That way, the interface designs are not judged too literally against the original functional requirements if the UX designers came up with innovative behavioral solutions.

What You're Looking For: The Create Action Funnel

At the end of the day, the product needs to help people change their behavior. It must put all of the prerequisites in place for people to act. We first talked about those prerequisites in Chapter 2, as the Create Action Funnel. Here's a quick refresher on what needs to come together, at the same time, for a person to take action:

1. *Cue.* Something needs to start the person thinking about the action. It can be something already in the person's daily life (whenever I see calla lilies, I think of hiking along the coast) or something the application does to catch attention (when I hear that particular buzz, I think about checking my text messages).

2. *Reaction.* The intuitive mind will automatically and rapidly react to the idea of taking the action. That reaction includes a basic sense about whether the action is interesting and pleasant, and it will also activate thoughts about other possible, related, ideas and actions. The product needs to get past this reaction without being rejected or having the person be distracted. I don't answer my landline at home, for example, because I intuitively dislike telemarketers.

3. *Evaluation.* The conscious mind will evaluate the costs and benefits of the action, including the value the product provides and the frictions or other challenges in using it. That evaluation is *relative*, not absolute—the action must be sufficiently worthwhile and better, on net, than the other things that person is thinking about doing at that moment. I check my text messages, for example, because it's easy, and the value I receive from them varies but is usually quite high.

4. *Ability.* The person actually has to be able to act *right then*. Potential barriers include not knowing what to do, not having what you need to act, or feeling that you'll fail. These can be overcome, but that takes time. And when the barrier is resolved, the funnel starts anew—all of the other factors still need to be in place. For example, if I want to check my text messages, but can't find my phone, I need to search for it. While searching, I might get distracted into a different line of thought.

5. *Timing.* There has to be a reason to act now, rather than doing something else that is more urgent. If I'm expecting a message from my wife telling me where to meet her in a few minutes, that's

urgent. But if the text messages can wait (and there's something else I need to do, like a report that's due), I'll put it off even if I want to check the messages and have the ability to do so.

These five things are needed for the person to then *execute* the action; together they spell the acronym C-R-E-A-T-E. Habitual actions short-circuit the process; the evaluation and timing stages aren't as important. But before the habit is fully formed, the user must still pass through the full Create Action Funnel.

As you review the interface design, ask whether each of these conditions is met *for each small step* the user needs to take (i.e., each page click and each form entry, along the way toward the final target action).

Fix any small, obvious problems you see—like the user not knowing what to do on the screen, or competing cues on a particular screen to do different things. There may also be larger problems, where there isn't an obvious solution—like when there's no apparent value *to the user* for taking a particular step on the way to the target action. In those cases, it's time to return to the core design process: action-environment-user.

How to Fix the Big Gaps: Action-Environment-User

Let's say you've identified large issues that need to be resolved. You can run through the design process from Chapters 6–8 to fix them. As a quick refresher, these tasks include the following:

- *Structuring the action* to make it feasible for the user and to shift the burden of work from the user to the product where possible;
- *Constructing the environment,* both the product itself and the individual's broader decision-making context to motivate, cue, and give feedback to the user; and
- *Preparing the user* to take the action through a combination of education, self-narrative, and building on existing positive associations.

These three tasks help you focus your attention on one part of the design process at a time so that you can best put the pieces in place for action. They provide guidance on "how" to go about the design process, after the Create Action Funnel provides "what" needs to get accomplished.

You can structure the process of generating solutions as a series of questions. Naturally, the particular questions you need to ask depend on the gaps in the application, but here are general ones to get you going:

Structure the action

- How can these screens be tailored to better leverage the existing knowledge and experience of the users?
- Do these screens present the Minimum Viable Action required of the user?
- What parts can be dropped to simplify the process? What parts can be automated or intelligently defaulted?
- Are they any repeated actions that can be turned into habits?
- Is each action required clearly communicated to the user, and does it appear feasible up front from the perspective of someone with scant experience with the product?

Construct the environment

- Does the user have a clear motivation to continue on each screen, and is she thinking about that motivation in that moment?
- Are you asking the user to take a single clear action on each screen?
- If the action takes longer than a few seconds, does the product provide clear feedback to the user of progress (or of the need to course-correct)?
- What distractions are there on each screen that would pull the user away?
- What distractions is the user likely to face given the time of day and location in which she will access this screen? How can you work around them?

Prepare the user

- How does each user persona likely see himself, and does that self-concept support action on this screen?
- Does this look familiar to what users already know, especially when it comes to taking action on the screen? Is it clear where and how to take action?

- Does the user know what is needed, especially when action is required outside of the application? Are there clear, physically specific instructions?

Look for Tactical Opportunities

By now, the overall flow of the application should make sense. It's time to fine-tune the content on each specific screen to maximize impact. Time and time again, behavioral economists and psychologists have demonstrated the significant effects that apparently minor changes in the presentation of a question can have on user responses; see the following sidebar for one of the many examples.

An Unusual Disease

One of the most famous examples of the power of small changes in wording is this study by Tversky and Kahneman (1981):

> "Imagine that the US is preparing for the outbreak of an unusual Asian disease, which is expected to kill 600 people. Two alternative programs to combat the disease have been proposed. Assume that the exact scientific estimates of the consequences of the programs are as follows.
>
> Program A: If Program A is adopted, 200 people will be saved.
>
> Program B: If Program B is adopted, there is 1/3 probability that 600 people will be saved, and 2/3 probability that no people will be saved.
>
> *Which of the two programs would you favor?"*

[And a second group was given this set of options:]

> "Program C: If Program C is adopted, 400 people will die.
>
> Program D: If Program D is adopted, there is 1/3 probability that nobody will die, and 2/3 probability that 600 people will die.
>
> *Which of the two programs would you favor?"*

In the first group, people overwhelming selected Program A (72%). In the second group, people overwhelming selected Program D (78%).[122] *All of the programs are exactly the same in terms of the expected number of people that will live and die.* One of the things they do differently is present the program as a loss or a gain.

Losses are a tremendous motivator for behavior, as described later in "Leverage loss aversion." If you can frame the target action as avoiding loss, without becoming too negative overall, you can greatly increase the chance of action.[123]

The best *strategy* to change behavior can succeed or fail because of the specific *tactics* the application uses (i.e., how, exactly, the application interacts with the user). It's essential to take into account how our minds react to content on the screen.

At first, the range of possible tactics can seem overwhelming. In Chapter 1, I mentioned that there are hundreds of different mechanisms that researchers have identified that affect how we make decisions; most can affect how the specific content is put in applications. Many of the books that already exist on psychology and the design process focus on these tactics—from Stephen Anderson's *Seductive Interaction Design* (New Riders, 2011) to Dan Lockton's website Design with Intent Toolkit (*http://www.danlockton.com/dwi*), to Susan Weinschenk's *100 Things Designers Need to Know* (New Riders, 2011).

We need a way to organize the impact that these mechanisms have, to categorize them and determine if that's what's needed on a given page.[124] The Create Action Funnel from Chapter 2 provides a useful structure for that purpose. You can think of each of the individual page-level tactics as affecting one or more stages of the Create Action Funnel—making it more (or less) likely that the person will take action on the given page.

So, here's a scenario. Your users have just loaded a particular screen on your website, web app, or mobile app. This screen represents one of a sequence of steps that lead up to the target action that the user wants to take (or there's only one step, and that's the target action). How can you speed the person through that particular page? Table 10-1 presents two dozen tactics you can use, organized by the part of the Create Action Funnel that they affect most strongly.

TABLE 10-1 Tactics to support action on a particular page

COMPONENT	TO DO THIS	TRY THIS
Cue	Cue action	Tell the user what the action is
	Increase power of cue	Make it clear where to act
	Increase power of cue	Clear the page of distractions

COMPONENT	TO DO THIS	TRY THIS
Reaction	Increase trust	Make the site professional and beautiful
	Increase interest and trust	Deploy social proof
	Increase interest and trust	Display strong authority on subject
	Bypass automatic rejection	Be authentic and personal
Evaluation	Increase motivation	Prime user-relevant associations
	Increase motivation	Leverage loss aversion
	Increase motivation	Use peer comparisons
	Increase motivation	Use competition
	Decrease cost of action	Avoid cognitive overhead
	Decrease cost of action	Avoid choice overload
	Increase motivation	Avoid direct payments
Ability	Increase logistical ability	Elicit implementation intentions
	Decrease constraints	Default everything
	Decrease constraints	Lessen burden of action and information (cheat)
	Increase sense of feasibility (self-efficacy)	Deploy (positive) peer comparisons
Timing	Increase urgency	Frame text to avoid temporal myopia
	Increase urgency	Remind of prior commitment to act
	Increase urgency	Make commitments to friends
	Increase urgency	Make a reward scarce

The following sections describe each of these cognitive mechanisms, and how you can deploy them to the user's advantage. While I've devoted a separate section (this one) to how you can apply behavioral tactics to an existing interface design, this should ideally occur simultaneously with the main interface design process.[126]

Tactics for Cueing

Many of the tactics listed here have been mentioned earlier in the book, under the discussion of behavior change strategies or the conceptual plan. In those cases, the text focuses on how that tactic can be employed, in particular, at the interface design level. The goal of this section is to provide a quick reference to each of the major tactics you can use to improve your interface designs, all in one place.

TELL THE USER WHAT THE ACTION IS (AND ASK FOR IT)

See also: Chapters 2, 7

Cueing users to act on a given page starts with something that should be obvious, but unfortunately isn't: making sure they know what action is desired. I know, you can't imagine that anyone would make such an obvious mistake. But we all do, all the time. Do you include a link to your website at the bottom of your emails? If so, do you actually ask people to look at your site, or do you hope it's obvious? Do you post your Twitter handle on your messages or blog posts, hoping people will follow you? Readers could figure out the action we intend (view website, follow on Twitter), sure. But the more mental leaps that are required between what we see (Twitter name) and the action, the less likely is it that the action will cross our minds before we're distracted by something else.

Dustin Curtis (2009) ran a set of experiments on how he presented his Twitter handle to readers of his blog. He started with a simple informative statement: "I'm on Twitter," in which "Twitter" was a link to his page, and 4.7% of readers clicked. Then, he did the obvious—which apparently isn't so obvious to the rest of us—he told people what the action was: "Follow me on Twitter." Boom—7.31% of users clicked. And, even clearer: "You should follow me on Twitter here"—12.81% of users clicked. There are multiple effects at work in the last statement (a personal request, specificity, etc.), but the effect of requesting the action is undeniable. One lesson is simple: *directly, and unabashedly, ask people to take action.*

MAKE IT CLEAR WHERE TO ACT

We scan, we don't read. Don't expect users to read lots of text on your page. The two-second rule is a good test—if you don't get the gist in a two-second glance at the page, you risk losing the reader's attention. Krug's *Don't Make Me Think* (New Riders, 2006) gives a great overview and practical examples, and Johnson's *Designing with the Mind in Mind* (Morgan Kaufmann, 2010) talks about the visual perception system and related psychology.

Some of the key things that we quickly recognize are the ways in which we can interact with a page (*affordances* per Norman 1988)—what looks like it is clickable, doable, or can otherwise get you off this page and quickly on to the next one. The lesson is simple: make buttons look like buttons, and make anywhere else people are expected to take action clearly a place where they *can* take action.

CLEAR THE PAGE OF DISTRACTIONS

See also: Chapters 2, 7

Since we're scanning, and trying to save work, we're all too likely just to click on the first thing that looks clickable. Make a single clear call to action, if your goal is to get the person to keep moving through the page. Remove extra links and buttons, or place them in a distinctly lower level in the page's hierarchy.

BONUS TACTIC: BLINKING TEXT

Blinking text is a really great cue. It never fails to catch our attention! And it's also darned annoying because it catches our attention and won't let go. Don't do it. Seriously.

Tactics Related to the Intuitive Reaction

MAKE THE SITE PROFESSIONAL AND BEAUTIFUL

We rarely consider unprofessional-looking websites to be credible (Fogg et al. 2001). If you're trying to help someone take an action, don't make them have an intuitive reaction of distrust. That's unnecessary friction on the action. Like it or not, we assume that scammers make bad websites and apps. We even find it easier to *use* clean, well-designed products (see Anderson 2011 for examples). So, even if your app is created to help people, it has to look good.

DEPLOY SOCIAL PROOF

If we see that other people are taking an action, we're more likely to feel that the action is valuable and worthwhile. It's a quick gut check—if everybody does this, it must be OK, right? This is one of the major ways that our minds save work and quickly make decisions in uncertain situations.

Using social proof is a key tactic in sales and persuasion, with a long research tradition behind it (Cialdini 2001), and can be valuable for page-level behaviors as well. You can convey the fact that other people are taking the same action by using people's faces, short testimonials, or even a brief statement like "90% of people finish this step" (this is similar to a peer comparison, explained later). For more information on this topic, refer back to Chapter 1.

DISPLAY STRONG AUTHORITY ON THE SUBJECT

People are more likely to trust those who they see as an authority on the subject. If you're telling your users that they have to do action X in order to build up to their goal of Y (and it's true), then speak with authority. Don't write wishy-washy text. Make sure your credentials can be seen without beating your users over the head with them.

There are great studies on how people wearing suits, or with professional titles, are simply assumed to be more credible and trustworthy. The use of (perceived) authority is also a favorite tactic in sales and persuasion. See Cialdini's discussion of the underlying research (2001).

BE AUTHENTIC AND PERSONAL

People pay more attention to personal appeals to act than to impersonal ones. If you receive a letter with a hand-written envelope, how likely are you to open it? How about one with a standard machine-printed address? The reasons are manifold, but we are more likely to ignore machine-generated, impersonal appeals than tailored, personal ones (Garner 2005; Noar et al. 2007). We have an almost automatic response of "this is spam" for any email or letter from impersonal sources.

Here's a great example of using personalization and authenticity to cut through the noise and get people's attention. In Oregon, there's a lottery for free healthcare for people that can't afford it. But some of the people who sign up for and end up winning the lottery don't open the letters notifying them that they've won. And so they miss their chance at free healthcare.

Ideas42, the leading behavioral economics consultancy in the United States, devised a simple outreach campaign to the winners of the Oregon healthcare lottery. They notify people that they've won with a postcard featuring the smiling faces of the people at Providence Health in Oregon who will help them sign up for their healthcare. The recipient's name and address is handwritten on the postcard. Figure 10-1 shows a sample.

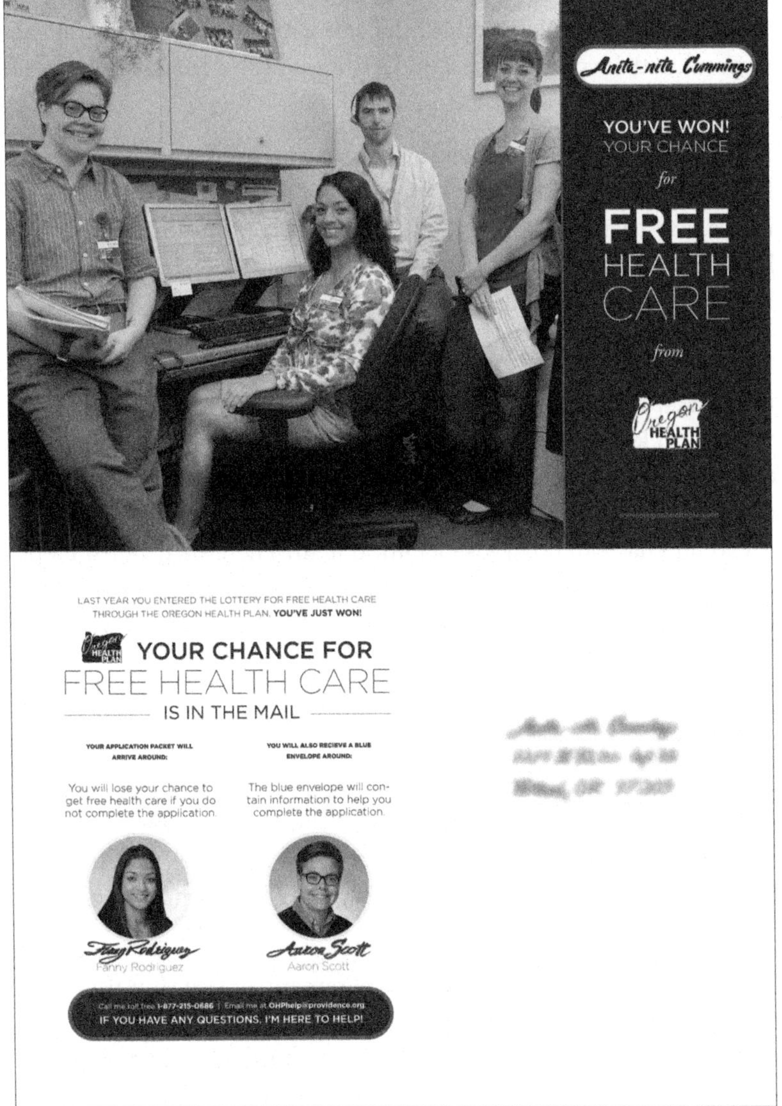

FIGURE 10-1.
A postcard developed by ideas42 to help winners of the Oregon healthcare lottery get past their automatic rejection of form letters, and read enough to see that they've won free healthcare

Remember, we've been conditioned to reject impersonal and computer generated appeals. Most of us have an intuitive reaction against them. To avoid that intuitive reaction, our products need to do something different, something that's good practice anyway: be authentic and personal.

Tactics Related to the Conscious Evaluation

PRIME USER-RELEVANT ASSOCIATIONS

We each have multiple possible mindsets with which we interpret and respond to the world. Those mindsets are selectively activated, based on our (very) recent experiences.

If you're asking people to commit to running once a week, get them thinking about previous times they've run, first (as long as that experience was positive)! When you ask them to commit to running, the benefits of running will be clearer and more salient in their minds. For more information on this topic, refer back to Chapter 1.

LEVERAGE LOSS AVERSION

People respond much more strongly to losses than to gains—they are "averse" to losses. In fact, in many scenarios, people will be willing to forfeit twice as much money to keep an item that they already have (and have no other personal attachment to), than they are willing to pay to purchase an otherwise identical item. There's a detailed literature on special cases of loss aversion, but that general rule holds true in many cases: *losses are roughly twice as motivating as gains* (Kahneman and Tversky 1984).

Loss aversion is a very powerful tool to help people change their behavior. By selectively framing the presentation of a desired action as *avoiding loss rather than gaining benefits*, the application can trigger a strong gut reaction to act. For example, it's can be much more persuasive to tell a guy that he'll lose sexual potency unless he gets in shape (Kolotkin et al. 2006), rather than telling him he'll gain a more attractive stomach.

When leveraging loss aversion, though, remember that your users can just stop using your product to avoid loss and negative emotions that come with it. The product must be seen as worthwhile and enjoyable overall—loss aversion should only be used on the margins.

USE PEER COMPARISONS

Being told about, and being compared to, the actions of our peers can be immensely powerful. Our behavior frequently conforms to what we believe our peers do (i.e., "descriptive norms"), compounded by the usually false belief that our peers are watching our behavior and judging it ("spotlight effect"). This effect has been shown in everything from energy usage (Cialdini et al. 1991) to voting (Gerber and Rogers 2009).

For behavioral products, the implications of peer comparisons are tremendous. Social norms are an incredibly powerful part of one's micro-environment and can encourage (or discourage) action. The same is true within the context of each individual screen that the user interacts with.

To use this technique, compare users' performance to a reference group that they care about (their friends, colleagues at work in a similar job position), and try to ensure that the reference group you choose is doing *better* than the user. Peer comparisons encourage people to move toward the norm (the average for the reference group). So, if you tell them they are already doing better than most people, they'll just relax and not work so hard. But that negative effect can be counteracted with an explicit social approval ("great job!") for exceeding the norm (Schultz et al. 2007). For more information on this topic, refer back to Chapter 1.

USE COMPETITION

We all have a natural competitive side—though it's much stronger in some people than others. Usually, you'd build a competition into the overall product (as described in Chapter 9, as one of the possible "design patterns for behavior change"), but it can be deployed at a page-level, too. For example, imagine a page that has people match Spanish words to their English meanings, to help the users learn Spanish. The page could include a counter of how many correct answers the individual has versus others on the page at the same time.

AVOID COGNITIVE OVERHEAD

Make it straightforward and clear what the user needs to do: each time the user has to make a logical leap from, "Oh, if I do this, then this will probably happen, but I'm not sure," that's costly. It takes time and energy away from the task at hand.

David Lieb (2013) gives a great example of a product that is physically easy to use, but still is costly to the user because of cognitive overhead. Here's his hypothetical user thinking through a QR Code: "So it's a barcode? No? It's a website? OK. But I open websites with my web browser, not my camera. So I take a picture of it? No, I take a picture of it with an app? Which app?" Forcing your users to think about what to do should be reserved for cases where their input is important and will shape their outcomes; don't force your users to expend energy because the product is confusing.

AVOID CHOICE OVERLOAD

A growing body of work demonstrates the difficulties individuals face when confronted with too many choices. Despite the common wisdom that more choices are better, two problems arise. First, people may refuse to make any decision at all. Second, people may regret the choices they made in an impossible search for the "optimal" choice (Iyengar 2010; Schwartz 2004).

For example, an often-cited study by Iyengar and Lepper (2000) placed two different displays of jam in a grocery store: one with 24 jams, and one with 6. The 24-jam display attracted 60% of customers, but only 3% of those shoppers ended up buying any of them. The 6-jam display attracted 40% of customers, but 30% of them bought one. Subsequent studies have also shown that satisfaction with one's choice, *whatever it is*, decreases with the number of options one had to choose among.

There is an obvious implication here when constructing individual pages in an app—avoid situations in which the user has to choose among a large number of options (if you want the user to make a choice and be happy with it). There is also a less obvious lesson: be wary of users (and fellow employees) who say they would really like more options. The person is probably telling the truth, at least from the perspective of that person's conscious deliberative self, but that doesn't mean providing more options is the right thing to do.

AVOID DIRECT PAYMENTS

You can always pay people to click on your button. But I don't recommend it. If you need to pay people to do something that's supposed to be a voluntary behavior change, you're probably not connecting that small action with the reason they want to change their behavior in the first place.

There is extensive evidence that financial incentives induce individuals to undertake behaviors that they would not undertake (Jenkins et al. 1998). People are motivated by money. No great surprise, right? However, when a person is already inclined to take the action, financial incentives can backfire by decreasing preexisting internal (intrinsic) motivations (Gneezy et al. 2011); the individual is more likely to stop the behavior after the incentive is removed. Similarly, other social, motivations are crowded out (see Ariely 2008 for examples) when we start thinking about our behavior in terms of being paid to act. Direct payments are less likely to cause problems with once-off behaviors, like signing up for the gym. But they can undermine long-term intrinsic motivation—like actually going to the gym over time! For more information on this topic, refer back to Chapter 7.

No Magic Wands

Throughout this book, I provide the tools you need to find the behavioral processes and product features that work in your particular context and verify their impact with your specific set of users.

What I can't do is give you the secret behavioral tricks that will always change user behavior in predictable ways. That's because such magical formulas simply don't exist (run away from people who tell you they do!). All behavior change interventions interact with an individual's desires, prior experiences, personality, and knowledge to produce their unique impact for that person. There is just too much variation across people for any approach to always work.

Most of the approaches and lessons that I talk about here have been tested either in a researcher's laboratory or in a specific product setting. In most cases, I've also observed these techniques in practice in my own work, or through the dozens of companies I've interviewed and learned from. Unfortunately, though, there are very few studies out there that apply and rigorously test theories of behavior change in ways that can be generalized to lots of other products. That's something we strive for at HelloWallet—but even then, it's very difficult to make the case that what works for us, in helping people take control of their finances, is going to work the same way for someone else's dieting software.

We are all still in the early stages of learning how to use products to help people change their behavior. So, in Chapter 14, I provide some guidelines on how to test specific interventions in your product and move the field forward at the same time. I encourage you to contribute your findings to the broader community so we can all learn and develop our skills together.

Tactics Related to the User's Ability to Act

ELICIT IMPLEMENTATION INTENTIONS

As you may recall, implementation intentions are specific plans that people make on how to act in the future (Gollwitzer 1999). They are a form of behavioral automation, telling the mind to do X whenever Y happens.[127] The person does the work of thinking through what needs to be done *now*, and then when the action is actually needed, there's no need to think, and no logistical barrier to action—the person just executes the action. Implementation intentions should include the event that triggers action, the context for that action, and the physical things the person should do. For example: "On Friday at work, if my supervisor yells at me about the project, I'll leave the room and take a short break rather than yelling back."

You can encourage the user to create a future action plan (implementation intentions) wherever the user is committing to take some future action, *especially* when that action is outside of the application. Making a specific, concrete plan of attack can help the person follow through with the action, even when the product isn't there as a reminder.

For behavioral products, deploying implementation intentions can mean adding text boxes where users describe how they'll take the action. The key is to make people think consciously about the concrete actions, and, if possible, visualize undertaking those actions. For more information on this topic, refer back to Chapter 7.

DEFAULT EVERYTHING

The power of defaults was touched upon earlier, when planning the overall behavioral strategy of the application. But it is also important to keep in mind for individual input fields within an application. In short, assume that many users will stick with whatever default value you give them. This occurs because people are in a hurry and don't fully read the questions posed to them, because they are unsure of what the question means, or because they simply do not have a strongly held preference.

This means that default values can be immensely useful (a) where the default response can move the individual closer to action, (b) where power users can fine-tune their responses, and (c) where everyone else can breeze past the defaulted values. However, default values should be used only where nonresponse is acceptable; it shouldn't be used where essential information is gathered. And, since users will make up fake answers (or simply disengage) when forced to answer questions that they can't really answer, it is better to altogether remove questions that users don't have answers to and can't be defaulted. When default values are provided, the answers should be interpreted as one part truth, and one part nonresponse.

For example, let's say your application asks users if they have kids. If there's special advice that's only relevant for people with kids, then default the answer to "no kids." Let those users who do have kids, and are paying enough attention, indicate it to receive the special content. For more information on this topic, refer back to Chapter 3.

LESSEN THE BURDEN OF ACTION AND INFORMATION (CHEAT!)

Part and parcel with defaulting is removing the need for users to do extra work. That's a high-level behavior change strategy, and it can and should be used as a tactic for particular interactions as well. If you don't need to ask a question of the user, don't. If you can save the user from scrolling down the page, excellent. That's just another small, but frictionful activity that the user needs to take on their path to action. Removing these frictions mean decreasing the cost of action, all else constant.

That isn't to say that users can't do work. There may be really important information below the fold, and the user really does need to read or act on it. However, if there is a choice between accomplishing the same task with or without additional form fields and user work, choose the route with less work. For more information on this topic, refer back to Chapter 3.

DEPLOY PEER COMPARISONS

If we think a task isn't achievable, we have better things to do with our time. On your pages, make sure not only that the person *can* do what's needed, but that they know they can do it, too. One way to accomplish that is through the peer comparisons described earlier: show the user that other people are successfully taking the action. For more information on this topic, refer back to "Use peer comparisons."

Tactics Related to When the Timing Is Right for Action

Ideally, the action on the page is inherently time-sensitive: people need to take the action immediately because of some existing, external rationale—like taxes on April 15. However, when that's not possible, there are a few other tactics that you can use.

FRAME TEXT TO AVOID TEMPORAL MYOPIA

We're wired to value the present far more than the future—that's our "temporal myopia." We talked about that earlier, when we looked at ways to motivate the user with immediate rather than future rewards. Well, what if you're stuck, and the basic structure of the application and its core motivation is already fixed? You can still avoid the curse of temporal myopia by crafting the descriptions you provide to the user.

When designing for behavior change, this means being very careful about the framing of time. Look for ways to frame benefits in terms of immediate or near-term gains; in the weight-loss example, reference how the dieter will feel and look better *almost immediately*. The opposite is true for *pain and effort*: effort that occurs sometime in the future is much easier to commit to than effort right now. So, if the pain and effort needs to be discussed at all, put it in the future as much as possible.[128] Benartzi and Thaler (2004) do this beautifully with their Save More Tomorrow plan—people commit now to saving (i.e., *pain*) at a future date. For more information on this topic, refer back to Chapter 7.

REMIND OF PRIOR COMMITMENT TO ACT

We don't like to be inconsistent with our past behavior. It's very uncomfortable, and we have a tendency to either act according to our prior beliefs, or change our beliefs so that they are in line with our actions (Festinger 1962). One way to achieve this is to have users impose urgency on themselves—promise to take the action at a specific time, then come back to them and remind them at that point. In addition to their other reasons to act, that will spur them to follow through, to avoid feeling inconsistent. For more information on this topic, refer back to Chapter 7.

MAKE COMMITMENTS TO FRIENDS

Another way to create urgency to act is to make specific promises to do so to one's friends. Social accountability is a powerful force—we don't want to let our friends down, or lose esteem in their eyes. The sidebar illustrates that point with a personal story from my friend Justin Thorp.

Our friends have a wide range of effects on our behavior, as we've talked about previously under the power of social proof and descriptive norms. But telling our friends what we're doing has a particular power to push us to act when we say we will. It's not just the action by which they judge us, but whether we kept our word overall—and that includes timing.

Our Friends Hold Us Accountable

I've always been a big guy. Back in the fall of 2009, I was clocking in around 280 and was getting fed up with being winded when I ran up a few flights of stairs. I knew it was time to do something different.

So I decided to get into running. That was a daunting task for me. I could barely run down the block. Being a nerd, my first thought was, what's better than exercising? It's exercising with technology. So I perused the app store and got RunKeeper—an app that used my phone's GPS to track how far, how fast, and where I ran. I was instantly hooked. It allowed me to see my progress throughout my running journey.

After a while, I noticed little Facebook and Twitter share buttons at the bottom of the RunKeeper report. With the press of the button, I could share my runs with my friends. I was like, "What the hell?" and hit the button not really thinking much of it.

A few days passed, and all of a sudden my friends and coworkers started noticing my runs. They were commenting on my Facebook posts. They were cheering me on via social media. When I wouldn't run, my boss would ask, "Justin, why didn't you go running today?"

When I got up in the morning and didn't want to go running, I'd hear the voices of my friends and supporters in my head. I didn't want to let them down. They believed in me and believed that I could do it.

And I did. I lost 50 lbs. I ran the Cherry Blossom 10 Mile Race. I gained a ton of confidence. And I still run regularly. It's become a great way for me to get exercise and clear my head.

—Justin @thorpus

Of course, it all depends on who we look to for support and accountability. If we turn to people who really don't care about us, or who don't value the activity we're trying to undertake, then their disinterest can sap us of motivation. Products can mitigate this by explicitly asking people to identify friends and colleagues who will support them, or by matching up the person with other users who are seeking to change the same behavior or have experience providing support (i.e., products can construct a local network of peers who *will* push us to succeed). Lift.do does something akin to that, as does Goal Sponsors, for a fee.[129]

MAKE A REWARD SCARCE

You can make a reward for the action scarce ("the names of the first 100 people losing 100 pounds will be featured on our website"), or artificially time-sensitive ("act in the next five minutes, and you'll get another 10 points"). This is another favorite sales and marketing tactic (Cialdini 2001; Alba 2011). It's best for once-off actions, and not repeated behavior. If you try to repeatedly push for a behavior with scarcity, people will stop believing you. Also, you run the risk of desensitizing the person to normal scenarios that aren't artificially scarce or time-sensitive.

Update the Interface Designs

After the interface designs have been evaluated for large gaps, and opportunities to leverage specific cognitive mechanisms have been found, you should make recommendations to the product manager for changes to the designs. These changes would then be considered in terms of their behavioral, engineering, and aesthetic impact. The end result is an updated interface design.

On a Napkin

Here's what you'll need to do

- Review the interface designs for the five prerequisites: cue, reaction, evaluation, ability, and timing.
- Apply specific tactics in each of these areas, leveraging the literature in behavioral science.
- If there are large gaps, you can repeat the exercises from Chapters 6–8, focusing on the action, the environment, and the user in turn.

How you'll know there's trouble

- Endless debates over wording and design details. Such questions should be tested in practice.

Deliverables

- Revised wireframes or mockups

[11]

Turning the Designs into Code

Put the Interface Design in Front of Users

When the interface designs are ready, the product team should test them in the field—before committing engineering resources to a full implementation. Ideally, that should be done with low-cost clickable prototypes—to increase the realism of the experience for users. But the team can gather rough and dirty feedback from graphic designs, aka *comps*, too. This process should iterate as many times as needed until the designs are solid and successful in the field.

Besides all of the excellent reasons one normally hears for user testing—to look for usability problems, to get gut reactions on aesthetics, to identify missing functionality—there's an additional reason in the case of designing for behavior change: you can never be certain the package will "work," behaviorally, until it does.

As I discussed in Chapter 1, behavioral social science, and with it, the process of designing for behavior change, is still developing rapidly. There aren't any simple formulas for behavior change. The previous chapters in this book have provided guidelines on leveraging the excellent research that's available, but field testing and refinement are still absolutely essential to the process.

As you gather user feedback, surprises will occur. The application may be quite engaging for some users, but completely uninteresting to others (or worse, it could be patently offensive). There are two issues in particular to consider as you gather this feedback:

- Keep in mind what the team defines as "success."
- Look for behavioral feedback.

Keep in Mind What the Team Defines as "Success"

Is success reaching 100% of users? Or, could success mean helping 10% of people immensely, and learning how to help the rest over time? If some of the users strongly dislike the product (but others like it), that's not necessarily a problem. We can easily focus on the negative cases—where the product doesn't work—and lose sight of the larger signal we get from our initial testing efforts that the product *does* work in many other cases. Think about whether the behavioral impact needs to be evenly distributed across the users, or whether you should *expect* diverging opinions and results among test users. Chapters 12 and 13 discuss the detailed metrics you'll need within the product itself to gauge success, but it's important to keep in mind your definition of success even when you're in this initial phase of gathering feedback from users on prototypes.

Look for Behavioral Feedback

People's *behavior* using the prototypes is much more reliable than their conscious, verbal feedback. Recall the discussion of choice overload (Chapter 10). People often say they want many options in their products but actually find those options paralyzing when confronted with them. If you present a screen that lets them customize every aspect of their exercise plan, they may express excitement and interest but be completely befuddled when trying to use it.

Other cognitive quirks also muddy the conscious verbal feedback that participants give. For example, we have a strong tendency to generate meaningful narratives for our past behavior even when luck and circumstance directed our actions. Instead of listening to what people say, look for what they do—do they spend a lot of time trying to make a decision on a particular page, do they actually complete a page sequence, or do they give up early?

Finalize the Designs

Based on the results of the user testing, you and the rest of the product team will have numerous ideas on how to further improve the product. If the schedule and product process allow it, it's ideal to repeat the design and review process (developing wireframes and specs, reviewing them from behavioral and engineering perspectives, and developing or updating the prototype) as many times as is feasible until the design looks solid. It's better to find the problems early—in the face of user feedback—than later.

In addition, throughout the user testing process, look for opportunities to *cut*. I've argued previously for targeting the Minimum Viable Action that the user needs to take to meet their behavioral goal. If the user testing process shows that certain interactions are confusing or difficult for users, the first response should be to remove that interaction altogether (if the product still meets its behavioral goals), rather than investing time into "fixing it." Simpler, shorter interactions will almost always be completed more often than longer, complex ones.

Build the Product

Plan and Prioritize Engineering Resources

In traditional product development processes, there is a point at which the engineering team reviews the proposed application design and comments on resource requirements for each component.[130] Engineers provide feedback to the product team on what is *feasible* to build in the desired time frame and help inform the prioritization of product features. The same process should occur when developing products to change behavior, but with one an additional stakeholder—the behavioral expert (the interaction designer, product manager, or other person tasked with designing for behavior change).

The behavioral expert's role is to evaluate the likely behavioral impact of each major change; if a proposed feature is not feasible from an engineering perspective, would the remaining functionality have the desired effect? The product manager should weigh the input of the engineering team, behavioral expert, the UX experts (on the usability of the remaining application functionality), and potentially the business/sales team (to inform the salability of the resulting application). For any element that the product manager decides to cut or substantially alter, then the behavioral expert should provide suggestions on how to still meet the behavioral aims of the application (i.e., how to ensure that the application is still effective).

Evaluate Engineering Trade-Offs

Next, the vetted, user-tested designs are taken up by the engineering team to build. Final graphic designs are made, and the coding of the software starts. As the product is engineered, naturally adjustments many be needed to the designs. The product team should work with engineering to track the implementation of the designs and adjust the designs as needed based on engineering roadblocks.

There are two things to keep an eye out for during the engineering process:

- Ensure that the Minimum Viable Action is still supported. Extraneous pieces can and should be cut, but you can't deliver psychology in pieces. Either the clear mechanism that helps users take action is there, or it isn't.
- Watch out for pauses and inefficiencies in the user experience that break the flow of user actions. Users need to feel that they will be successful at each step, in a reasonable amount of time, and that each step meaningfully builds toward the goal, or else they will give up.

Test It

Software bugs take on a special meaning in a behavior change world: they cut into the credibility, perceived reliability, and sense of immersion that is necessary for many psychological mechanisms to work. The last thing you want is for your users to be consciously thinking about how buggy the product is, or build up a strong association between your product and low quality.

Paraphrasing Dave Ramsey's guidance about where to seek financial advice (2009): you wouldn't trust a finance teacher who was broke, and you wouldn't trust an application to help change your life if the app can't even function properly.

Go Lean If Possible

Thus far, I've intentionally avoided making strong recommendations about product methodology. As I've stressed earlier, designing for behavior change can work with any methodology. Thinking about the psychology of your users can happen in a sequential development model just as it can in an agile development approach. But if you're not sure what to do, the lean startup approach provides a firm foundation.

The lean startup approach (Ries 2011) teaches that each iteration of the product should generate validated learning about what the market actually wants. It recommends building the Minimum Viable Product that can test whether product concept will work and getting it into people's hands as quickly as possible. From a practical perspective, that means taking the most basic, testable part of the designs and building that before anything else (and, of course, not spending more time on the initial designs than is necessary).

The approach is very much in line with the philosophy of designing for behavior change. While you can (and should) design your product thoughtfully, you never really know if the psychology will work until it does. So, though it's not required when designing for behavior change, it certainly helps to take a lean startup approach when designing and building the product.

On a Napkin

Here's what you'll need to do

- Get the designs in front of users—preferably in the form of a clickable prototype, but graphic designs can work, too.
- Watch for user *behavior* as people interact with the prototype, and pay less attention to what they *say*.
- As the product is built, evaluate engineering trade-offs for their behavioral implications.

How you'll know there's trouble

- The final product is feasible to build from an engineering perspective, but is disconnected from the behavioral plan and doesn't provide a compelling story for behavior change.

Deliverables

- The product!

[*Part V*]

Refining the Product

You've built one heck of a product. It looks good, it's engaging, and it incorporates the best of behavioral science. After testing and gathering feedback on the wireframes and prototypes, and building the first versions of the actual product, you're ready to deploy it. The following chapters cover what comes next: figuring out how much of an impact the product actually has, and generating ideas on how to improve it (see Figure Part V-1).

In terms of the iterative product development process first presented in the Preface, these chapters are about *impact, insight, and measuring changes to the product*. Chapter 12 gathers data on the product's current impact and sets a benchmark for future changes to the product. Chapter 13 gathers additional data on user behavior to find the places in the application where users get stuck and develop potential solutions. Chapter 14 further develops those potential solutions and integrates them into the next round of the product development cycle. Those changes to be measured could be fundamental changes to the outcome, actor, or action, or additions to the behavioral plan or user stories that are added to the product's backlog of tasks to complete.

FIGURE PART V-1. Part V covers the *impact assessment, insight and ideas,* and moving deeper into the spiral with changes to the product and *measurements of each change* in future iterations

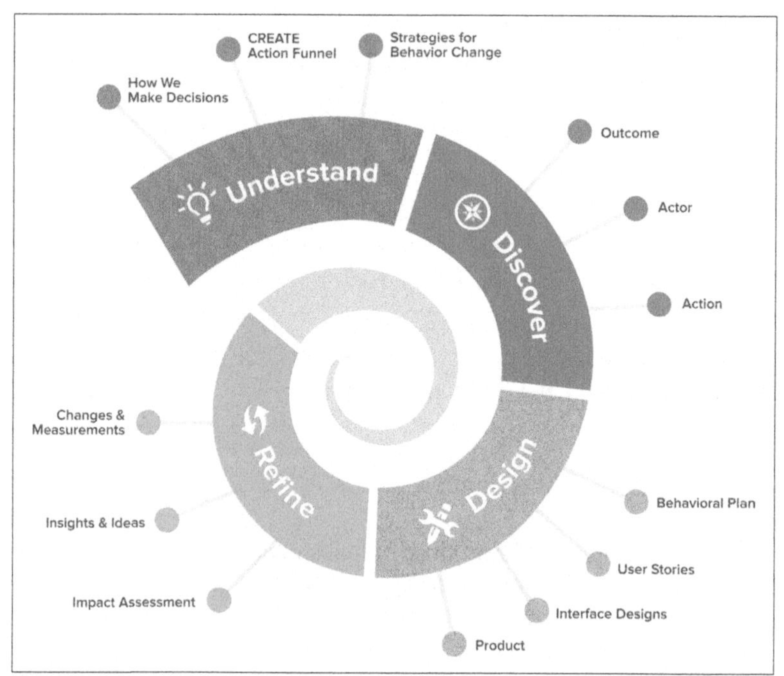

[12]

Measuring Impact

Opower, an energy-efficiency company based in Arlington, Virginia, runs some of the largest experiments in the world about how products can change behavior. Millions of people have participated in their studies—simply by opening a letter from their utility company or fiddling with their thermostat.

Opower is best known for delivering monthly reports to utility customers, showing them how their energy usage stacks up against their (anonymous) neighbors. It's a well-studied technique in social psychology called peer comparisons, which we discussed a bit in Chapter 10. Figure 12-1 shows an example of one of its comparisons.

A host of government, private, and academic publications have shown that Opower's simple comparisons help consumers cut their energy bills by roughly 2% on average (Alcott 2011). That may seem small, but it adds up to over 2.6 terawatt-hours of electricity—enough to power 300,000 homes for a year, or roughly $300 million in consumer savings on energy bills (Opower 2013).

Opower constantly runs experiments to measure their impact and tests ways to improve it further. Rigorous measurement and testing has been a key factor in their success.

This chapter and the next two provide the tools you need to measure your product's current impact and improve that impact in the future.

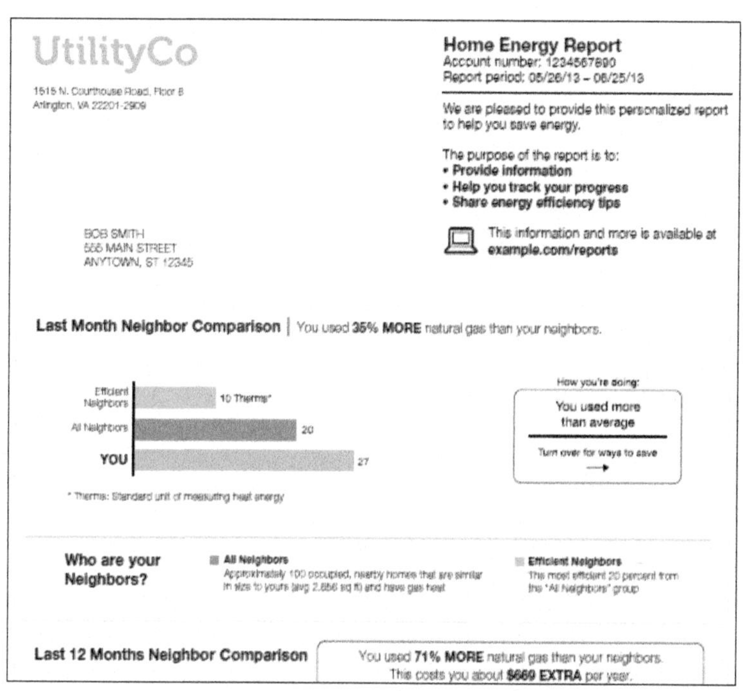

FIGURE 12-1. Opower energy report, comparing the reader's home heating usage to that of his neighbors

Anyone Can Measure Impact

When you read the title of this chapter, do you imagine arcane symbols and inscrutable formulas? That's not what you'll find. Instead, you'll find common-sense explanations of how you can measure your product's impact.

For software products, there are numerous powerful and user-friendly tools that handle the underlying math and statistics for you. For most impact experiments, that's all you really need. You usually don't need an econometrician to understand if your product is working or not and how to improve it.

Some techniques are more advanced though; I'll mention that up front and explain what is going on in nontechnical terms. If you don't have a statistical background, and you decide that you need those techniques, that's a point at which you need to get some expert assistance. For readers with a statistical background, those sections will quickly tell you which tool to pull from your toolbox so you can get to work.

Why Measure Impact?

The ultimate goal of this book is to help you design products that support behavior change. This chapter is about measuring how effective the product really is, right now. Naturally, both you and I know that the product is impeccable. But there are a few good reasons to carefully and precisely measure its impact anyway:

To share with the finance department
: Precise measurements of product impact allow a company to determine its return on investment. That's important for the company's internal finance department—to justify future design and engineering work—and for any external funders (from grant makers to venture capitalists).

To share with the team
: One of the most rewarding experiences I have in my daily work is when I send out messages to the staff about positive research results—showing how we're quantifiably helping people. The thank you notes are deep and heartfelt. Seeing the real impact the product has on users helps the folks in the trenches, who develop the product day in and day out, to see the value of their work.

To share with the world
: When you have something that works, show it off. You know you want to anyway. Just *saying* that your product works isn't news; no one has a reason to trust you. If you can demonstrate your impact, especially with an independent, third-party experiment, that's news.

To improve the impact
: With a benchmark of the product's current impact, the team can experiment (formally or informally) with changes. The team can then tell whether the changes helped or hurt, and come up with even more ideas to move the product forward.

To learn what's hindering impact
: Properly deployed, measurements of impact can help the product team understand where, exactly, users are facing behavioral challenges and where the product is failing to deliver on its promise.

To settle arguments

Rather than relying on the loudest member of the team, or the Highest Paid Person's Opinion (HiPPO), impact measurements turn arguments about what the product should do and what it should look like into a dispassionate look at the data. Instead of arguing about what *might* work, see what *does* work with quick tests. Computer scientist and Admiral Grace Hopper said it well: "One accurate measurement is worth a thousand expert opinions."

Now that you're suitably convinced, let's talk about how to actually do it.

Where to Start: Outcomes and Metrics

Make Sure the Target Outcome Is Clear

The first step in measuring the impact of your product is to be absolutely clear on the impact you care about (i.e., the intended outcome of the product). In Chapters 4 and 5, we identified the target outcome, actor, and action that would determine whether the product was a success or not. Here's a quick refresher on defining the *outcome*:

- The outcome is *what will be different* in the real world when the product is successful.
- The outcome should be something *tangible*, and not something in the user's head. Often the user's head is just a proxy for what the company really cares about—a tangible outcome that occurs because the user's knowledge or emotions have changed. For example: lower BMI, or time spent exercising each week, instead of knowledge about the importance of exercise and maintaining one's weight.
- The outcome should be something *unambiguously measurable*. For example, your product is supposed to decrease government corruption. But what is corruption exactly?
- The outcome should be able to *signal success*. If you can say, "Well, if X didn't happen, the product would still be a success," then X is not the outcome we're looking for.
- The outcome should be able to *signal failure*. You must be able to think of a plausible case in which the outcome would indicate that the product is failing.

Vanity metrics—metrics that make a company feel good but don't give an accurate sense of whether the product and company are on the right track—fail on these criteria. For example, consider page views—the stereotypical vanity metric. Let's say a company had *zero* revenue from its flagship consumer product but had lots of page views on the product's website. That usually wouldn't be considered a success. (And, vice versa: if the product brought in lots of revenue, but for some reason it had few page views, that *would* be considered a success.)

Define Metrics for the Outcome and Action

With a clear outcome in mind, you should define two metrics: one for the *outcome* and one for the *action*. You need to know, unambiguously, whether the target outcome has occurred (and at what level) and whether the user has taken the action that is supposed to be causing the outcome.

The outcome metric should flow directly from the target outcome itself. It's how you determine if the outcome is there or not. You should define and write down a formula, even a dirt simple one, which says how the outcome is measured. Here are some easy ones:

- Company income = money received from clients over the course of a month
- User weight = body weight without shoes, measured in the morning after breakfast

And here's one that is a bit more complex:[131]

- Neighborhood connectivity = number of times users attend social gatherings with their neighbors over the course of a month

The metric should make clear *what* is measured, *how* it is measured, and for *how long* it is measured. For example, one way to define company revenue for a particular product is: money received (not money booked) because of product sales (not investment earnings or sales of fixed company assets), over a 30-day period.

Why so specific? Because if the value of the metric changes over time, we need to be sure that it changed because of your product, and not because the metric's definition was unclear, and two different ways of measuring it over time caused a *fake* change in the data.

Ideally, the metric should be:[132]

Accurate
: It actually measures the outcome you want to measure.

Reliable
: If you measure the exact same thing more than once, you'll get the exact same result.

Rapid
: You can quickly tell what the value of the metric is. Rapidness encourages repeated measurement, and makes it easier to see if a *change* in the product was effective.

Responsive
: The metric should quickly reflect changes in user behavior. If you have to wait a month until you can measure the impact of a change (even if it only takes a minute to measure it; i.e., even if it is rapid), that's 29 days wasted that you could have been learning and improving the product.

Sensitive
: You can tell when small changes in the outcome and behavior have occurred. For the developers among you: floating-point values are great; Booleans are not.

Cheap
: Measuring the outcome *multiple times* shouldn't be costly for the organization or it will shy away from measuring the impact of individual changes to the product and have difficulty improving it.[133]

Quite a lot there, right? Yes, but that doesn't mean you need to obsess over the perfect metric. What we're really looking for is a quick check of sufficiency. Treat this list like a checklist—for a given outcome metric, ask the following: is it specific enough that there won't be too much disagreement when it's measured? Is it reliable enough that it won't fool the team into thinking the product isn't working when it actually is?

Defining a metric for the *action* is similar. The action metric tells you whether (and to what degree) the user is taking the target action, the action that is supposed to drive the desired outcome. If the desired outcome is a specific BMI level, and the action is exercise, a sample metric would be: how much is the user exercising, and how often? A good action metric must pass the same tests as the outcome metric: accurate, reliable, rapid, responsive, etc. Here are some good and bad action metrics:

ACTION: USER EXERCISES

Bad metric

User exercises = how much the user reports walking each day. This is a bad metric because (a) the user may not know how far he or she is walking without the help of a pedometer or other tracker and (b) the user may stretch the truth.

Good metric

User exercises = how much a pedometer automatically tracks the user walking each day

ACTION: USER STUDIES NEW LANGUAGE

Bad metric

User studies = an expert evaluation of language proficiency on a lengthy written exam. This metric is problematic because it focuses on the intended *outcome* rather than on the *activity* that we assume, rightly or wrongly, leads to that outcome. It also takes a long time to measure and can't be measured frequently (without annoying the users!).

Good metric

User studies = time spent within the application, or number of exercises completed with a minimal level of accuracy

Clearly, there are trade-offs when creating outcome and action metrics. The most accurate metric may take too long to gather, or the cheapest metric may not be reliable. Again, there's no need to obsess over it—we're looking for an action metric that is sensitive enough to tell you when there is a problem, and accurate enough to not mislead the team.

Set the Thresholds for Success and Failure

There are always opportunities for new products, new problems to solve, and new markets to tap. At some point, the company needs to determine whether the product is "good enough" to move on to something else, or that it is failing so badly that it should be discontinued or major corrective action should be taken. To support that assessment, the company should determine the specific threshold for "success" and "failure," up front.

For a new company, new product, or new market, it can be difficult to know what *should* be labeled a success or a failure. The company can turn either inward (this is what *we* need in order to sustain the business and not pursue the next most promising product), or outward (this is what *other* similar products are achieving; if we aren't achieving that, we won't gain traction in the market). I haven't seen any hard-and-fast rules here—it's up to the company to decide what it needs to accomplish with the product.

The thresholds of success and failure should be set *before* they are measured (and ideally, before the product is even built, as we talked about briefly in Chapter 5). Many of us have been in companies where we've spent months (or years!) developing a product, deployed it to the market, and gotten a lackluster response. Then, the spin starts: looking for things that are positive, looking for things that indicate it might possibly get better if the team put in another few months of work. That's a moment of truth, when a dispassionate, spin-free analysis is needed. Maybe it's just not the right product, maybe it's actually good enough and the team is being too hard on itself. Setting up clear definitions of success and failure beforehand helps combat the temptation to spin the numbers after the fact.

Defining success and failure ahead of time doesn't mean that we can't change the goal posts now and then. As we learn more about the market, product, and the company's other opportunities, our understanding of what's "good enough" will change. But make sure the team knows about the change, and understands the rationale. No one likes a moving target—especially when that means making the job harder for the team midstream and without explanation (raising the standard) or it seems like accepting failure (lowering the standard).

How to Measure Those Metrics

You know what you want to measure. Now, you need to measure it: by instrumenting the product or otherwise gathering data about your users' behavior and the target outcome. How you gather this data depends on the type of product and behavior change you're working with: whether the target behavior is within, or outside, of the product.

Measuring Behaviors Within the Product

If the behavior that the product is trying to change is part of the product itself, you're in luck. There are tools to help you gather the data. For example, let's say your application aggregates user contacts and helps users keep in touch with them regularly, like Contactually.[134] The behavior change problem entails helping your users figure out how to best organize their contacts within the app.

You can code your product to automatically record the actions that users take (organizing contacts) to see if they are successful. In that case, you can code your product to automatically record the action and outcome or push events out to a third-party platform like KISS Metrics or Mixpanel[135] (that's what Contactually uses). That's the ideal. When your product is online, you can even gather the data in real time and see what's going on immediately.

Measuring Behaviors Outside of the Product

It can be much more challenging if the behavior change problem is outside of the product. First, look for ways to pull in existing real-world data. At HelloWallet, one of our primary goals is to help people save money for the future. But they can't actually do that within our application—they move money into their savings accounts through their bank. Early on in our product development, we realized that we needed to ask our users for read-only access to their bank account information. With the bank account information, we could provide them with better guidance, and, very importantly, we could tell if our guidance was actually working or not.

You'll need to be creative, and search for datasets you can pull in. Opower's main product, described at the beginning of this chapter, is a piece of paper—a physical mailer sent to utility customers. There's no way to reliably measure people's real-world behavior with that mailer. But they have built relationships with the utility companies to access utility records on how much energy people actually use. And, with that data, they can reliably tell what impact their mailers are having on behavior.

Tools for Gathering Data Within the Product

To measure your product's impact, you'll need to look beyond basic tools that track page views and conversions. Often the impact you're looking for isn't just a simple event in the application, like a page view. For example, if your product helps users form the habit of updating their budget each month, measuring the habit means more than the pages they've seen. Second, you'll need access to raw, per-person data for statistical modeling. Third, in order to assess changes in impact, you'll probably need to run A/B tests.

If you're not familiar with them, A/B tests take a randomly selected group of users and show them one version of the product (version "A"), and show another randomly selected group another version (version "B"). Tools that support A/B testing or its cousin, multivariate testing, will advertise that fact; the mechanics of A/B testing and multivariate testing are discussed in the section "Determining Impact: Running Experiments."

There are a variety of tools that can handle the A/B testing for you. For example, Google Analytics has taken the old Google Website Optimization package (with A/B testing support), and integrated it as the Google Analytics Content Experiments Interface.

Getting individual-level data—what each person is doing in the system—requires more horsepower; it's something that Google Analytics doesn't provide. There's an open source version of Google Analytics that does what Google Analytics does (though a few versions behind), and provides that individual-level data: Piwik.[136] It can be a bit clunky, but it gets the job done if you know how to analyze the raw database records.

Other tools, such as KISS Metrics, provide per-person tracking and also provide a nice GUI for doing some of the analyses you need. You'll need to access the raw data (available via Amazon's S3 service) to really dig into the details. Companies can also readily implement their own per-person tracking by pushing the events that occur within the system out to a database for later analysis.

Your company may need to *consider adding functionality to the app to make real-world measurement possible*. Let's say you have an app that helps people eat healthier. It provides meal plans for easy and healthy home cooking, so users don't need to eat out as much. That's great, but how do you know if the product is successful? Creating a meal plan isn't enough. You need to know if people are actually acting on that advice. One way to measure behavior outside of the product (actual use of the meal plan) would be to add a feature to link to the person's grocery store loyalty card. The grocery store knows what the user is buying, and has a financial incentive to have people buy more there, instead of eating out. Users can be rewarded for following the meal plan, and get greater insight into what they are eating.[137] There's a benefit for the user, the grocery store, and for you—since you'll be able to measure impact.

Sometimes however, there simply isn't a dataset you can draw upon, or the dataset is too imperfect or infrequent to use. For example, let's say your application encourages people to vote. The act of voting is outside of the product, and it takes months to get official data on whether someone voted or not.

In such cases, where you really don't have a way to regularly gather real-world data, there's a three-part strategy for benchmarking your product's impact:

- Benchmark the impact your product has on an intermediate user behavior that you can measure regularly, even though it isn't the final real-world outcome you really care about.
- Determine how to accurately measure the real-world outcome *at least once.*
- Build a bridge between the intermediate user behavior you measure regularly and the real-world outcome you care about.

The data bridge is basically a *second* benchmark—connecting the regularly measured behavior (usually in the app) and the irregularly measured real-world outcome. To make the explanation clearer, let's start with the first benchmark: the link between your product and regularly measured in-product behaviors. We'll return to the data bridge after we've learned the basic benchmarking procedure.

Determining Impact: Running Experiments

You know what you want to measure and can measure it. Let's determine the impact your product is currently having.

The gold standard for measuring the impact of a product is to employ randomized controlled experiments, otherwise known as A/B tests or split tests. You select a random sample of potential users then divide the sample into a control group and a treatment group at random. The control group doesn't receive the product (or, if the team is developing a new feature, the control group doesn't receive that feature). The treatment group receives the new application (or feature). You would then measure the outcome for each group. The impact of the application is simple to calculate, once you know you have a strong signal from your data:

Average outcome with treatment group – average outcome with control group

And yes, that's it. Basic experiments are very easy and straightforward to analyze if they are designed correctly. The beauty of experiments is their simplicity and power. It allows you to focus on what you care about (impact) and not worry about all of the other things that can give misleading results or lead to endless arguments about interpreting the data. For example:

- "Aren't the people who appear to benefit from your product just the people who would have done well on their own?" Impact experiments show what happens *above and beyond* what people would normally do; you measure "normal" behavior with the control group, and subtract it out.
- "Couldn't the good results you're seeing be caused by something else?" Impact experiments show the unique impact of the product, above and beyond external impacts (i.e., anything else that might be happening at the same time to cause good outcomes). The difference between the treatment group (external impacts and product impact) and the control group (external impacts only) is the unique product impact.

While this type of experiment is excellent for telling you *what* impact you're having, it can't tell you, at least not directly, *why* the product has that impact. We'll talk about that in Chapter 13.

In order for your experiment to be successful, there are a few things you need to be careful about:

Make sure you have enough people
: How do you know how many people are enough? There are books on the topic, but for most people a simple online calculator is enough. There are two versions of the calculation: to estimate how many people you need *before* you run the experiment (a "sample size" or "power calculation" test), and to determine if you really

can tell the two apart after the experiment ("statistical significance" test). I will explain how these tests work in the common scenarios.

Ensure a real random assignment

Make sure that the treatment and control groups are actually randomly assigned. Use a random number generator, and generate a new number for each person. If you have an existing list of people, and it "looks" random, it almost never actually is—there's some ordering there, but you can't know how it influences the results. *This is the most common way I've seen product-based experiments go awry, and it completely destroys the experiment.* As a sanity check, you can verify that the random assignment process was done correctly by checking whether the two groups have similar averages on things that the product couldn't impact—like age or gender. If so, great. If not, it wasn't a true random assignment.

Make sure you're only varying one thing

Only the product should vary across the two groups. Don't treat the two groups differently or measure their outcomes differently in any other way. You *can* test multiple versions of the product at once (the only thing you're varying is the product) with an "A/B/C test" or a multivariate test; they are discussed in "Running Multiple Versions at Once."

Compare results for everyone

Make sure that when you compare the two groups, you compare all of the people in each group. In the treatment group, for example, there will be some people who are offered the product, but don't actually use it. Count the nonusers, too; otherwise the results mix up the effect of the product, with the effect of who chooses to use it or not.

Know who you're working with

Check whether users have previously had experience with the product. For example, let's say you're trying out a product or feature on a population that already has experience with a previous version of the product. The test is still valid, but that limits how much you can *generalize* the results of the test to people who have *never* had experience with the product.

Measure the same thing for both groups

If you are testing the impact of the entire product (instead of just a new feature), and the product tracks the outcome, how do you know the outcome for the control group? They don't have the product! That's a challenge. There are two main options: find a way to measure the outcome outside of the product (and use the same method for both the treatment and control), or use a crippled product with the control group that only tracks the outcome, and nothing else. Or, if that fails, you have to use statistical models to estimate causal impact (that's covered later on in this chapter).

How Many People Do You Need?

When you're benchmarking your product, you're trying to figure out how much impact it normally has on your target outcome. The quality of your benchmark depends on how much information you have: you need to pass a certain threshold in terms of the number of people you examine for the results to be meaningful.

Here's a simple example of why the number of people in the experiment is important. Let's say your product helps people eat less ice cream. You try it with one person. Poof! He doesn't eat any more ice cream! The second person, well, he doesn't do so well. He actually eats more ice cream and hates you for it. The third person cuts back a lot. So does the fourth, and so on. That's actually a pretty normal variation across people.

Overall, the product is a success. It helps people cut their (unwanted) ice cream habit by 50%. If you'd only looked at the first person, though, you'd have thought it was magic. If you only looked at the first two people, you'd be really confused. If you looked at the first four, then the picture would be clearer—overall, it seems to help, but there are exceptions. Adding additional people makes the picture clearer and clearer. But by the time you add the thousandth person, that person's data isn't going to help much. You'll already have a very good idea of what the impact of the product is. You don't need more people.

In many cases, it's straightforward and easy to estimate how many people you need in an experiment, or the desired "sample size." Intuitively, your desired sample size depends on how big of an impact you're looking for, relative to the baseline outcome, and how much noise there is clouding that impact.

Here are the specific numbers you'll need:

- The average outcome for people who don't have the product (or who don't have the new feature you want to test). That's the *baseline.*
- The variance (difference from the average) in outcomes among people without the product (or new feature). That's the *noise.*
- The smallest *meaningful impact* on the outcome. Or, how much of change in outcomes do you need for you to justify rolling out the new product or feature to more people? Be conservative: hopefully the product will have a much *larger* impact, but here you want the smallest change that would tell you it's a success.

You'll plug these values into an online calculator, like the ones on the DSS Research site.[138] If the product's outcome can have many evenly spaced values, like weight, height, or number of cigarettes smoked in the month, then you'll use a calculator that can handle the average value for the population. If the product's outcome can only be one of two things, like either the patient is alive or dead, then you'll use a calculator that handles percentages.

You'll be asked for two parameters that indicate how sensitive the test should be:

- Confidence level or, equivalently, an alpha error level (alpha error level = 1 – the confidence level). Usually the default confidence level is 95% (alpha of 5%). That roughly means you can expect to incorrectly say there *is* an impact when really there *isn't* one, 5% of the time. *That's a false positive.*
- Statistical power, or, equivalently, a beta error level (beta error level = 1 – statistical power). Usually the default statistical power is 80% (beta of 20%); that roughly means you can expect to incorrectly say there *isn't* an impact when really there *is* one 20% of the time. *That's a false negative.*

These default parameter values are built around the assumption that you want to be very careful not claiming that there's an impact when there isn't. It's important, but not as important, to avoid missing an impact that really is there. Each study is different, but those are pretty good assumptions to use when you're testing whether your product works or not. It will be very embarrassing (and costly for the engineering team) to claim you've found an answer, pursue it, then find out it was a mirage. So, generally, keep these defaults.

You may also be confronted with a question of whether you want a "one-sided" or "two-sided test." In a two-sided test, you're looking to see whether the product causes any change, positive or negative, in outcomes. In a one-sided test, you're assuming that if the product has an effect, it will be positive. If the effect is actually negative, the test won't work correctly. There's always debate around this issue, but I prefer to take the more open minded route—a two-sided test that could show me the product actually makes things worse.

Once you enter these values into the calculator (and checked that the confidence level, statistical power, and type of test are correct), the calculator will tell you how many people you need in the treatment and control groups. If you have more, that's great. If you have fewer, look for more users!

Instead of an online calculator, you can also use any statistical package for this, like R, Stata, or SPSS.[139]

Is There Really an Impact?

If you have a strong signal in the data, then it's dead simple to determine the impact: subtract the average impact of the control group from the average impact of the treatment group.

What does it mean to "have a strong signal," though? Researchers refer to this as statistical significance, but I prefer the more obvious description: there's a strong indication that the two groups you're looking at really do have different outcomes (i.e., that the results can be reasonably trusted).

The trustworthiness of your results depends on the same things that we looked at when calculating the desired sample size—the impact of the product relative to the baseline, and the amount of noise in the data—plus the number of people who were actually in the test. When we calculated the desired sample size, we were effectively trying to figure out, beforehand, how many people we would need *in order to trust the results*. Now that we have the results, we do a quick test to double check that we really did get what we expected.

For most experiments, there are two tests of statistical significance, depending on how you measure the outcome (just like when we were determining the sample size). If the outcome is something binary (people log into the application or not), then you'll run a test on the percentage of people in each group that have the outcome. If the outcome is a floating-point number or integer, then you'll determine the strength of the signal based on average outcomes.[140]

Unfortunately, I've too often seen people check a raw impact number without looking at whether the data can be trusted. They can get really excited about unreliable results, and, most importantly, they take the wrong lesson from the test and waste time building the wrong new features. So, save time and resources. Check that the signal is strong. It's not hard, and it needs to be integrated into the daily routine of the company.

Running Multiple Versions at Once

Earlier I spoke about a single treatment and a control group. However, you can have many different treatment groups running at the same time—if you want to test the impact of multiple versions of the product (or product feature). When running multiple tests (aka A/B/C test):

- Calculate the number of people you need *for each treatment*. Add them all up, plus the control group.
- You don't need, necessarily, to keep the treatment and control groups all the same size. (It makes things simpler but can also mean you unnecessarily include extra people in the test.) As a general rule, you need more people where you think the difference from the control group is small. Otherwise, you'll end up with some tests that give you a solid result, and others that are inconclusive. Run the power calculation I described to determine how many people you need in each group.
- Always assign people into one and only one group.

This type of experiment allows only one thing to change at a time—having version A of the product versus version B (versus C, versus D, etc.) versus not having the product at all. If you want to test multiple interacting variables at once, you'll need a *multivariate testing tool*. Multivariate tools allow you, for example, to test multiple buttons with a call to action, and multiple blocks of text explaining the action, all at the same time.

Underneath the hood, multivariate testing is just a different experimental design—it's a type of randomized control trial experiment, like A/B testing. However, analyzing the results of those studies is more difficult.[141] So, use an off-the-shelf tool instead, like Optimizely or Maxymiser (they also do the simpler version, A/B testing). These tools take care of the math for you.

How Do You Do Random Assignment in Practice?

Previously I mentioned that you should do a random assignment to determine what group each person goes into. How do you actually do that in practice?

The simplest answer is that you can use a tool to take care of it for you. In various languages, there are packages that make testing easier, such as Ruby on Rail's "Vanity" package[142] or the Javascript library Genetify.[143] Additional packages that don't rely on (much) coding and that you can just hook up an existing website include Optimizely and Google Analytics's Content Experiments.[144]

But it's not difficult to do yourself. It just depends if you already know who your users are, or not. Start with the number of people you need in each test. Let's say you have one control and three treatments, each of which needs 250 people, for a total of 1,000. Divide the number of people in each group by the total. Here: 0.25, 0.25, 0.25, .0.25. The resulting proportions must add up to 1. Take your proportions and label them on a 0–1 scale, creating a "roulette wheel" of probabilities like this:

> 0.00–0.25: Control
>
> 0.25–0.50: Treatment 1
>
> 0.50–0.75: Treatment 2
>
> 0.75–1.00: Treatment 3

For each user, you're going to spin this virtual roulette wheel (by generating a random number) and seeing which section it lands on.

YOU ALREADY KNOW YOUR USERS

If you already have a list of users you want to assign, then it's easy. Generate a random number for each person on the list, 0–1 (exclusive of 1). If the number is in the first section of the roulette wheel, assign the person to the control group. If it's in the second section, assign the person to the first treatment group, etc. The person falls into a particular section when this is true: lower bound of section ≤ random number < upper bound of section.

YOU DON'T KNOW THE USERS YET

If you don't already have a list of users in hand, then there's a slightly different approach. You'll need this if you are testing new users in real time (i.e., people are constantly signing up for your system, and you assign them to the experiment once they join).

You should either pick a fixed number of people you want to include in the experiment, and wait until the target is reached, or pick a specific time at which you'll look for the results. In either case, you assign people in the exact same way as before: generate a random number for each person. Then, assign them to a group according to the roulette wheel. Make sure that repeat visitors keep their original assignment; don't reassign them to a new group each time they come back (for a web app, set a cookie on their browser that will tell you they've been there before).

If you don't pick a specific stopping point, then there's trouble. If, instead, you constantly check the results of the experiment, waiting for something that looks promising, you'll be misled. You'll increase the likelihood that you'll say there's a difference between the two groups when there actually isn't one (List et al. 2010).[145] The problem is that things tend to jump around a while until they settle down and give you a solid answer. Even if you pass a "solid signal" test (statistical significance), it can still jump around. If you accept the first promising result that comes along, you'll often get the wrong answer.

So, pick a point at which you need the answer: either a specific number of people or a specific date. Make that the final stopping point for the test, instead of getting too excited along the way and killing the experiment early.

More Advanced Experimental Designs

STAGGERED ROLLOUT

Let's say you have a product that your users want, and *you can't withhold it from them*. This happens in many international development projects, where the funder strongly believes in the success of the project before it is tested and feels it would be morally wrong to withhold the product from potential recipients (Karlan and Appel 2011). You can still do an experiment and measure the true impact of the product—with a staggered rollout.

In a staggered rollout, everyone gets the product (or new product feature); they just get it at different times. Take the full set of people who want it, then randomly assign them to an "early" or "late" group. Track the outcomes for *everyone* from the moment the early group gets the product. The treatment group is the "early" people; the control group is the "late group," from the time when the first folks receive the product until they do. Staggered rollouts are thus limited in how long they can run—the experiment ends when the late group also gets the product. But they have the benefit of not leaving anyone out. Everyone gets the product, eventually.

A clever way to do a staggered rollout is to ask for people to pre-commit to buy or receive the product when it's released. Then, use a rolling schedule for the release—only make enough units of the product, or give out enough access credentials, to supply to a randomly selected subset of the enrollees. Then, later, supply it to the rest of the people who signed up.

MATCHING AND QUASI-EXPERIMENTS

Where random sampling is not possible, special techniques can match individuals from a treatment group to similar people in another group. The matching procedure can be used to approximate the experimental environment (i.e., "quasi-experiments"). These are second-best options to running an experiment but are better than nothing—and statistically can yield very similar, solid results if done correctly. You'll need an econometrician, though.

Build It In, Hook It Up

Ideally, companies should build the ability to run experiments into their application, or hook up an off-the-shelf product to help them do so. This is the best way to learn, and avoiding friction in the deployment of an experiment will speed up the process of refining and improving the effectiveness of the application. Even if the final impact your company wants to measure is outside of the product, like exercise, enabling experiments within the application will be immensely helpful for quickly iterating and testing the steps that are within the app. The assignment process itself is generally very easy—as the description of the roulette wheel indicates—and is something that most development shops can integrate into their code (that's what we did at HelloWallet).

Determining Impact: Unique Actions and Outcomes

Experiments are the best general-purpose and accurate way to measure the impact of your product. But there's an important case in which they aren't needed to accurately gauge impact. That's when there is no conceivable way that the outcome would occur without the product being there.

For example, imagine a new and highly effective cancer treatment. A team is developing a product to make people aware of it: the target outcome is for people to use the new cancer treatment. Without that awareness, no one would know. There's no comparison group needed—any impact that occurs is because of the product.

Similarly, it's easy to measure the *baseline* impact of the product when the action only exists in the product itself—which often occurs where the behavior change process entails the user learning to use a new product. For example, remember Speek from Chapter 8? People don't make Speek conference calls (and provide revenue to the company for premium features) without the application itself. If you want to know the impact of the product *as a whole* on Speek calls and on company revenue, just measure them. That's the benchmark you can use to compare against future changes. After that baseline has been established, you'll still need to run experiments (or use other means) to gauge the impact of new features and other *change* to the application to distinguish the impact of the new feature from that of the existing functionality.

Other Ways to Determine Impact

Experiments take care of all of the nasty details of figuring out whether the application, or something else, changed the user's behavior and outcomes. The random assignment process, properly done, ensures that nothing is different between the two groups except for what they want: the product itself. So, any difference in outcomes is caused by the application.

As an academic, I could make the case that experiments are really the only way to measure *causal impact*, because of these benefits. But in real-world products, that's unrealistic and too restrictive. If you aren't using experiments, then you have to face the nasty details of estimating the causal impact of the application head on. It can certainly be done, but it should be done with open eyes.

The easiest and most common way to look at impact is a pre-post analysis.

A Pre-Post Look at Impact

In a pre-post analysis, you look at user behavior and outcomes before and after a significant change. For example, if users on average walked 500 steps a day before using your product and 1,500 steps a day after using it for one month, then the product *may* have increased their walking by 1,000 steps a day.

In a pre-post analysis, you take the difference you see, and then you try to adjust it for all of the other things that could have caused the change that weren't part of your product. This can be done informally, or formally. The formal version requires running a multivariate statistical analysis like estimating a regression model. The informal version means carefully thinking through what else could have impacted the users and their behavior.

Personally, while I was trained in the formal, econometric approach, I find that starting with an informal analysis is immensely valuable (even if you later do the econometric analysis as well). Also, you'll probably need a stats person to handle the econometric analysis, but anyone can do an informal analysis to help gauge how important further analysis is, and as a reality check on the stats. So, here's how to run an informal analysis of a pre-post study.

You have measurements of user behavior and real-world outcomes before and after a change: either when you gave the users the product for the first time, or added a new feature, etc. Subtract the *pre* from the *post*: that's your working impact number. You also should have a sense of how big of a change you need for you to care. If you get people to walk two more steps a day, is that relevant? No. Maybe you only care if the product can get people to walk at least 100 more steps a day—it's not much, but at least it's something to build upon. That "when do I care?" number is your threshold.

Now, look for non–product-related things that would have caused the impact you're seeing. With pre-post studies, there are a few very common factors. I'll use the example of an exercise tracker to make things concrete:

Time
: Would the time of year, day of month, day of week, time of day, etc. matter for this outcome? For example, if you saw that users were walking more in the spring than in the dead of winter, would that surprise you? No. So, it's unlikely that your *product* would have caused a change you see in walking between winter and spring.

Experience
: Let's say you launched you product last month. You've just added a new feature that puts a smiley face on the tracker when users do well. In a pre-post study, it will be difficult to know if the smiley face caused increased exercise, or if users just gained experience with the product from its initial launch and slowly exercised more because of that experience (rather than the smiley face). *Gradual changes over time are often caused by experience; sharp changes in behavior are more likely to be caused by a change in the product or another external "event" you can search for.*

Data availability or quality
: Let's say that in the new release of the tracker, you added a smiley and someone in the engineering department fixed some bugs in the analysis of accelerometer data. Walking is up! Hmm. That could be because of the smiley, or because you're simply getting better data about the users. I've found that data quality issues in particular are often invisible and therefore often misleading—someone changed something, and didn't think it was important or didn't want to admit the previous problem. Like product changes, data quality and data availability changes are sharp, sudden changes, so they are very hard to distinguish in a pre-post study.

Composition of the population
: Let's say that with the new release of the tracker, you've added lots of new features and made a big announcement. You see that average walking is up! Excellent. But that may be because the product caused people to walk more, or it may be that the announcement of the new features caused new users to join who were already

walking more—and the new users brought up the average. This occurs in sudden ways (like product announcements) or through the slow addition and attrition of users over time. You should counteract this by looking at a specific group of people before and after the change.

In each case, you're looking for a gut check—is this a big deal? Measuring walking behavior in the dead of winter versus in spring is a big deal. Measuring it from one Tuesday to the next usually isn't (barring holidays). A big deal is anything that looks like it's going to have a large impact on behavior *relative to what you're seeing pre-post* and *relative to the threshold at which you care.* If the combination of many small things push the likely impact of your product below the threshold at which you care, then you can usually stop—and move on to something more promising.

If the pre-post impact is so large that nothing else seems to explain it other than the product, excellent. You should check your work with a statistical model and prepare to be surprised; but if you can't, at least you've gotten an initial estimate of impact.

This informal analysis feeds into formal statistical modeling. Each of the factors you identify that might be important become variables in the model—things that you are trying to control for, in order to isolate the unique impact of your product. You'll need to identify data that measures them, and run the model itself. That's beyond the scope of this work—but a good stats person can help.

Seem complex? It can be. That's why experiments are wonderful, because they remove these complexities. But we can't always run them or get enough users into the system to get a solid result. And so we sometimes must use pre-post analyses. When the product has a big effect, and there aren't many other things going on that confuse the result, that's enough to get a signal for further product development. Another option is cross-sectional multivariate analysis, which is up next.

A Cross-Sectional or Panel Data Analysis of Impact

In a cross-sectional analysis, you look for differences among groups of users at a given point. You want to see how their usage of the product impacts their behavior and outcomes, after taking into account all of the other things that might be different about the users. For example, you might look at the impact among frequent users of the application versus infrequent users. As with pre-post analyses, I usually start with an informal, logical analysis, then feed that understanding into a formal statistical or machine learning model if it looks like there's enough of an impact from the product to care.[146] Cross-sectional analyses usually pull together diverse groups of people; in order for the analysis to be valid, you'll need to control for all of the factors that make those groups different *other than the product.*

As before, there are some common differences you need to take into account. Most importantly is this: why are some people more frequent users than others? Age, income, prior experience with the behavior, prior experience with the product's medium (mobile versus web), self-confidence, sufficient free time, etc. All of these are factors that affect the users' behavior above and beyond the product.

If there aren't obvious candidates that explain the difference in behavior across users, then take the list of factors you generate, and plug them into a statistical model. Again, it's beyond the scope of this work, but a good stats person can help.

In addition to cross-sectional and pre-post analyses, one can (and should) also look at models that examine changes in behavior and outcomes among many users, over time. These models, using "panel" datasets (or time-series cross sectional datasets with many people, but shorter time frames), provide a much more fine-grained look at behavior. They can pull out impacts of the product that pre-post and cross-sectional models can't, because they can control for other differences across the individuals. However, they require much more data and statistical knowledge.

What Happens If the Outcome Isn't Measurable Within the Product?

You can safely skip this section if users take action directly in your product and you can easily measure the outcome there.

As we already discussed, sometimes the target outcome, and even the target action, may not be directly measureable in the product. For example, think about a website that helps users set up an urban vegetable garden with video tutorials. The target outcome is more vegetable gardens; the target action is that users set them up (rather than, for example, contractors being paid to set them up).

Each person who uses the urban garden site is tracked with a cookie or authenticated login. Each step in the "how to set up an urban garden" tutorial is tracked. When users complete the tutorial, are they "done"? Did they complete the action? No. The action that the company wants to drive is setting up vegetable gardens, not completing a tutorial about setting up vegetable gardens. The difference between those two could be slight, or it could be massive if no one actually follows through. Without further information, there's no way the company can know if the product is successful at driving behavior change. Similarly, it has no way of knowing that the product has caused more vegetable gardens to be set up than there otherwise would have been.

So, what can a company do? If the action or outcome is not directly measurable with the product, then a *data bridge* is needed. A data bridge is something that convincingly connects the real-world outcome with behavior within the product. There are two basic strategies for building a data bridge:

Build it yourself
: Find a reliable way to measure the target action and outcome. Then, build a model of what behavior in the product relates to that action and outcome.

Cheat
: Find an academic researcher who has already established the link between something you can reliably measure in the application and the real-world outcome. For example, there are numerous studies that document "overreporting" (lying) about voting when people actually don't vote (Silver et al. 1986). If there isn't an existing research paper on the topic, work with researchers to generate one (ideas on how to partner with researchers are discussed in Chapter 15).

For the rest of this discussion, I'll assume that you haven't been lucky enough to find an existing research paper or interested researcher to do the work for you—and so you have to build the data bridge yourself.

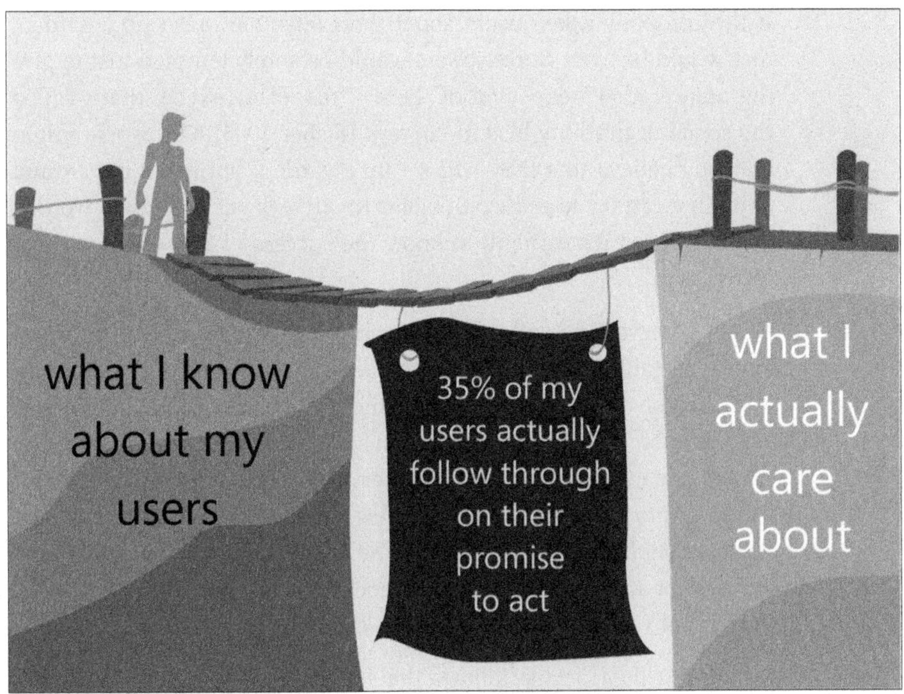

A data bridge, connecting what you know with what you care about, with measurements about the relationship between the two.

Figure Out How to Measure the Outcome and Action, By Hook Or By Crook (But Not By Survey)

For our sample company that's encouraging users to set up urban vegetable gardens, it will need to measure the number of vegetable gardens, plain and simple. An obvious route would be to ask the participants, with a survey. Not ideal. Surveys are good for gathering facts when people have an incentive to actually answer the survey but don't have an incentive to lie. Imagine that the vegetable garden company asked users of its website, after a week, whether they set up a garden. Most people wouldn't answer—especially those who didn't set one up. Some would answer truthfully. And some would answer with "what will be truthful when they get around to it" (i.e., they'll tell a white lie). The company can't really know which is which; at least, not without doing additional field research to verify if people aren't telling the truth.

If the company asked users about their *intention* to set up a garden, that would be even worse. Users would be sorely tempted just to give the answer that's expected of them ("Yes, of course!"); that's called the social desirability bias in surveys (Fisher 1993). Or, people might honestly believe that they will set up a garden, but never get around to it. One can try to reduce this bias in surveys with carefully worded questions, but it's difficult to know the success of that effort without verification.

Direct observation is often the best option: either observing the number of vegetable gardens themselves, or other things that uniquely indicate that the action was taken, like the number of people buying special vegetable garden supplies within a city. The company doesn't need to measure every single action or every time the outcome changes—it just needs to be able to measure a few times so it can understand the relationship between the product, the action, and the outcome. So, a small pilot study where an intern goes out and manually counts the number of vegetable gardens in an area is fine.[147]

Building a data bridge follows the same rules as creating a benchmark for the product, described earlier in this chapter. In this case, you're looking for the causal relationship between something easily measurable in the application, and a real-world outcome that's hard to measure, but is what you really care about. If the real-world outcome is unique to the product (i.e., if *no one* normally creates vegetable gardens in the area you care about), then you can do a simple observation of the real-world outcome, after people use your product, as your metric. If the real-world outcome has multiple possible causes, then you'll need to use an experiment, statistical model, or pre-post analysis.[148]

In either case, there are three factors to keep in mind when measuring the real-world outcome itself. These determine how sturdy the resulting data bridge will be:

Representativeness
: You want to observe cases that are representative of what "normally" happens; if you decide to count vegetable gardens in Portland (very rainy), and most of your app's users are in Phoenix (rather dry), that won't help you generalize much about vegetable garden creation. The most solid results come from taking your user base and randomly selecting some of them to directly observe.

Getting enough data points

You need to ensure you have enough information to get a solid signal about what the real-world outcome really is. For example, if you make only one observation of whether people make a vegetable garden after saying they will in the app, that's not going to tell you much about whether *other* people will. You need the general percentage of people who create gardens when they say they will. So, how many observations are enough? There's no hard-and-fast rule—it depends how important the accuracy of the estimate is to the company. For experiments, we discussed in detail how you compute sample sizes. If you're not using experiments, you can use online tools for computing "confidence intervals,"[149] which tell you how confident you can be in your estimate; if you build a statistical model of the relationship, that will also provide you with confidence intervals.

Getting a baseline

Sometimes things happen in the real world that have nothing to do with your product. I know, it's hard to believe. Some people will create vegetable gardens on their own, even without the vegetable garden app. So, when you're observing your real-world outcome, include some cases in which people don't use the app. This is important if you're doing a simple model in Microsoft Excel, or if you're running a full experiment to build your data bridge.

If these options fail, and there's really no way to measure the product's real-world outcome, then the rest of this discussion about impact can't help. That signal—what's actually happening in the world—is essential for keeping the whole process honest.

Find Cases Where You Can Connect Product Behavior to Real-World Outcomes

Now you have measurements of actions taken within the product and of real-world outcomes (though perhaps imperfect measurements). How can you connect the two? You can connect them at the individual level, or at an aggregated level. At the individual level, for example, the urban gardening app could ask for users' names and addresses to connect their behavior in the product to whether or not they actually have a vegetable garden (send the intern to their home, and mark it down in the record). Getting data about individual users is the ideal—as long as the data meets the standards (representative, sufficient in size, and with a clear baseline).

Alternatively, the action and outcome can be measured as an aggregate: a known geographic area or a known group of people. If you know that a certain set of users in the product correspond to the known area or group (even if you don't know who is who), and you can measure the actions and outcomes reliability in that area or group, you're in business. As we'll see, it'll be more challenging to figure out exactly what is going on, but you can do it.

Build the Data Bridge

A data bridge brings together something you know and can measure frequently—user behavior within the application—with something you have only measured a few times—the impact of the product on the real-world target outcome. It allows you to estimate how much the target outcome has probably changed based on behavior within the product. You'll estimate that relationship by running a pilot project that gathers both datasets:

1. Take a circumstance in which you can reliably connect user behavior in the product with the real-world outcome or action, as we've just described.
2. Measure the causal impact of the product on the real-world outcome or action—using an experiment (ideal), statistical model, pre-post analysis, etc.
3. Analyze the various user behaviors that occur within the application, and identify one or more that is strongly related (correlated) to the application's causal impact. If a statistician is available, use a mediation analysis.
4. When the indicative user behavior occurs within the product, build a model (in Excel, or in a statistical package) of how much that changes the target outcome. That's the data bridge.[150]
5. In the future, whenever you see the behavior in the product, use your model to estimate the likely impact on the target outcome.

For example: the urban gardening site runs a pilot study, where it takes two sets of randomly selected people and offers its program to one group and not the other. Some of the people in the first group completed the training program; some did not. An intern visits the homes of everyone in the study and measures the truth. The company finds that 65% of people who were offered the program created a garden, and 90% of those who were offered the program *and completed their training within the application* created gardens. Meanwhile, 15% of those who weren't offered it nevertheless created a garden. Those three stats provide a basic understanding of how to interpret user behavior on the website in the future.

The company would improve the chance that a person will set up a garden by 50 percentage points (from 15% to 65%) if it *offers* the person its training program. It will improve the chance that the person will set up a garden even more if it can convince him to complete the training program.[151] The company can get a precise estimate of that impact using what's known as a mediation analysis on the experiment.

A quick review: if your target outcome is something outside of the product, and not directly measureable, then you'll need to build a data bridge. The easiest way to do that is to find an existing research study that documents the relationship you're looking for—like between the intention to plant a garden and the actual act of doing so. If not, look for a case in which your team can directly observe the users' behavior, and compare the things they do or say in the product to what they actually do in the real world. That's your data bridge. In the future, you can use that relationship to estimate how much of an impact you're having based on what you see in the application, and iteratively improve your product for greater impact.

On a Napkin

Here's what you'll need to do

- Define two metrics that say how you'll measure the product's target outcome and target action.
- If the outcome and action are within the application, great. Measure them directly. If not, try to find creative ways to get that data from someone else or build it into your application.
- If both of those fail, you'll need to build a model of how behavior with the product affects the outcome and action: a data bridge.
- Measure the impact itself. The gold standard is A/B testing; you can use off-the-shelf tools that don't require a stats person.

How you'll know there's trouble

- The team can't decide on a reliable, accurate metric of the product's outcome, or doesn't define success and failure by that metric.

Deliverables

- A clear measurement of the product's impact!

[13]

Identifying Obstacles to Behavior Change

You've built a solid product. You've established a baseline for the product's impact. Now, you want to improve it. This chapter will help you discover problems, develop potential solutions, and generate additional ideas for how to make the product better.

I think of debugging a product's behavioral impact as a five-step process:

1. Watch how your users are actually using your product, and see what's stopping them from changing their behavior.
2. Check your data to find other problems in the product and to gauge the severity of the issues identified through observation.
3. Devise potential solutions by understanding the psychology of why the problem occurs and what's feasible in your product.
4. Prioritize proposed changes to the product and integrate them into the product development process.
5. Test the behavioral impact of high-priority changes.

This chapter walks you through the first three steps; the next chapter covers prioritization and testing the impact of changes.

Watch Real People Using the Product

To understand your product and how it's impacting people's lives, there's no substitute for actually watching people use it. They will use it in ways you won't expect. They'll uncover assumptions the team had while designing and building the product. Some of them will also get frustrated, curse a bit, and stop using the product. Reams have been written about the importance of directly observing your users with your product to improve its usability. It's doubly true when trying to improve the behavioral impact of your product.

When you observe your users with the product, you're looking for two main things:

- Where they get stuck, distracted, or discouraged
- New ways for them to take action that are more natural for them

The first one is straightforward. You're looking for the places where things go wrong. Where do they give up using the system? Where do they get diverted into other areas or thoughts that aren't related to the task at hand? Where do they get discouraged or frustrated, putting them in a bad mood that taints their interaction with the rest of the system?

The second one entails revisiting the knowledge gathered in Chapters 4 and 5: about user motivations, prior experience, relationship to the product and company, and barriers to action. Maybe you can come up with new ways to tailor the product to user needs. You can also generate new ideas for targeting the product based on what users try to do in the system (but the system doesn't support) or what they say they want to do in interviews.

While I'm a big fan of direct observation, it's insufficient on its own. Direct observation provides the team with vivid stories and anecdotes about their users and their challenges in the product. These stories can be easy to remember and rally behind, which is vital for coordinating the team's efforts and getting everyone behind a common vision for improvement. However, the more vivid and the more consistent these stories are with our own experiences and beliefs, the easier they are to remember. Vividness and memorability aren't the same thing as severity. The team needs quantitative data to assess the importance of various obstacles for users and to systematically discover other obstacles that are more subtle and wouldn't show up under direct observation.

Check Your Data

Gather Additional Data About Your Users As Needed

Previously, we talked about the quantitative data you need in order to assess the overall impact of the product. To find obstacles along the way, we'll need to add additional data collection throughout the product.

We've outlined the real-world *outcome* the product seeks to engender, the user of the product that does something to create that outcome (aka the *actor*), and the *action* the user undertakes. We've also broken the *action* down into a sequence of steps that leads up to the target action. Building on these concepts, here are the data points we'll need to find obstacles to impact:

- Who is using the product? Give each user a unique ID that is tied to all of the user's data and behavior in the system, if at all possible.
- Is the user taking one of the steps in the sequence? Link that event record to the user's ID.
- Is the user completing the target action? Link that information to the user ID. If the user completes the sequence, tag it.
- What is the current state of the target outcome (covered in Chapter 12)?
- If possible: What changes occurred after in the target outcome over time? Link that information to the user ID.

In order to make this explanation clearer, we're talking about data collection that is used for debugging purposes (this chapter) separately from data collection for impact assessment (previous chapter). But to save yourself time, you should do the actual coding to instrument the product all at once!

In addition, when measuring who is using the product, the more you know, the more you'll be able to improve the product. That doesn't mean you should ask lots of unnecessary questions—users will just get annoyed and stop using the product. But if the product can glean useful information about the users while they use it—great; that will make targeting improvements to the product easier. One metric in particular that isn't essential but will help with targeting is the user's "persona." Identify which of the personas identified in Chapter 5 the user best fits into, and store it.

Use the Behavioral Plan to Find Bottlenecks

In previous chapters, we planned out something like this:

Step 1 → Step 2 → Step 3 → Step 4 → Target Action → Target Outcome

The next step in improving the product's impact is to focus on everything that happens before the target outcome. We want to determine if the sequence that leads up to the target action is actually working. By this point, you should have instrumented the product to measure user behavior at each step in the sequence. Treat the sequence of steps like a conversion funnel in marketing: look at the percentage of users who make it to each step, up to the target action. For example:

Step 1 (100%) → Step 2 (50%) → Step 3 (45%) → Step 4 (12%) → Target Action (11%)

Wherever there is steep drop-off in the number of users completing a step, the product clearly has a problem. In this case, there are serious problems finishing step 2 and step 4. That's where you would devote additional analysis to understand what's going on—with user testing, and with a deeper look at the quantitative data to see if there are signs of what's going on.

If you're dealing with a target action like "exercising," you may notice a limitation of this approach. If someone exercises, it could be because of the product, or it could be because of other reasons. If you're not running an experiment, then those "other reasons" could make it difficult to figure out where the *product's* bottlenecks lie. To figure out what's going on in these cases, it takes a more advanced technique, a causal map, which we'll talk about shortly.

Check Whether the Action Is Actually Working to Drive Outcomes

Test the fundamental assumption that the target action actually drives the target outcome. In some products, the link between the two is trivial—for example, for a product that helps people keep a regular sleep schedule, the action is waking up on time (like Clocky, the rolling clock). Even then, it behooves us to check that assumption (perhaps users set the morning wake-up time too aggressively, are tired during the day, and have irregular, unhealthy sleeping times).

In the last chapter, we determined the benchmark impact of the product. If there's no impact, you know there is a problem somewhere. But that only gets us part of the way. We want to narrow in on the relationship between the target action and target outcome.

How can you test this relationship? You can find a way, by hook or by crook, for people to take the action and do *nothing else* with the product. Pay them to do it. Look them in the eye and ask them to do it. Or, you can look at the overall data you have on people using the product and deploy statistical tools to look for the particular role of the action on the outcome: in an experiment, that's a mediation analysis (like we used in the last chapter to build a data bridge between behavior within the product and events outside of the product). In a statistical world, structural equation models are one way to do it. Sorry, you need a stats person for that—and honestly, it's not my expertise either.

Note: this is ideally something that you've already done some preliminary testing of, very early on in the process and before the product is actually built. I don't mean to imply that testing the core assumption of the product should come this late. But the particular way that people take the action, after the product is built, may change the impact. So, double-check the relationship between action and outcome to avoid encouraging an action that doesn't actually cause what you care about.

Segment the User Population

You may want to (and should) look beyond how the average (or median) individual is doing—and look at the product's impact on specific subpopulations. The obstacles that users face may be confined to a specific subset of the users, and that knowledge can help the team identify the problem and resolve it.

Segment the user base into groups of people that are relevant for your team. These segments can overlap, and are driven by distinct needs:

- Segments of users who are of interest to the product's key constituencies. For example, the marketing team may want to segment users by buying power
- Segments of users who the team expects will behave differently in the application and respond differently to application's incentives (family status, age, and income bracket)

- Segments of users who empirically break the population up according to how well they actually change their behavior (or not)

The first method of segmentation is designed for effective description of what is occurring within the application—using the categories that key stakeholders within the company expect. The latter two methods are used for effective analysis of how the application is successful (or not), and for guiding future changes to the application.

In each case, place individuals into groups that are unambiguous and unchanging—like initial age when enrolling, etc. For this purpose, we do not want segments that depend on user behavior—like "active users versus inactive users"—because it is very difficult to measure *changes* in engagement-related behavior of those groups.

Advanced Technique: Creating a Causal Map

Our behavioral plan is the ideal path that we want users to take:

Step 1 → Step 2 → Step 3 → Step 4 → Target Action → Target Outcome

However, in reality, often there are lots of other reasons why an individual might, or might not, be changing her behavior. Some of them will be in the application, and some not. To figure out what needs to change, you need to understand what's happening, both on and off the ideal path.

By drawing out the "other reasons" that user behavior might change, we can get insight into what's happening into the application. I like to illustrate them using a simple flowchart, then annotate it with the data we have at each step along the way. I refer to it as a *causal map*, for lack of a better term. I haven't seen other examples of this approach in product design,[152] so I'll use an example from my own work.

One challenge we faced at HelloWallet was to increase the amount of money that people had set aside for emergencies. The majority of users hadn't set aside enough; in fact, roughly half of all Americans don't have enough emergency savings, according to a survey by Bankrate.com (Steiner 2011). Only half of Americans could come up with $2,000 for emergencies with 30 days' notice (Lusardi and Mitchell 2011).

The application provided clear guidance on how much, and how, users should have saved. That formed the ideal path:

Enroll → load bank accounts → see advice in our "Guided Approach" sequence on saving → set up an automatic transfer of the money → have more emergency savings

But let's say someone does put aside money for emergencies, and *we don't know why*. Logically, is the application, and that particular path through the application, the *only possible cause* of that action? Certainly not. The person could have already had a plan to save for emergencies. The user could have received a windfall, like a tax refund, and decided to put some of it away for the future. Or, maybe something else in the application—like budgeting—helped free up the money for savings. One can generate a list of these various scenarios (and estimate how likely they are). But from the perspective of improving the product—many of them are tightly related to one another.

Based on this logic, you can create a map of what can happen within and outside of the system. In particular, look for the *discrete actions or bits of data that are measurable that lead up to the person taking the action*—on the ideal path or off of it.

In our case, we had a wealth of quantitative data. For example, we could measure whether someone actually went to the budget screen, freed up money to save, etc. We could also measure whether people were already saving money (based on their existing savings balance), and even if it looked like they had a windfall of income.

But even without quantitative data, you can trace out the *major* ways that a person would come to the same outcome (more saving for emergencies) and get a rough measurement based on user testing and user research, to determine if the unintended paths are something that people normally do.

Either way, the goal is to tell a story of what users do on the ideal path, and beyond. It's like taking the behavioral plan from Chapter 6 and embedding it in a larger story of the other major things that could be going on in the user's life, with respect to the target outcome. Figure 13-1 shows what the causal map looked like for this project.

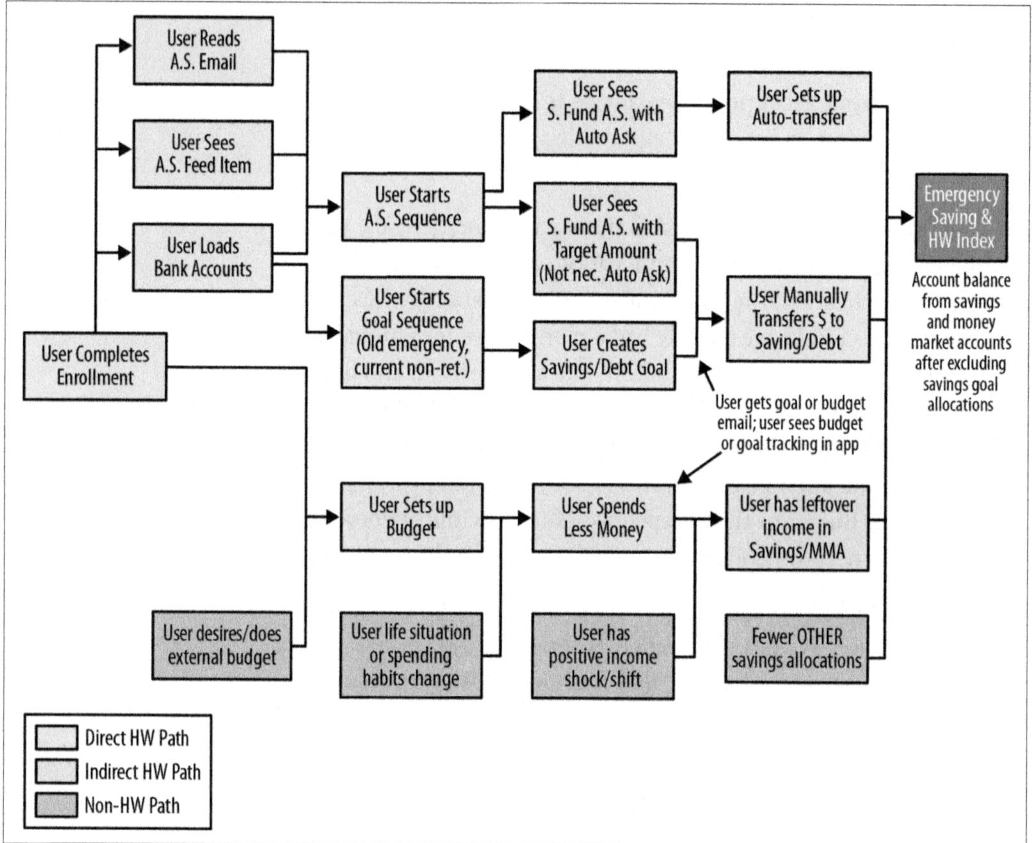

FIGURE 13-1. A causal map showing the various reasons a person might put aside money for emergency savings (HW stands for HelloWallet; A.S. stands for Action Steps—a guidance module in our system at the time)

In your causal map, you should distinguish between:

- The ideal path(s). Here, we had two different features that supported the same target outcome, each with its own ideal path. The ideal paths are in light blue.
- Other actions that user might take within the system that impact the target outcome; that's in green.
- Actions that have nothing to do with the product and the company can't claim to have caused but still cause the target outcome; that's in red.

Each action within the system should be measurable. In the case of actions completely outside of the product, and not directly measurable, don't bother mapping out all of the possible things that a user could do that affects the target outcome. Just examine the most immediate prior action that the user takes, right before doing something measurable. The target outcome is, by definition, measurable, so you might just have a single "external" box leading into the target outcome. But try to find earlier points in the map where the external action will have a footprint in the data that you can see and understand. Like, for example, if someone stops saving for other things (and "frees up" money for emergencies), we should know.

USING THE CAUSAL MAP TO DETERMINE BETTER WAYS TO TARGET THE APPLICATION

The causal map tells us two things. First, it can tell us where outside forces will hinder action. In the previous example, a *negative* income shock will significantly decrease emergency savings (that's what emergency savings are there for, in fact). Sometimes the product can be tweaked to help people handle those obstacles; sometimes it can't.

Second, the map can help reveal other ways to achieve the same outcome. If something other than the ideal path is successfully causing people to take the target action, that's not a bad thing! Figure out ways that the product can capitalize on it. Maybe the product initially focused on restricting fatty foods to help someone lose weight but found that exercise was more decisive, and the product could encourage that instead.

USING THE CAUSAL MAP TO HELP ASSESS THE IMPACT OF THE APPLICATION AND MARGINAL CHANGES IN THE APPLICATION

Remember in Chapter 12, where we discussed using statistical models and pre-post analyses to figure out the causal impact of the application? The causal map provides variables to consider in that analysis. If it looks like something outside of the application causes the target action, you'd better control for it when benchmarking the product (this is automatically taken care of with experiments, but is essential otherwise). The same holds true for testing the impact of *changes* in the product. If you aren't running an experiment, make sure the factors identified in the causal map have been accounted for.

USING THE CAUSAL MAP TO FORECAST THE IMPACT OF FUTURE CHANGES

Finally, the causal map can be used to roughly estimate how important future changes to the product might be on user behavior. For example, with the causal map illustrated in Figure 13-1, we analyzed how much savings contributions would decrease if we took away the goal module, or if we increased the percent of people who loaded their accounts in the system.

Figure Out How to Fix the Obstacles

After you've determined where there are problems in the app, try to figure out why there's a problem—what's going on with those particular pages or interactions that makes them obstacles and what might resolve them.

In many cases, the problem and solution will be obvious. For example, in your quantitative data, you see a steep drop-off on a particular page, or during qualitative testing, users often complain about that page. When the team takes a fresh look at the page, they themselves can't figure out what users are supposed to do. There's a huge block of text with a link in the second to last sentence that they are supposed to click on. Solution: make the call to action clear, and get rid of some of the overwhelming text around it.

When the problem or solution isn't so clear, there are a couple of paths to take. First, you can try to avoid the problem altogether. Before tackling a nasty behavioral problem head on, see if you can sidestep it. If there is a problem with a particular screen or interaction, is there anything wrong with dumping that content altogether? Is it absolutely necessary for the person to see/do that thing? If not, cut it. Return to the lessons of Chapter 6—simplify, automate, and default where possible to remove user work. You resolve the problem, and get a less complex product at the same time. For example, if users balk at entering their age into your diet tracking app, do you absolutely need to ask them? Can the application function perfectly well without it, or can it use a proxy?

If you can't avoid the problem, you need to really understand it. Start by asking your users what's going on. You can often include these questions at the end of a direct observation period you used to initially find the problems. You can also dig into the quantitative data and see if there are signals there. For example, let's say you have a problem with drop-off over time in your time-management app (like a Nozbe, Asana, or OmniFocus). They use the app for a few days, and then never come back. When you interview users, they may tell you what's going on (they started using a different program). Or, the data may show that they stopped coming back after hitting an error message in the app and getting frustrated.

If you find solutions with these straightforward, common-sense approaches—avoiding the problem, interviewing users, and reviewing the data—excellent. If not, you can use the Create Action Funnel from Chapter 2 to generate testable hypotheses.

Using the Create Action Funnel to Debug Problems

Let's continue the example of a time management and organization app. You have a nasty problem, like app abandonment: many people use the app for a bit and then never come back.

Many things could be going on. Users might be turned off by what they saw in the app. They might be perfectly happy with the app, but after an initial period of testing, they determine it's not relevant for them. They might have switched to a different app. They might love the app but have difficulty forming the habit of regularly managing their tasks after the initial excitement and exploration phase is over. And so on.

Not only are there many possible explanations, but users might say one thing (they were too busy to use the app) and the real reason was something different (the value proposition wasn't compelling, and so they didn't *make* time to use the app).

In these uncertain, confusing situations, you need something to help structure the process of searching for solutions and point you in the right direction. The Create Action Funnel from Chapter 2 is one way to do that. In order for people to take action—like logging back into your task-management application—they need the five prerequisites that make up the funnel.

1. *Cue*. The idea of logging into the app needs to cross their minds. Are you reminding your users to log in? Have you built a strong association between something they see or interact with in their daily lives and the thought of using your app? For example, when they are prepping for work on Sunday nights, that's the time to check in and organize the tasks for the week.

2. *Reaction.* Do your users viscerally dislike something about the app? Did they have a frustrating experience that sticks with them? Do they not trust you with their data?

3. *Evaluation.* Is the app actually of value to users? Do they see it that way? Have they had first-hand experience of the value that's relevant to them, or is it buried somewhere and haven't found it yet?

4. *Ability.* Do the users know where to log in? Do they have their phones or access to a computer at the time when they want to manage their tasks? What if your app requires Internet access to manage tasks, but users want to use it in places where there is no reliable Internet access (e.g., on the subway)? (I had this problem with a task management app, by the way.)

5. *Timing.* Do users have a compelling reason to use the app at a particular time? How easy is it to procrastinate?

By going over these five prerequisites, the team can generate a set of hypotheses about what is going wrong. And, with those hypotheses, a way to *test* whether that potential problem is truly what's happening. For example, "Hypothesis: users want to use the app, but don't have reliable Internet access at the right time. Test: log *failed access attempts* from the mobile app and upload them for analysis to the company's servers when an Internet connection is available."

Often, we look for obvious problems: like the app doesn't do want people want. The Create Action Funnel reminds us that there is much that could be going wrong. I like to generate at least one hypothesis for each of the five prerequisites to make sure that I'm keeping my investigation open-minded. Ideally, the tests for each hypothesis *should be quick and simple.*

If you're looking for ideas for potential solutions in each of these areas, check Table 10-1 in Chapter 10. That table, and the sections that follow it, list two dozen techniques from the literature on how to encourage action, organized by where they affect the Create Action Funnel.

Testing: Small, Light, and Incremental

Generating hypotheses about what's going wrong with the application and testing out potential solutions doesn't have to be a big, formal affair. Before devoting lots of engineering and design time to changing the application, look for early signals about whether or not you're on the right track:

Check the data
: You've hypothesized that people have a frustrating experience, and that's what's causing them not to come back. Check the last thing that people do in the system. Do the people who don't return have errors more often than those who do?

Generate a prototype
: If you can quickly generate a graphic design or clickable prototype of the potential solution and try it out with users, great. For example, try field testing a simple email design that helps people plan a regular time to handle their tasks (i.e., use implementation intentions, as discussed in Chapter 10 and Table 10-2—they increase the likelihood that people will act at the time they've committed to).

Investigate logical implications
: Look for *other* things that would also be true if the hypothesis were true, but are easier to test. This is a common technique in the analysis of formal theoretical models and can be applied here, too. For example, let's say you believe the problem is a lack of trust. It can be hard to measure directly and takes time to investigate. Instead, if some people didn't trust the company, what *else* would they have done? They would have skipped optional data gathering questions, more than other users. They would have been more likely to click on the privacy policy and terms of use. Both are easy enough to find out.

You're not necessarily looking for the final, definitive answer (if you can get one, excellent). Instead, you're looking to quickly identify and remove answers that are clearly wrong. Then, you can devote further design and engineering resources to investigating and testing the possibilities that are left.

On a Napkin

Here's what you'll need to do

- Study how your users are actually using the product, to see where they struggle, and especially what obstacles they face on the path to behavior change.
- Examine the application's data, and find out whether users are falling off for each step of the process that leads up to the target action.
- Avoid obstacles by simply removing the problematic functionality, where possible. Otherwise, use the Create Action Funnel to diagnose what's happening at a particular obstacle.
- Use small, quick tests to evaluate potential solutions before devoting significant design and engineering resources.

How you'll know there's trouble

- The team doesn't see any obstacles hindering users from changing their behavior.
- Qualitative and quantitative data about a potential obstacle strongly disagree.

Deliverables

- A list of issues to address in the application, their severities, and sketches of potential solutions

[14]

Learning and Refining the Product

Determine What Changes to Implement

At the end of each cycle of product release and measurement, the team will have gathered a lot of data about what users are doing in the product and potential improvements to it. Obstacles to behavior change, the subject of the last chapter, are only one source of those product improvements. Business considerations and engineering considerations must also be reviewed. It's time to collect the potential changes from these diverse sources and see what can be applied to the next iteration of the product. I think of it as a three-step process:

1. *Gather* lessons learned and potential improvements to the product.
2. *Prioritize* the potential improvements based on business considerations and behavioral impact.
3. *Integrate* potential improvements into the appropriate part of product development process.

Gather

First, look at what you learned in the last two chapters about the current impact of the product and obstacles to behavior change. What did users struggle with? Where was there a significant drop-off among users? Are users returning to the application, or only trying it once or twice? Why does that appear to be happening?

- Start by picking the low-hanging fruit. List the clear problems with a crisp follow-up action; for example, no one knows how to use page Y.
- Then, write down the lessons that are more amorphous; for example, users don't trust the product to help them to change behavior. Maybe the team has started thinking about potential solutions, but there's more work to be done. The next step is to further investigate what's going on and settle on a specific solution to resolve the problem.

Next, gather lessons about the core assumptions of the product:

- Does the target action actually drive the real-world outcomes that the company seeks? For example, maybe walking a bit more each day isn't enough to reduce heart disease among the target population, and a stronger intervention is needed.
- Are there other actions that appear to be more effective? These lessons can come from the causal map (optionally) developed in the last chapter. Could the product pivot to a different action that is more effective?
- Are there major obstacles in the user's life, outside of the product, that need to be addressed? Looking again at the causal map, what major factors that are currently outside of the product's domain are counteracting the influence of the product? If exercising more leads the person to also drink more alcoholic beverages (as a "reward"), is that defeating the product's goals? To design for behavior change, we care about the net impact of the product, not just the intended consequences. Is there anything the product can do about that countervailing force, or is it just a fact of life?

Finally, look beyond the specific behavioral obstacles and impact studied in the last two chapters. The team has probably generated numerous ideas for new product features or even new products. Collect them. Other parts of the company will also suggest changes to the product as well: changes designed to increase sales, improve product branding, resolve engineering challenges, and so on. Behavioral considerations are just one (vital!) element in the larger review process.

Lessons and proposed improvements can come at different times during the product development cycle—from early user research to usage analysis after the product is released. Some lessons will only come at the end, during a formal sprint review or a product post mortem. I suggest creating a common repository for them, so that ideas don't get lost. That can be someone's email box, a wiki, or a formal document of lessons. In an agile development environment, they should be placed in a project backlog.

Prioritize

In any product-development process, there is a point at which the team needs to decide what to work on in the future. In an agile environment, that process occurs frequently, at the start of each sprint. In a sequential development world, it often occurs separately from the release schedule, as managers plan for future iterations of the product. In either case, the team needs to prioritize the long list of specific changes to the product and problems to investigate further.

The prioritization process should estimate the behavioral impact of major changes to the product: how will the change affect user behavior, and how will that affect the product's outcomes in the real world? Since the product is designed for behavior change, these behavioral impacts will likely have knock-on effects on sales or the quality of the company brand. Naturally, the prioritization will also incorporate business considerations (will the change directly drive sales or company value?), usability considerations (will it make the users happy and reduce frustrations, hopefully driving future engagement and sales?), and engineering considerations (how hard will it be to implement the change?).

The team should ground its assessment of behavioral impact in real data: the drop-off numbers at each step of the user's progression and the causal map from Chapter 13 allow the team to make a quick estimate of how large of an impact a change in the product should have. That helps the team answer: how big of a problem does this change really address? What *very rough* change in the target behavior and outcomes do we expect from it? Even if the proposed change to the application wasn't driven by a behavioral concern—for example, if it came from a client request during a sales conversation—it should be evaluated for its possible behavioral impact. It may have the added benefit of helping improve user success at the target behavior, or *it may distract the user and undermine the product's effectiveness.*

The weight of each of these considerations—business, behavioral, engineering, etc.—in the company's prioritization will vary, and there's no hard-and-fast rule.

Integrate

Your company has a prioritized list of changes to the product (including open questions that need to be answered) and a sense of how difficult each piece is to develop. Now, separate out changes that require adjusting core assumptions about product and its direction, from less fundamental changes that keep the same direction. If the change entails targeting a different set of users (actors), a different target action, or especially, a different real-world outcome, then those go into the first bucket. If the change entails a new product or new product feature, where there are major unknowns, also in the first bucket. Everything else can go into the second bucket.

Here's one of the few places I take a strong stand on the product-development process—items in the first group, with changes to core assumptions or major new features, need to be separately planned out by the product folks before they are given to the rest of the team. Even in an agile development process, core product planning shouldn't be done in parallel with the rest of the process; that's the same dictum that Marty Cagan, in *Inspired* (SVPG Press, 2008), gives in his analysis of product management. It's just too much to determine what to build and how to build it at the same time.

When designing for behavior change, core changes to the product require updating the behavioral plan. They may also require updating the product's outcomes, actions, and actors. In other words, they require another cycle of the full discovery or design process, starting with Chapter 4 or 6 of this book. Everything else can go directly into a user story (agile) or product spec outline, starting with Chapter 9.

Each time the core assumptions—actor, action, and outcome—are changed, they should be clearly documented, as described in Chapters 4 and 5. Then the behavioral plan should be updated. This formalism helps the team pull problems into the present—rather than let them lurk somewhere in the future, only to be found after significant resources have been developed. Making the assumptions and plan clear up front is intended to trigger disagreements and discussion (if there are any underneath). It's better to find those disagreements sooner rather than later.

When a core problem—like a particular step in the sequence of user actions is confusing users—there's a natural tendency to settle on a proposed solution, and just get it done (i.e., a "fix" is often implemented before vetting and testing the problem). But human psychology is tremendously complex, and trying to build a product around it is inherently error prone. There's no reason to think that the *proposed solution* is going to be any more free of unexpected problems than the previous solution. The discovery process—documenting the outcome, action, and actor, and then developing the behavioral plan—is one way to draw out the unexpected and provide opportunities to test assumptions early. It'll never be perfect, but it's a whole lot better than just shooting from the hip.

Measure the Impact of Each Major Change

Each major change to the product should be tested for its impact on user behavior; measuring changes in impact should become a reflex for the team. It's not always easy to stomach, but it's necessary. That way, the team is constantly learning and checking its assumptions about the users and the product's direction. As we've seen, small changes in wording and the presentation of concepts can have major impacts on behavior; if we're not testing for them, we can easily and unintentionally undermine the effectiveness of our product. But without a reflex to always test, testing the marginal impact of changes can raise all sorts of hackles and resistance. Let's look at some of the issues that can arise and how to handle them.

Most tests will (and should) come back showing no impact

Many people get frustrated at test results that come back with no clear difference between the versions they're testing and call that "failing." Assuming you designed and ran the test correctly, a "no difference" result should be celebrated. It tells you that you weren't changing something important enough for the test to have found a difference. Either be happy with what you have, or try something more radical. It saves you from spending further time on your current approach to improving the product.

What's a well-designed test? It's one where you've defined success and failure beforehand. It's not one where you go searching for statistical significance (or a "strong" qualitative signal). For example, let's say you have a potential new feature/button color/cat video. How much of an impact does it need to have before you care? If you improve impact by 20%, is that your threshold for success? Is it worthwhile to work on this further if you're only getting a 2% boost? That definition of success and failure, along with the amount of noise in the system, determines how many people you need in the test. If you get a result of "no difference" from the test, that doesn't necessarily mean "there's no effect"; it means there's no effect *that you should care about*. You can move on.

A/B tests in particular seem to mean you're showing a "bad" version of the app to some people

If you have a good UX team, then most of the time, no one really knows if a *change* in the app will improve it. You can't accurately predict whether the new version will be better or worse. You usually are showing a "bad" version; the problem is that you don't know which one it is! Our seemingly solid hunches are usually random guesses, especially when we have a good design team. There are two reasons why.

First, a good UX team will deliver an initial product that is well designed, and will deliver product improvements that are also well designed. We all make mistakes, but a good design team will get you in the right ballpark with the first try. By definition, further iterations are going to have a small impact relative to the initial version of the product. Don't be surprised that new versions have similar results (impact, etc.) to earlier versions—celebrate the fact that the earlier version was a good first shot.

Second, human behavior is just really confusing. As we've seen repeatedly throughout this book, we just can't forecast exactly how people will react to the product. In familiar situations, we can and should use our intuition about a set of changes to say which one is likely to be better—like when we're applying common lessons we've learned in the past. But when you have a good design team, the common lessons have already been applied. You're at the cutting edge, and so your intuition can't help anymore. That's why you need to test things, and not rely (solely) on your intuition.

Does planning for tests imply you're not confident in the changes you're proposing?

This is another issue I've heard, and it's a really tricky one. You naturally expect that any changes that you're planning to make to the product will improve it. But that's often not the case (since it's hard to make a good product better, and human behavior is inherently complex).

That sets up a problem of cognitive dissonance, though. It's very uncomfortable to think that some of the changes you've carefully planned out, thought about, and *decided will help* are actually going to do nothing—and you don't know which ones those are! It would be like you're admitting a lack of confidence in the changes that you've already advocated. So, a natural (but dangerous) response is to plough ahead and decide that testing is not needed.

There's no simple solution to address this situation—the need to confidently build something you shouldn't actually be confident in. The best approach that I've come across is to move the testing process out of the reach of that cognitive dissonance. Make testing part of the culture of the organization; make it a habit that's followed as standard procedure and not something that the organization agonizes over and debates each time a new feature is added.

Alrighty. Those are three of the major issues I've confronted as teams explore testing incremental changes to their product. Thankfully, it's not hard to actually measure incremental impact. If you created a benchmark of the product's impact in Chapter 12, then all you need to do is to reapply the same tools here: experiments, pre-post analyses, and statistical models. Shifting from epistemology to the practicalities of testing, the next sections describe how each method can be used to measure incremental impact.

How to Run Incremental A/B Tests and Multivariate Tests

If you're changing the content of a screen or adding/removing user interactions, then it's straightforward to run an experimental test to see the impact of the change:

1. Create two or more parallel versions of that part of the product: the existing version (control) and new version(s) (treatment).
2. Estimate how many people you need in each group using online power calculation tools, as described in Chapter 12.

3. Randomly assign users, also as described in Chapter 12.
4. Run the test and measure the target behavior and outcome.
5. Check that the signal is strong enough to make a solid comparison, using one of the online tools listed in Chapter 12, or using a statistical package like R. If so, compare the averages for each group.

And that's it. That tells you the impact of the change. An experiment like this is the best, most reliable way to measure the *effect* of a feature. If you find that the new feature or change hurt the impact of the product, then the team will need to determine if it makes sense to cancel the change. If it helped, celebrate!

However, it can be very costly or difficult to run A/B tests when you're making a small change to the system: you may not have enough users to get a strong signal, or it may be costly for engineering reasons to keep two versions of the feature (old and new) at the same time. In that case, there are less expensive (but less precise) tools one can use.

How to Compare Incremental Pre-Post Results

Whenever the engineering team makes changes to the application, the company can look at user behavior before and after. As discussed in Chapter 12, numerous other factors could cause changes in behavior, so the results of a pre-post test need to be interpreted carefully. But if there is a major difference between the two versions, and nothing else that appears to have changed for the users at the same time, then a simple pre-post comparison is good enough. It can provide a reliable and easy way to gauge if the change helped or not.

How to Find Incremental Effects in Statistical Models

Another way of looking at the effect of a change in the application is to rerun the statistical models used to establish the product benchmark in Chapter 12. You do this by:

1. Comparing people who used the new changed feature versus those who didn't
2. Comparing the impact of the application before and after the change

In the first case, look for people who simply didn't see the change in the application, because they didn't log in, for example. If the reason people didn't see the change in the application is completely random, then you have a *natural experiment* and can treat the change like an A/B test. Check that the signal is strong, and then just compare the average behavior of each of the two groups.

If you don't have a natural experiment, then you look for statistical controls that account for *other reasons* that those people didn't see the change in the application (like their being overall less interested in the application, less likely to take the action at all, etc.). The challenge is that it is very difficult to control for all of the possible reasons that someone wouldn't interact with the changed part of the application. So, just like with pre-post analysis, there's a risk that you'll get misleading results. But if there is a major change in the outcome, and nothing else appears to explain it, the statistical model can point you in the right direction even if it isn't exactly perfect.

In the second case, when you compare the impact before and after the change, you're effectively running a pre-post analysis (but with a statistical model to control for additional factors). You'll need to think through the other things in the application and in the users' daily lives that could have been different before and after the feature was changed. It's certainly risky, but it may be the only practical option. The same rule applies: if it's a big change (one that you actually care about), and nothing else seems to explain it after a careful analysis, then the model can point you in the right direction.

Running Qualitative Tests of Incremental Changes

I didn't mention qualitative research in Chapter 12, when we were establishing a benchmark of the impact of product on user behavior and real-world outcomes. That's because it's difficult to generate a repeatable, reliable ROI metric of real-world impacts using most qualitative methods. But qualitative research can be quite valuable when you want to quickly judge how users are responding to a change in the application.

Put the revised application in front of users during user interviews, user testing (speak out-loud methods), or even focus groups. If you get a clear signal about whether the change has caused problems, you've just saved a lot of time. You can get feedback and insight in a fraction of the time it would take to test the product change with an experiment or pre-post analysis. While I am a big proponent of experiments (and statistical modeling), the benefit in terms of speed and depth of understanding from qualitative testing is too much to ignore. Of course, the team should have already performed a round of qualitative testing on the prototypes before the change was made to the product itself, too.

Deploying Multiarmed Bandit Techniques

There's been a lot of interest and attention given recently to multiarmed bandit techniques. These procedures dynamically adjust what content is shown to users based on the content's past performance. The process starts with two (or more) alternative versions of a page or product and an initial estimate of how effective each version of the page is for driving a target outcome, like conversions. As users reach the page, most of them (say 90%) receive the version that appears to be most effective. The rest of the users receive the other version(s), just in case the initial estimate of its relative effectiveness was too low. The system recalculates the effectiveness of the various versions on the fly. As more users come into the system, most are directed to whichever version is *currently* seen as most effective. It *exploits* the best performing version by giving it lots of users, *explores* other versions just in case it's wrong, and *learns* over time. The technique is dirt simple to code and can be found in this provocative 2012 blog post by Steve Hanov, "20 lines of code that will beat A/B testing every time" (*http://stevehanov.ca/blog/index.php?id=132*).

Multiarmed bandits are generally good at driving users toward the version of the page that is most effective. That's excellent. But that benefit comes at a cost. The first cost is time. Because the algorithm basically assumes it knows what's right based on early indication (and, to be fair, it often is), it takes a long time for the exploration part to test that assumption (i.e., it takes a much longer time to determine if one version of the page is actually better, or it just looked like it was better initially). The second cost is related: risk. If the early data gives a false signal, or the *type* of users in the system changes midstream, it takes a much longer time to discover that error and show the right version of the product to users than an A/B test would.

Both A/B tests and multiarmed bandit are forms of experiments, and both are scientifically valid. Both can tell you the impact of a change in your product. I'll leave the choice of which to use up to you, depending on how confident you are that one version of the page or product clearly is better than another, and that the multiarmed bandit algorithm will be able to pick up that difference early on. There's a nice summary of the pros and cons of multiarmed bandit techniques versus A/B testing on the *Visual Website Optimizer Blog* (Chopra 2012 [*http://bit.ly/19RJU2r*]).

When Is It "Good Enough"?

Ideally, the outcome of any product development process, especially one that aims to change behavior, is that the product is doing its job and nothing more is needed. When the product successfully automates the behavior, builds a habit, or reliably helps the user make the conscious choice to act, then the team can move on. There are always other products to build. And, for commercial companies, there are always other markets to tap. So, how can the team tell when it is good enough?

Return to the product's target outcome, and try to stop thinking about the product itself. The target outcome should be measurable, by definition! What's the target level (or change in the target) that the company decided would count as success? If the product currently reaches that threshold, wonderful. Forget the product's bugs. Forget the warts in the design. Move on. If the current product doesn't yet meet that threshold, what is the best alternative use of the team's time? If the alternative is more beneficial to the target outcome and can be achieved with similar resources, the team should switch its focus.

Expending effort on building a product or anything else warps our judgment of value.[153] Designing for behavior change is about final, objective outcomes—so that means taking a dispassionate look at what's really in the best interest of the company and users. Ideally, the person taking that dispassionate look wasn't involved in building the current product at all. Sometimes it means letting a somewhat broken product remain somewhat broken so the team can work on something else, in the name of helping your users.

How to (Re-)Design for Behavior Change with an Existing Product

Thus far, I've presented the process of designing for behavior change in terms of what it takes to build a new product or product feature. What should you do if you already have a product and are just starting to formally target and assess its impact on user behavior? The process isn't so different than if you were starting with a new product, but you have much more information to start with!

Here's how to do it:

1. Document the target outcome, actor, and action. (See Chapters 4 and 5 on how to record existing targets or develop new ones.)
2. Develop a rough behavioral plan using the product's current sequence of steps—what does the product actually encourage people to do?
3. Instrument the product to measure user behavior at each step of the way, if it hasn't already been instrumented.
4. Dig into the data (Chapters 12 and 13), to see what your users are doing, what impact the product is currently having, and what obstacles users are facing.
5. Generate ideas for product changes, large and small. Prioritize them as necessary.
6. In parallel, sketch out a blue-sky version of the product that wasn't constrained by the current implementation. Knowing what you know, how would you design the product for maximum impact? You don't need to do this too formally—just run through the "On a Napkin" exercises given in Chapters 4–8.
7. Check if that blue-sky idea is either:
    a. So promising that it might warrant a new development effort. If so, *test the idea first, don't build it yet.* After the initial testing, if everything pans out, consider switching products. I know that's not what product teams want to hear (see "the Ikea effect"), but it might be the best thing for users and company.
    b. *Promising and similar enough to the current product* such that incremental changes can be made to the current product to try out the ideas and improve the impact over time. Add the new ideas to the list of proposed changes, and prioritize them (along with all of the other proposed changes) as necessary.
8. Take the list of prioritized changes, integrate them into the product development process, and get crackin'.

Alternatively, you can take a more focused, but less open-minded, "fix what's broken" approach. In that case, you'd start with the discovery process (Chapters 4 and 5) to make sure everyone is on the same page about what the product is supposed to do. Then, you'd go straight into a diagnosis of known problems—using the Create Action Funnel to identify the underlying psychology that's driving the problems. That's described in Chapter 13. And, with the problem diagnosed, you'd jump to Table 10-1 to identify behavioral tactics that can resolve the problem.[154]

If you have a product with a narrow problem, then the "fix what's broken" approach is great. Otherwise, I suggest going with the more detailed approach; that helps you test your assumptions and potentially reenvision the product to make it far more effective.

On a Napkin

Here's what you'll need to do

- Gather together all of the proposed product changes—changes to improve the behavioral impact of the product and other changes suggested by sales, marketing, or other parts of the company.
- Prioritize the changes based on the company's and user needs and their likely impact on the user behavior.
- Measure the impact of each major change to the product, using the same tools outlined in Chapter 12. Make incremental measurement part of the culture of the company.
- For existing products, start with discovery, then skip the design stage and dive into the data to see where refinements should be made.

How you'll know there's trouble

- Major changes are planned for the product without assessing their likely impact on user behavior.
- The team is afraid to test the new feature, because the tests usually come back negative or testing would imply a lack of confidence.

Deliverables

- A new and (hopefully) improved product!

[*Part VI*]

Putting It into Practice

We've covered how the mind makes decisions, how to design products that leverage that knowledge, and how to test and refine those products over time. We're almost done.

At each step of the way, this book has provided guidance on how to apply these lessons in your daily work. But there may be some places you still have questions you aren't sure about. Part VI tries to answer some of the most common questions and reinforce how the whole process works to help orient you at each stage.

Chapter 15 covers a range of questions about the decision-making process, what that means for product development, and how products that change behavior affect a company's bottom line. It also provides a simple, start-to-finish example of using this process for a new product.

Chapter 16 wraps things up. It summarizes the major techniques learned in the book and the common themes that underlie the book's approach to behavior change.

[15]

Common Questions and a Start-to-Finish Example

An Example of the Approach

The method described here comes from our practical experiences at HelloWallet and from the inspiration we've gained talking with other companies in the field. Throughout this book, there are examples of particular companies that we've learned from and how they, and we, have applied this approach. But there hasn't been an opportunity to analyze a single, start-to-finish scenario. Let's do that here.

For this scenario, let's move past the standard examples used in this book of exercise trackers, personal finance apps, and such, and show how the approach can be used in a novel context—working with contractors on your home.[155] Not all behavior change is sexy and socially important. In fact, as I mentioned in the Preface, mundane changes in everyday life are the most numerous, but the least obvious, targets for behavior change. So without further ado, here's the scenario:

Jake has a software company that develops apps for building contractors, helping workers with a range of tasks, from avoiding injury to making efficient use of building materials.[156] One day, some of his clients approach him and want him to develop a new application that will improve the *quality* of their work, decreasing the rate and severity of errors on the job site. Most errors are caused by people making careless mistakes, so Jake recognizes that the success or failure of this new application will depend on helping contractors and their workers change their behavior. It's something they already want to do, it's something the contractor's customers (the homeowners) want, and there's always room for improvement.

So, let's walk through the four stages of designing for behavior change—*understand, discover, design, and refine*—for Jake's new application (see Figure 15-1). At this point, all Jake has is an initial request from his clients and a hazy vision of what the product will do.

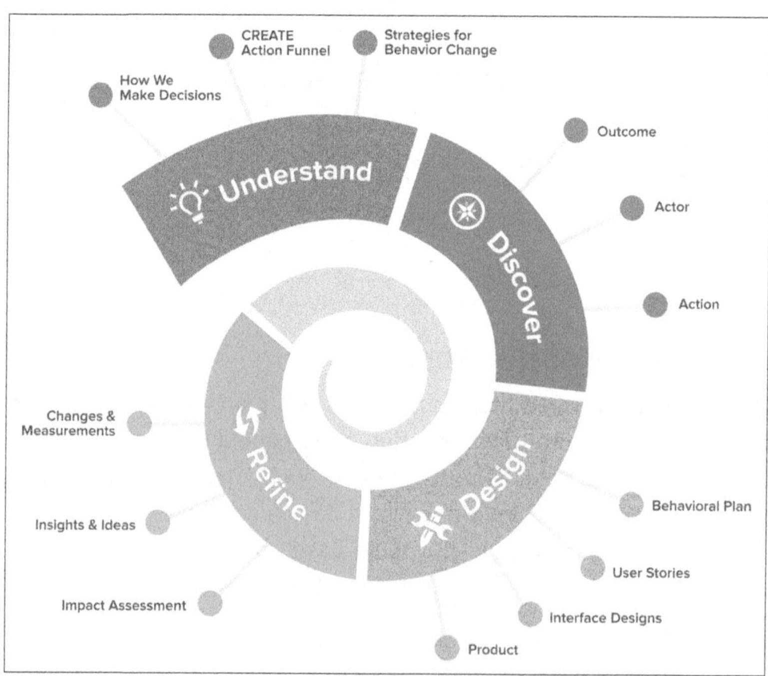

FIGURE 15-1.
The four stages of designing for behavior change

Understand

As the foundation for designing for behavior change, Jake learns about how the mind makes decisions. The most important lessons can be summarized in the Create Action Funnel (Figure 15-2): in order for the proposed application to be successful at changing the behavior of the contractors, he needs to ensure that they are *cued* to think about the app regularly; don't have a strong negative *reaction* (e.g., getting angry at being told what to do); *evaluate* the situation and see that the benefits of taking action will outweigh the costs; have the *ability* to actually make those quality-control changes; and feel that the *timing is right for action* (because of urgency or setting aside time to do it) to use the app and improve the quality of their work.

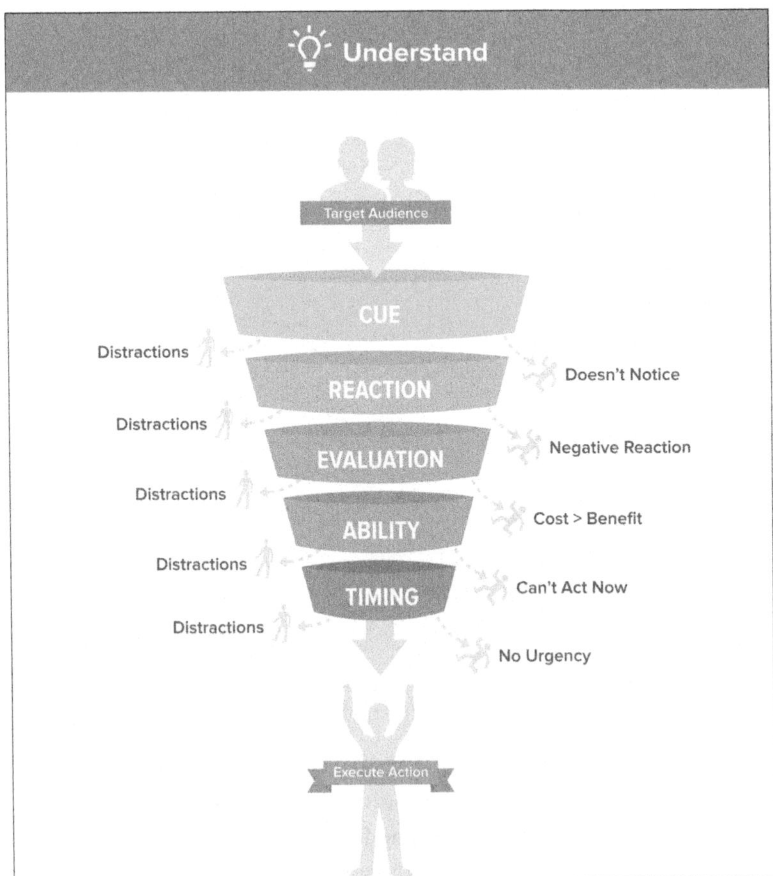

FIGURE 15-2.
If you remember one thing from the "Understand" phase of designing for behavior change, remember this: the Create Action Funnel

Discover

Next, Jake will start planning out the new product (Figure 15-3). Jake already has a vision of what he wants to do: improve building quality. He'll flesh out that vision to clearly define the real-world outcome that he wants to achieve. After talking with potential clients for this application, he realizes that what they care about most is decreasing the number of problems that are euphemistically known as "nonconformities." That's when the contractor doesn't end up building what had been agreed upon, leading to arguments with customers (i.e., the homeowner) and problems with the building inspector. Often, the contractor has to tear out the nonconformity and redo the work, at his own expense. No one is happy in that situation.

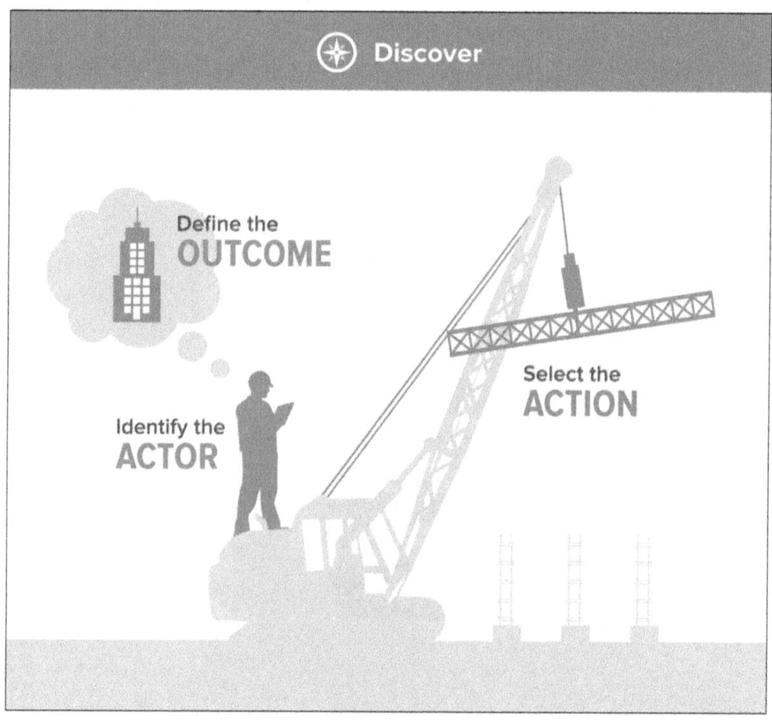

FIGURE 15-3. The discovery phase: your goal is to clarify the outcome, actor, and action

Jake works with his team and other experts in the industry to generate a list of potential actions that the contractors can take to decrease nonconformities. For example, taking additional training courses, adding additional supervision, and using testing and monitoring devices to ensure that the weather and other conditions are right for each task (weather conditions can significantly affect the quality of newly poured concrete, for example).

As part of the brainstorming, Jake discovers that sometimes contractors don't follow the building plans because they don't have the most up-to-date version, don't have the opportunity to check it regularly, or look for shortcuts to save time. Jake adds an idea to the list of potential actions: helping contractors frequently refer to the building plans.

He does user research in the field and discovers that both the foreman and the individual workers have the ability to decrease nonconformities. But the foreman is most likely to be receptive, and have the necessary skills, to use Jake's app. The foreman is thus the actor who will take action to decrease errors.

Putting the actor, outcome, and list of possible actions together, he evaluates the costs and benefits of each option—in terms of how difficult it will be to change the behavior, how effective that change will be at ensuring contractors keep to the building plans, and the revenue that his company can make from selling the application. The action of "helping the foreman frequently refer to the most up-to-date building plans" is the best option.

Design

With a clear sense of the behavior that the product hopes to change (outcome, actor, and action), Jake and his team start designing the product (Figure 15-4).

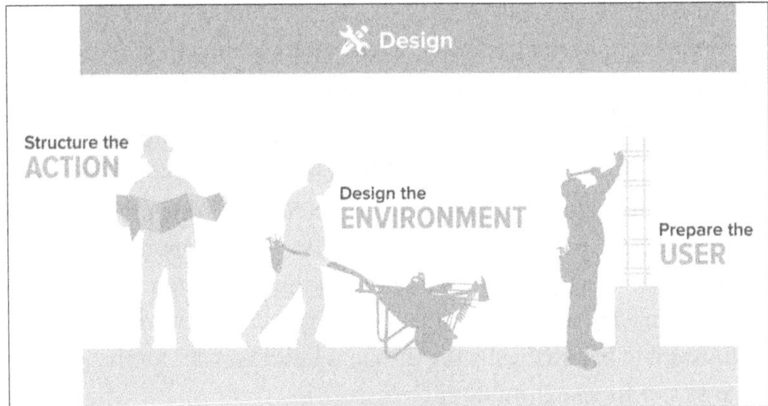

FIGURE 15-4.
The design process focuses attention on changing the action, environment, and user preparation, in turn, to support behavior change

The first task is the conceptual design, or behavioral plan—a narrative that describes how contractors will change their behavior over time, using Jake's product. He breaks the action into its component steps so that he can *structure the action* to ensure success. In order to regularly refer to the building plans (action), the user will need to (a) bring a device (a phone or a tablet) with the app to the job site, (b) load the correct building plans, (c) make the time to review them, (d) actually review them, and then (e) build in accordance with the latest plans.

Jake looks over this list for places he can simplify the process or tailor it to the existing skills and experience of his target users, the foremen. For example, he can use GPS to automatically load the correct building plans, and simple database logic to ensure that only the most up-to-date version is shown by default. He can schedule the review process to align with consistent cues in the user's environment—arriving at the job site, taking a break, etc. Those consistent cues also lay the foundation for building a long-term habit out of the behavior.

Next, he designs the environment in which the user acts. Part of that is the application itself, and part of it is on the jobsite. He looks for ways to cue action (reminders within the product, or papers taken to the site) and highlight the users' existing motivation (e.g., using loss aversion to highlight the cost of fixing nonconformities after the fact).

Finally, he looks at how to *prepare the user*. He adds a short training video within the application for first-time users, and integrates the application into the quality-control procedures the users already follow (to create a narrative in which using the product is a natural extension of their work). Thankfully, some of those procedures already occur on the foreman's smartphone, and so Jake plans to directly link the new application to the ones that they are already using.

The resulting behavioral plan tells Jake's team what the product should do. Next up, the team will work on the interface designs—the look and feel of the product that delivers this functionality. The team chops the behavioral plan into specific user stories for their agile development process, like, "As a user, I want to quickly learn how to use this software, so I don't need to waste time figuring out how it works" or, "As a user, I want to automatically see the right building plan for the job I'm on, to save time searching for it."

The interaction designer develops wireframes based on these user stories; along the way, she will use the numerous behavioral tactics in her toolbox—priming the user to activate thoughts of quality, avoiding choice overload by restricting the complexity of decisions that need to be made at one time, and eliciting implementation intentions around how to resolve nonconformities if they are found.

Afterward, Jake reviews the wireframes using the same process that he used for the behavioral plan—focusing on the action, the environment, and the users's preparation in turn. For each interaction the user has with the system, Jake checks whether the action could be simplified, whether the product delivers a single, clear call to action, and whether the user is properly prepared for action and knows what to do.

When the wireframes are solid, the team does qualitative testing with potential users, generates a clickable prototype for additional testing, and refines the designs accordingly. When the designs are done, the team builds the product.

Refine

No product is perfect, especially one that tries to change deeply ingrained, real-world behavior for people on the job. So, Jake and his team *assess the impact* of the product by doing a simple comparison between clients who were randomly selected to receive the trial version of his product, and those who weren't (Figure 15-5). He compares nonconformities across the two groups, and finds that yes, the product works—it substantially reduces errors. But there's room for improvement.

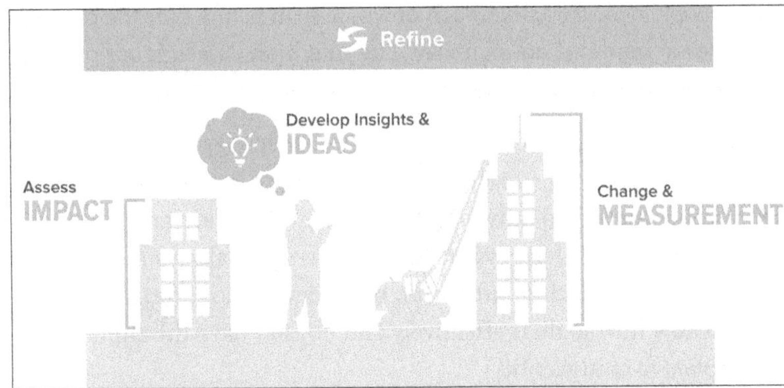

FIGURE 15-5. Refining the product starts with a clear sense of its current impact, finding ways to improve it, then testing those changes in the field

During data collection, Jake realizes that many of the mistakes that occur on the job happen in the late afternoon when workers are tired and hurrying to get home. He has some *ideas* on how to fix that, such as having the app recommend breaks, and making the foreman consciously aware of that problem. He evaluates these behaviorally informed changes along with additional requests from his current clients and from his marketing team.

Finally, he develops a plan to change the product that should improve its impact and increase revenue. He makes the change, measures it, and it works. Nevertheless, he continues to gather data about the performance of his app and iteratively improves it in the future.

Questions About How and Why We Act

Now, let's turn to a set of questions that I've encountered about how our minds' decision-making process works. There's no strict ordering or relationship here; these are just some of the most common issues that people have wanted to better understand. Feel free to jump to those questions that are relevant to you.

What Happens Before People Take Action the First Time?

The Create Action Funnel provides the five preconditions for action, and the design process puts those five preconditions in place with a product. But how do people normally progress from inaction to action over time?

There's no consensus in the literature about how individuals move from inaction to action on their own. There are many pathways by which people become active, each of which brings together the preconditions for action in their own way. The intentional design of products to support action, described here, is just one of those pathways.

Consider the example of a person who wants to clean the house. He has a positive intuitive reaction and decides that the benefits (girlfriend won't leave him) outweigh the costs (an afternoon of TV watching lost) after a conscious evaluation. But there are always more pressing things to do (no time pressure), he forgets to do it (no cue), or he doesn't know how to do it effectively and doesn't have the right cleaning supplies (lacking ability).

Here's a quick overview of different pathways by which this person could move from failing to take the action to successfully doing it:

Self-directed action

He thinks about cleaning a few times, and it doesn't happen. When he's at the grocery store, he remembers to pick up cleaning supplies, but doesn't set aside time to use them. One day, he says enough is enough and plans out a specific day and time to do it, sets a reminder, and removes other distractions.

Intentional help from another person

A friend hears him complaining about his dirty house and decides to push a bit to get it done. The friend reminds him at the grocery store to get supplies and makes him commit to cleaning on a particular day.

Directed help from a product

He downloads a task-management app based on David Allen's book *Getting Things Done* (Penguin Books, 2001). He records all of the things he needs to do (cleaning and otherwise), and, with the help of the app, works out the logistics and timing to finally clean up the house.

Sudden change in environment

He wants to clean the house, but just doesn't get it together. For other reasons, he changes jobs and moves. His new house is much smaller, and he gets rid of most of his stuff. It's also much easier to clean, and he finds it's easy to continue a habit of keeping the house clean once he's started.

Sudden change in life circumstances

The guy gets married. His wife won't put up with his messiness and lays down the law for him. He shapes up.

Social drift

For various reasons, he gets to know new people at work, and some of them become friends. He visits their houses, which are pleasantly clean. When he goes home, he looks at his house differently. This happens a few times, and he's ashamed of bringing other people over. He gets up the gumption and does it.

These are common pathways, but of course there are many more. The point is that there simply isn't a single route by which people change their behavior over time. Sometimes there's a single, culminating event that forces change (marriage); at other times, things move more slowly (social drift).

While these examples point to multiple *possible* routes, anecdotes aren't science. Thus far, researchers haven't established clear, generally accepted rules for how individuals move from inaction to action over the course of time. There's a great deal of activity in the addiction and health space, with models such as the Transtheoretical Model[157] (Prochaska and Velicer 1997) and Health Belief Model (Janz and Becker 1984), but their general applicability is unclear. We know a lot more about what happens at the moment of action (a cue, a conscious choice to act, etc.) than we do about what happens before that action.

> **Lessons for Behavioral Products**
>
> This section speaks to the transition from inaction to action, but it's especially relevant when you're trying to increase adoption of your product. There's no simple answer to how people will decide to adopt, but you can improve your chances. If possible, identify life transition points for your users, and ensure your product cues them then. Beyond that, you can use open-ended campaigns to gather data about unknown entry routes, and subsequently focus efforts if major opportunities are found.

How Do the Preconditions for Action Vary From Day to Day?

Each of the five preconditions can vary from day to day and moment to moment. In Part III, we discussed how the five preconditions are characteristics of the action, the environment, and the actor (the "context" of the user's decision to act, or not). Both the actor and the environment vary over time, and thus so do the conditions for action:

Environment

: As a person moves through the day, the environment generally changes. The different environments shape whether the person will take a particular action or not. For example: someone may have Internet access while waiting for a meeting, and can use mobile apps, but not while driving. The person may see reminders to exercise at home, but not while at the bar.

Actor

: Over the course of the day, *people* also vary in themselves. Their wakefulness varies, their tendency to be distracted varies, and of course, so do their emotions. An action that seems interesting and worthwhile to a rested, well-fed person can seem overly complex, too much work, and not urgent to someone who is hungry and tired.

This variation is a mix of happenstance and structure. Day to day, a person's work schedule may be too irregular to identify stable moments of opportunity for engagement with the product. But the commuting schedule may be stable and clear. Where feasible, the product should align with the moments and situations of opportunity, in which some of the preconditions for action are already naturally in place, and then fill in the gaps.[158]

From the perspective of product design, look for structure within this day-to-day (and moment-to-moment) variation, and build on it to encourage action. Are there particular times and places when the user of the product is least distracted? Or most motivated to act? Where are the cues to act in the person's daily life?

> **Lessons for Behavioral Products**
>
> You have two main options to harness the natural variation in people's days. You can do user research, and try to find structured opportunities for engagement that are common across the user base. Alternatively, you can prompt users to self-identify the best times for them—when they want to receive reminder messages, when they want to be motivated with uplifting stories from other users, etc.

How Do the Dynamics of Using a Product Change as the User Gains Experience With It?

There are many ways in which people can change as they start using a product. There's no guarantee that over time, people will become experts or master the product and behavior. For example, some people keep using a product they love indefinitely, and others stop after the first time, or after a few weeks.

Rather than a proscriptive pathway, there are different states that users can be in, relative to the product. In each of these states, the dynamics of the Create Action Funnel (cue-reaction-evaluation-ability-timing) and the context that supports it (action-environment-actor) are somewhat different. These states are:

- *Not a user of the product*
    - *Dynamics.* For someone that has never used the product before, its very newness is a benefit and a curse. Cues are likely to be noticed. Newness can increase motivation to explore. But newness can make the user unsure about the logistics of actually using it, and that person's ability to succeed. Also, our intuitive reaction to the idea is based on our experiences with similar activities, which could be good or bad.

- *What the company should do.* Ensure the user knows about the product at all (cue). Make sure the value is clear (evaluation), and associate the product with familiar, pleasant things (reaction).

- *A one-time user of the product who had a positive experience*
  - *Dynamics.* Once we gain experience with a product, our future intuitive reactions take that into account. If we liked the product the first time we used it, excellent. We gain knowledge of how to use it (decrease costs, increase logistical ability).
  - *What the company should do.* Keep cueing the user; it's unlikely that the user has built a strong association between the product and an existing cue in his environment. Highlight the positive experience (evaluation and reaction). Use knowledge gathered during the first use to try to align the product with times and situations when the user isn't distracted and can take action (ability and timing).

- *A one-time user of the product who had a negative experience*
  - *Dynamics.* If the first experience was negative, we have two obstacles to overcome—the allure of newness is gone, and we have an intuitive negative reaction. It is much harder to bring these users back.
  - *What the company should do.* Honestly, focus attention on other users. This is a tough group to win back. And focus attention on improving the experience of first-time users in the future.

- *A user who's returned to the product one or more times*
  - *Dynamics.* When a user has successfully returned to the product, that's a sign that the conditions are ripe for future use. Something in the user's context has pulled him back. However, it's not clear yet how *stable* that something is—it might be a temporary assignment at work that makes the user think about or need the product. It might be a core desire. At this point, minor disruptions to the user's context (a different routine at work, etc.) can easily stop him from returning.

- *What the company should do.* Keep cueing the user until there's a strong association between the product and an existing environmental cue. Highlight prior positive experiences and successes. With user research, try to understand the user's context: are there temporary factors pushing him to use it for which the product must find a substitute?

- *A user who regularly uses the product*
  - *Dynamics.* When the user returns to the product repeatedly, then there's a stable context that pulls him back. Only major changes in the user's context are likely to disrupt continued use—the user changes jobs, gets divorced, takes on significant new activities that pressure his time, or the product suddenly drops the particular functionality he loves.
  - *What the company should do.* Don't screw it up. Be very careful when changing functionality that's driving usage. Look for regular users who drop off—if the context disruption is temporary, there's a very good chance you can win them back (but don't take it for granted; see Milkman et al. 2013). If you are working with a potentially habitual behavior, make sure the cue and routine are constant over time.
- *Habitual user*
  - *Dynamics.* If the user returns on a regular basis and responds automatically to an environment cue, you've successfully built a habit of use. (You can see whether it's a habit by looking at the usage pattern in the data and through user research.) Since the behavior is largely on autopilot, it's highly resistant to change. Only major changes in the cue or a lack of ability to act are likely to break it.
  - *What the company should do.* Don't mess with the cue or change the fundamental learned routine that users enact.

In addition, Nir Eyal talks about how to leverage the initial usage of an application to build future interest and make it easier or more valuable for users to return. He refers to it as the "investment" step that occurs right after an individual has had a positive experience with the product. He focuses on investment in the formation of habits, but it's an insight that can be applied for non-habitual behaviors as well (Eyal 2013).

> **Lessons for Behavioral Products**
>
> As users gain experience with a product, the type of support they need changes. The most critical periods for adopting a new product to change behavior is the first experience (when curiosity and newness is replaced by an evaluation of the product), and in the transition from a returning user to a regular user (when minor changes in circumstance can disrupt the new behavior).
>
> Does the product provide an excellent first-time user experience? Does it provide a compelling, ongoing reason to return to the product—especially on a regular schedule with a stable cue to facilitate habit formation?

Questions About the Mechanics of Building Behavior Change Products

How Can a Company Get Help Testing Its Product, Especially from Outside Researchers?

Experimentally testing a product, especially when the target behavior can't be measured within the product itself, can be an intimidating endeavor. Believe it or not, academic researchers would probably love to help test your product's impact on behavior. Many of them can't be "hired" in a traditional sense—because they have full-time jobs in academic institutions and for professional reasons can't accept consulting contracts. But you can build partnerships of mutual benefit if you have enough users of your product to support a scientifically valid study.

Here's how you can go about building research partnerships:

- *Find researchers in your field.* This is a lot easier than it used to be; you can start with Google Scholar (*http://scholar.google.com/*) to search for the topics you work on, and see whose names are in the most commonly cited articles (the results are sorted by the number of citations). Academic conferences on your topic are another good way to start but take more investment of time and energy.

- *Contact them*, asking for suggestions about academics who might be interested in studying the topic with your user base. In particular, ask who might be interested in testing the impact of interventions. Follow-up and contact the suggested researchers; the researchers you initially contacted may be interested, of course.
- *Discover what they need to aid their work.* Describe your product and user base. Ask them what they need. Depending on the person, and their status in relation to their career and field, that will vary. Here are common options:
  - *Access to unique data.* In some disciplines, it is extremely costly and difficult to obtain detailed information about individual users, from demographic information to observed preferences, and especially about changes in behavior over time.
  - *Access to a large user base.* The power of scientific tests increases with more users, but it is costly for most researchers to gather a large enough test population on their own. If your product already has them, excellent.
  - *Access to funding.* Financial support from companies to academic social science researchers can be highly problematic; it can taint researchers' independence and undermine their ability to publish the results of a study with the company. However, if the company is looking for expert advice, and not academic publication of the results, some researchers certainly can be hired for paid consulting arrangements. Other options include providing grants for research on the topic, and supporting grant proposals submitted by the researchers to third-party grant agencies.
- *Develop a shared research plan.* With a small, trial project, try working together. Set clear expectations on access to data, funding (if any), staffing (on both sides), and timing of the study and analyses.
- *Don't try to restrict the results or ideas.* Academic research runs on innovative ideas and the data to back them up. Companies can't lock down the ideas learned from the study—they must be shared between the company and researchers. Similarly, if there is a whiff of restriction on the publication of negative results, that will undermine the reception of the study and turn away most researchers. Paid consulting arrangements work differently, of course.

- *Respect the need for specific testing protocols.* In order for a study to be scientifically valid, researchers will have to execute the study according to specific rules. For example, they may require very specific wording for questions asked of users. That's part of the bargain; and, it will often help the company formulate much more solid conclusions than if it had informally developed slapdash surveys.

Lessons for Behavioral Products

If the testing process seems overwhelming, don't despair. First, look to off-the-shelf tools for testing applications (discussed in Chapter 12). If those aren't useful, look for professional research partnerships with the academic community. If your company is doing innovative things to help users change their behavior (which of course you are!), researchers may be interested in working with you.

How Can You Sustain Engagement With Your Product?

Products that hope to actively change long-term behavior can't do that if people start using the product, then drop off. Sustained engagement with a product requires an act of behavior change just like the product's target behavior. At a high level, *continued usage of a product follows the same rules outlined throughout this book.*

There are five preconditions to (re-)engaging with a product. A cue to do so, a positive intuitive reaction, a positive conscious evaluation, the ability to do so, and reason to do so at a particular time (rather than endless procrastination). These preconditions can be met with the three big strategies for behavior change:

1. Helping the user make a conscious choice to reengage each and every time
2. Building a consistent habit of logging into the application, with a cue, routine, and reward
3. "Cheating"—making the product a required part of the person's daily life (like a time-keeping app at work) or making it a default behavior (like a home page on a browser)

To support the conscious choice to reengage,[159] companies can design around the behavior of reengagement:

- Tailor the action to the user. Make it dirt simple to log back in again (e.g., by using a single sign-on procedure with Facebook instead of a unique username and password).
- Design the product and overall environment to support it, by making sure the motivation is there (i.e., that the product is worth using!), providing a clear cue, and removing distractions.
- Prepare the user by ensuring that prior experiences with the product were worthwhile and enjoyable and by making use of the product seem a natural thing to do, and removing any logistical barriers to actually using the product.

Too often, companies just focus on providing value and wonder why users don't come back. Value is clearly important—users have to want to use the product (i.e., they must have a positive conscious evaluation of the product), or they won't voluntarily use it. But there's much more involved, and much more that companies can do.

Of the five preconditions for reengaging with a product, it's the cue that I think has received the least attention and thought in product development circles outside of growth hacking (where it is an essential part of the discussion). Perhaps it's because we think that if we build the greatest product in the world, people will naturally come and use it.

To cue individuals to reengage with a product:

Provide value

Absolutely, this is essential. If users don't think your product is worthwhile, you aren't going to be able to grab their attention repeatedly (they'll change their environment to avoid you). So, value is the first step. But it's only the first step.

Uniquely become part of the person's environment

One way to remind people to use a product is to ensure it's seen—by placing the Nike+ FuelBand by the side of the bed or by making your application the home page on a browser. By *uniquely*, I mean that there aren't other shiny things the person is seeing at the same time; that's a real problem with tweets and emails, for example—they are extraordinarily crowded channels.

Uniquely become part of the person's expected routine

At a particular time of day (or situation), train the user to uniquely think of the application as a way to do something or relieve boredom. "Training" isn't happenstance: ask the user to plan out a particular time to use the product (i.e., as part of implementation intentions). If you're providing value, then help users form a habit around getting that value.

Be so darn cool and memorable that people think of you, on their own

We all aspire to this, and we think that a beautiful product will make users dream about us. I don't know about you, but I've seen a lot of beautiful artwork in museums. I don't dream about them, and neither do I dream about more than a handful of products. So, invest in other ways to get attention.

Build strong associations with something that is part of the user's environment or daily routine

If you can't get in front of users' eyeballs directly or reserve a slot on their daily calendar, build on what's already there. For example, whenever there's a crisp spring weekend day in D.C. (an existing aspect of my environment), I think of the bike trailer my kid loves riding in and head to the garage to get it.

Be useful each and every time they see you

Don't train the user to ignore you. Does your carpet catch your attention? No. It's in your line of sight, and you step on it as part of your daily schedule. But it does nothing for you most of the time. Same thing with sending lots of emails to users. *Don't be the carpet.*

Be new and different each time

One way to avoid being the carpet is to make sure that each attention-grabbing piece of content contains something new (or potential for newness)—social network notifications do this beautifully with their teaser emails about friends doing stupid stuff. It's more than a random reward for logging into Facebook or Twitter—the attention grabber itself is different each time.

Lessons for Behavioral Products

You can think about behavior change as a two-stage problem. First, there's the behavior of engaging with your application. Second, there's the behavior that the application seeks to support. The same tools taught throughout this book for the latter behavior are also applicable to the former.

Pay particular attention to how the application is cueing people to log in—is there a consistent reminder in the user's environment that either you can construct uniquely for your product, or that you can associate with your product?

When You're Seeking to Change Behavior, How Do You Avoid Going Too Far?

There is sometimes a fine line between *helping* people take an action they want to take, and pushing them to take the action they wouldn't otherwise take. How do you avoid going too far into coercive tactics? I'm not your mother, and I'm not judging you. But here are some ways to think about the issue.

Personally, I approach the issue pragmatically. In the end, we are trying to change behavior. But we're trying to change behavior in ways that (a) people want and that (b) are beneficial. At the extremes, we can all reasonably distinguish products that are *enabling* from products that are *coercive*. For example, an arm band that automatically tracks exercise and reports the data to the wearer—that's enabling. An ankle bracelet that shocks you and reports you to the police whenever you leave the perimeter of your house—that's coercive. However, in the middle, things get fuzzy.

One reason it's fuzzy is that we all want many things. And we want different things over the course of our lives and even over the course of the day. Our self-control waxes and wanes, we change our behavior in subtle ways at work and at home, and, let's face it: we all have "moods." No person, and certainly no product, is smart enough to judge what another person's "true" desires are in a given moment.

Things also get fuzzy because "beneficial" behavior change is in the eye of the beholder. There are trade-offs in every action we take, especially as we build products to change our own and other people's behavior. I might think that it's a reasonable trade-off between privacy and beneficial behavior change to use an app that monitors my credit card for cigarette purchases and then alerts my spouse. You might not.

While there are gray areas, I don't think that the ethics of behavior change are relative, squishy things. There are clear lines we should not cross if we claim to help users take action (and not to be forcing them to do so): involuntary actions; not telling users what we're doing; and manipulating people's emotions so they make poor choices. Around those lines, we need to be a bit humble and find ways to check ourselves and our motivations. Here are some approaches you can try:

- *Tell users what you're doing.* If the person wants to take the action, at least at some point in the daily ups and downs of life, great. Telling the user what you're doing shouldn't cause a problem and is a good, simple check on excess.
- *Make sure the action is optional.* Leave it up to the user to decide whether or not to use the application, and don't hide behind false options—for example, an app that monitors employee productivity at work isn't optional (the job may be "optional," but the app isn't).
- *Ask yourself* whether you'd want someone else to encourage you to use the product. Is this product really designed to help you?
- *Ask others,* especially strangers, if they would *trust* the application.

Avoiding coercion doesn't mean that you encourage users to do anything they want to do. The company will have, and must have, a stance on the behaviors it wants to encourage. "Dieting" and "eating everything you want" aren't two equally valid options for weight loss. One works (sometimes) and the other doesn't. You can talk about and be up front about that stance. If you're helping people diet, don't be ashamed about it. Do it, and do it proudly, but be transparent and make participation optional.

Many types of products, even those that are explicitly coercive, can be good and useful. The ankle bracelets used for home detentions probably fall into that category. On net, society is better off because of their use. But that's a different type of product, which deserves scrutiny and thought. Here, my goal is to spur thought about products that enable voluntarily behavior change so that we are clear about what we're doing and the means we're using to affect user behavior.

Lessons for Behavioral Products

Talking about product ethics may be an unusual topic for a book aimed at practitioners. But we can't outsource ethics. We should feel proud of our work. Part of that means double-checking that the product is truly voluntary, is up front about the behaviors it tries to change, and seeks to make a beneficial change for its users.

How Does Designing for Behavior Change Affect My Business Model?

Helping users voluntarily change their behavior can directly support the core business goals of a company, but these types of products do raise special business considerations.

Recall from the Preface that there are two main targets for behavior change:

- Behaviors that users want to change *within their daily lives*
- Behaviors that occur *within the product itself* and are required to use the product

In the latter group, the business impact is clear and straightforward. Let's say the behavior change task is learning how to better organize email in an email client. If you help users do this more effectively, they are more likely to (a) buy later editions of the product in the future (or renew, if the product is on a subscription model) and (b) recommend it to others. In both cases, behavior change means more revenue.

For behavior that users want to change in their daily lives, there are a variety of options, depending on whether the behavior is frequently repeated or occurs once. Let's say the behavior change task is exercising. It's a repeated behavior that people often want to change in their daily lives. Standard business models work perfectly well for this type of product and align user success with business success:

- *Revenue increases with the time users spend using the product.*
    - *Subscriptions and reoccurring fees.* For example, a product that helps people set, track, and compete with friends over exercise goals. If the product is successful, both exercising and revenues are sustained. A similar model exists for products

that automate user tasks altogether—like target date funds in the investment space, which charge an ongoing fee for automating the process of asset allocation.

  - *Advertising*. For example, the same exercising tracking/competition product could be free to the user but advertise fitness products. If the product is successful, it continues to deliver an interested, engaged audience for advertising.

- *Revenue increases with new sales.*

  - *Market penetration*. For example, an exercise tracker like the Nike+ FuelBand. People don't really need two exercise trackers. But if the product is successful at changing behavior, then current customers refer others, and sales grow. If the market becomes saturated, that's a nice problem to have, and the company can move on to new product lines (up-sell).

  - *Cross-sell and up-sell*. For example, the company has multiple exercise products (a tracker, shoes, clothing, etc.). If one product is successful at changing behavior, then the customer is more inclined to buy other products from the company.

- *Revenue increases with the success of users at changing their behavior.*

  - *Incentive-aligned third-party support*. For example, a third party benefits from the same thing that users benefit from: behavior change. The third party would then pay for the product on the user's behalf. Employers benefit from their employees being physically healthy and pay for products like Keas to help employees exercise. Energy companies benefit from their customers being energy efficient, and pay for products like Opower.

As you can see, products that change repeated behaviors follow the same business models as any other product—plus the somewhat unusual option of third-party support.

Products that change a one-time or infrequent behavior have a more difficult time aligning user success with business success. Consider, for example, the behavior of getting a mortgage, and products that help people shop around for a better one. Thankfully that's not something that most people do very often. Here's how standard business models become problematic:

- *Revenue increases with the time users spend using the product.*
    - *Usually not relevant.* Customers just want to find a good mortgage; they won't pay more if it takes longer to find one.
- *Revenue increases with new sales.*
    - *Cross-sell and up-sell.* This is feasible if the company offers related services—like banks that offer mortgages and checking accounts. However, customers have a hard time assessing the quality of one-time services like mortgage-buying assistance; that uncertainty leaves room for chicanery. In the mortgage market, there's a significant temptation (financial incentive) to shift from providing unbiased decision-making support to pushing mortgages that generate high, lead-generation fees.
    - *Market penetration.* Generating new sales based on high-quality decision support for mortgages is possible. However, because customers have difficulty assessing quality, the same temptations exist for the companies that seek to "help" users make that decision. Hence, businesses use gimmicks that made customers excited up front, but leave them loaded with significant fees and risk, like balloon mortgages.
- *Revenue increases with the success of users at changing their behavior.*
    - *Incentive-aligned third-party support.* A one-time change in behavior would need to be very significant to attract (incentive-aligned) third-party support. In the case of decision-making support, Fannie Mae and Freddie Mac have appropriate incentives for end users to receive optimal mortgages, but few other entities have incentives aligned with the end user for such a product.

And, of course, there are business models in the behavior change space that clearly are not aligned with the interests of user. Gyms are the classic example of businesses that profit because their users fail to change their behavior. Many gyms rely on fees paid by users who plan to exercise but never do.

Lessons for Behavioral Products

This probably isn't in the domain of designing for behavior change per se, but the company should think about how a focus on behavior change affects its bottom line. Does the company rely on subscriptions and would lose money if users simply solved their problem? That's a misalignment of the company's goals with the user's goals and spells trouble. Thankfully, there are numerous incentive-aligned options, especially for repeated behaviors.

[16]

Conclusion

Four Lessons

We can design products that help people take action. We've seen it done—in exercise, in energy usage, in personal finance, and in many other domains. It requires four things:

1. An understanding of how the mind works
2. Clarity about the intended outcomes of product, and about its users
3. A detailed plan for how the product will help the user act
4. The willingness to accept that the product won't be perfect, and needs to be tested and refined over time

Each of these maps onto one of the major processes of designing for behavior change, and the corresponding parts of the book: understand, discover, design, and refine. Throughout this book, I've tried to provide the background information and the practical tools needed to make this happen in your own business, government agency, or NGO.

Here's a quick recap.

Understand: How the Mind Makes Decisions

When we're awake, we're always doing something—whether it's reading, running, or resting. We tend to think that the things we do are *intentional*: I run at 7 p.m. each day because I really want to; I read the newspaper every morning because I want be informed about world news. We believe that our conscious minds think carefully about what to do and decide on a course of action. But the reality is a little more complex:

- *Most of the time our behavior is on autopilot,* driven by the automatic, reactive part of our brain. Habits are a key type of autopilot behaviors and work in predictable ways, with cues, routines, and, sometimes, explicit rewards. But habits aren't the only type. We intuitively react to situations based on our past experiences and the *mindset* we're in—the particular facet of self has been activated to respond to the current situation.
- *Even when we're not on autopilot, our minds are constantly looking to save work.* We have terribly limited attention, limited short-term memory, and limited and easily depleted willpower. That's not to say we're stupid or weak—instead, our minds find creative ways to work around our biological limits. We substitute simple problems for hard ones. We look to our peers to guide us when we're not sure what to do. We look for solutions that are "good enough" rather than trying to find the absolutely optimal answers.
- *The simple, obvious stuff matters.* Designers have known this for a long time. We like products that are easy and beautiful. We're more comfortable with familiar things and familiar actions than new and strange ones. We like good experiences, and we really don't want to fail. We try to do urgent things before things that aren't urgent.

Given this quirky decision-making process, why do we end up taking one action rather than another? We're each unique, and there's no simple formula that says person X will always do Y. But we can extract lessons from the research literature to identify the preconditions that need to be in place for a person to take a specific action:

- *Cue.* The thought of taking the action needs to somehow cross the person's mind. This can occur because of an external cue (the phone rings) or an internal one (the stomach growls).
- *Reaction.* In the blink of an eye, the automatic, intuitive self reacts to the idea. It checks whether the action is relevant and interesting at all. It generates an emotional response. It activates and starts to consider *other* possible actions that the person might take.

- *Evaluation.* If the action isn't intuitively discarded, it can bubble up to conscious awareness for a cost-benefit analysis: how hard will the action be to take, what's the action's value for the user, etc. The mind would evaluate other alternatives as well and determine the most promising action.
- *Ability.* If the action is worthwhile (benefit > cost, and more than the alternatives), the person must actually be able to act. Ability has many levels: the person must know logistically what to actually do, have the resources to do it, and must not be dissuaded by the assumption of failure. If the user faces obstacles, often they can be resolved, but that process takes time and leaves the person open to distraction.
- *Timing.* The person needs to have a reason to act now, rather than doing something else that is more urgent. That reason can range from external emergencies (the car is about to crash) to internal disequilibrium (hunger, thirst).

If all of these are in place, then a person can *execute* the action. Together, they form the C-r-e-a-t-e Action Funnel. For any given action, you can think about people leaking away at each step, either intentionally deciding not to take the action, or becoming distracted by other things. Designing for behavior change entails helping people pass through all five stages, from inaction to action.

There are three main strategies that products can take to help people through the Create Action Funnel:

1. They can use the brute force method, supporting the user's conscious decision to act, each and every time the user should take the action.
2. They can build habits, which rely on the automatic, intuitive part of the mind. With habitual behavior, the evaluation and timing parts are usually skipped over, making it more likely that the person will take the action.
3. They can "cheat"—by shifting the burden of work from the user to the product, so that after the user gives consent, the *user doesn't need to act.* That inverts the Create Action Funnel and makes inaction work to the user's benefit.

Discover: How to Clarify Goals and Understand Your Users

Designing for behavior change builds upon a clear understanding of the target outcome, action, and actor:

- The *outcome* is what will be different in the real world when the product is successful;
- The *actor* is who will cause that change (the actor is usually the user of your product); and
- The *action* is how the actor will do it—the behavior the actor will undertake.

You elicit and clarify each of these three things in order to find problems early on in the development process: problems where the team disagrees on the actual purpose of the product, or who the target audience is, or how the product will be judged for success or failure.

Ideally, the outcome should be a tangible, real-world impact. There's a natural tendency to think about the impact on users' emotions, awareness, or knowledge—things that are inside users' heads. We want to move beyond that, into the practical impact on people's actual behavior and the world around them. Often, it's the application of a user's newfound knowledge that companies really care about, and not the knowledge itself. For example, if a product taught people about the dangers of smoking but did absolutely nothing to change smoking behavior, that would be a failure. It's the real-world impact that matters.

Next, the company should clarify exactly how the actors (usually the users of the product) are going to make that outcome happen. If the outcome is improved health, then are users supposed to exercise more or eat better? If the company isn't sure what the best action is for their users, this process can help:

1. *Generate a set of ideas.* The team can brainstorm ideas on its own, or use questions like these to spark thought: "What does someone do right before the outcome occurs?," "What actions do users already take that are related to the outcome?," "What's stopping users from making the outcome happen?" Direct observation of users to learn how they are already making the outcome happen (e.g., how they are already losing weight) is invaluable.

2. *Learn the about the target users.* What's their existing motivation to act? What blocks them? Do they have prior experience with similar actions or with similar products?

3. *Generate user personas.* For each potential action, segment the user population based on who is going to respond differently to an appeal to act. For example, people who exercise regularly are going to respond differently than couch potatoes to an appeal to run a half marathon.

4. *Evaluate the potential actions.* Rate each action according to four criteria: *impact* (how effectively it will drive the outcome, like health), *motivation* (how much users currently want to take the action), *ease* (how familiar the action is to users), and *cost* (how costly it will be for the company to build a product that supports the action). Then select the best action given the particular resource constraints of the company and the realities of the users.

If the company already has a target action in mind, that's great—all it needs to do is specify what the action is, learn about its target users, and generate the personas.

Design: How to Design for Action

Designing a product to support behavior change can seem like a daunting task. There are countless choices that you need to make, and hundreds of different cognitive mechanisms at play. You can think, in turn, about the three different parts of the decision-making *context* that come together to shape behavior: the action itself, the environment, and the user's preparation. These three elements are *how* you influence behavior, and the Create Action Funnel tells you *what* needs to happen here.

ACTION

Start by breaking the target action into discrete steps that the user will need to complete. For example, in order to eat healthy dinners at home, the user will need to decide what to eat, know how to prepare it, plan out the ingredients, buy those ingredients, budget enough time to cook, and cook. Given this list of small, discrete steps:

1. Tailor each step to the user's level of expertise and interest.

2. Simplify each step to reduce the amount of work required of the user. Ideally this means removing steps altogether.

3. Make each step easier to complete by making it understandable to the user, ensuring the user can see it as feasible, and providing feedback of progress during long-duration actions.

ENVIRONMENT

Shape the user's decision-making environment in two senses—by designing the product itself to support action and by helping the user change the broader environment, outside of the product. In each case:

1. *Increase motivation* by reminding users of their existing reasons to act and, potentially, by providing additional incentives.
2. *Cue action* by directly asking users to act and encouraging them to set up a cue in their environment.
3. *Generate a feedback loop* by providing ongoing status updates about how users are doing so they can adjust their behavior accordingly.
4. *Remove competition* for users' attention and behavior by removing distractions within the application, coopting and building upon existing behavior, or competing head-on for users' interest.
5. *Remove obstacles* by ensuring that the product is accessible and meets the particular constraints (e.g., handicaps, reading ability, platform access) of the users.

USER PREPARATION

Now the behavior has been tailored to the users, and the environment has been set up to support that behavior, look at how to best prepare the user to take action. There are three tactics:

1. *Narrate.* Change how users see themselves. Help users see the action as a natural extension of who they are by having them recall similar things they've done in the past and by linking the action to their self-identity.
2. *Associate.* Change how users see the action. Make it clear how this action builds upon, and uses knowledge from, other things they've done before. Make a strong connection between the action and other positive things they enjoy—like smelling the fresh cut grass after mowing.

3. *Educate*. Change how users see the world. Show them logistically what's required to complete the action. Make sure they have all the information they need to act. However, it can be ineffective to use education as a tool for motivation (people probably already know the action is important).

Use this three-step process, focusing on the behavior, then the environment, then the person, to develop a *behavioral plan*—a narrative that describes what the user might do to progress from not taking the action to taking it. That plan can be articulated in a customer experience map, journey map, textual narrative, or a simple list of bullet points with annotations.

The behavioral plan provides the core functional requirements for the product's behavior-changing aspects. It's a conceptual design for the product. The product team converts that plan into the raw material for the team to consume and act upon. In agile development, that is a set of user stories; for sequential development, it's a functional spec.

The interface designer and other members of the product team then develop wireframes or mockups of the product. If the product team is stuck and not sure how to structure the application flow itself, they can use one or more *design patterns for behavior change*—such as trackers, gamification, or how-to tutorials.

While the wireframes are being developed, you can deploy specific tactics from the behavioral social science literature to increase the probability action—ranging from social proof, to reminders, to competition, to loss aversion. Table 10-1 provides a list of two dozen, high-impact tactics, organized by the part of the Create Action Funnel that they affect.

Finally, the team should test the concepts with potential users, using either wireframes, or ideally, prototypes. If everything checks out, it's time to build the full product.

Refine: How to Iteratively Improve the Product

Whenever we design a product that interacts with the vagaries of human behavior, we're going to get some things wrong. The goal of the design process is to make the initial product *less wrong*.[160] But there will still be significant room for improvement. Improving the product proceeds like this:

1. *Define clear metrics* for the outcome and target action.
2. *Measure the impact* of the product on the outcome and action. If the outcome isn't directly measurable within the product, develop a *data bridge*—a statistical relationship between something that can be measured in the app and the outcome the company cares about. The data bridge can come from existing research or a small pilot study conducted by the team or third-party academics.
   a. If possible, run an A/B test or another type of controlled experiment to measure impact. That's the gold standard, and there are numerous tools to help companies run them with online products. Statistical knowledge is not required (though it can help).
   b. If experiments aren't feasible, the team will need to measure overall impact, then formally or informally control for other things that might influence the users' behavior. Statistical techniques such as matching and the analysis of panel datasets can mitigate these issues but require statistical expertise.
3. *Find obstacles to impact* by directly observing your users and checking the data for places in the app where users get stuck. A causal map, showing the various pathways by which users can decide to take the target action, can help the team figure out what users are doing and how to best interpret the data.
4. *Identify potential solutions*, either through user feedback or a set of small, quick tests to diagnose why the problems are occurring. The team can use the Create Action Funnel to target and interpret those quick tests.
5. *Prioritize proposed changes* to the product designed to improve behavioral impact alongside other proposed changes meant to support business goals, engineering goals, etc.
6. *Test each major change*. Regardless of whether everyone on the team thinks it's a good idea, check the impact of that change on behavior. Human behavior is just too complex to accurately forecast, and a culture of testing can help check everyone's assumptions.

Themes

Stepping back from these detailed lessons, there are a few basic themes that I'd hoped to express here. These themes provide some additional color and guidance on how to design for behavior change.

We've learned a great deal about how the mind makes decisions, but our knowledge is still limited

The behavioral social science literature provides the foundation for this book, and there are numerous field experiments that illustrate how our decision making works. The research on biases and heuristics is well established, but research on how products can help change behavior is still in its infancy. This book pulls together the best of what's known currently, but our knowledge is certainly not complete.

Understand your users

Changing behavior is a highly personal affair. Our products should meet users where they are in their daily lives and help them take action—that starts with understanding their needs and interests, constraints, prior experiences, and levels of expertise.

There are no magic wands for behavior change

There's no sure-fire way to *make* people take an action. Even if we fully understood the decision-making process, we each have unique personal histories and environments that shape our behavior. While we can't dictate behavior, we can facilitate it. If someone wants to act, well-designed products can help him do it.

Be intentional

If the goal is to help people change behavior, then do it. Don't hide behind wishy-washy recommendations or "raising awareness" among users; that leads us to design and build products that are internally conflicted and ineffective. Be up front and proud of products that help users take action.

A behaviorally effective product must first be a good product

The product must be well designed, pleasant to use, and solve a user need. Any considerations about changing behavior need to build on top of that foundation—otherwise, people will simply choose not to use the product.

Avoid user work

Look for technical solutions to avoid user work; it's much easier to engineer a solution than it is to change behavior. We can and should celebrate user triumphs—but those triumphs should occur where hard work was unavoidable, and not where the product was poorly designed.

We don't need to get fancy

Look for the Minimum Viable Action that a user can take to reach their goal, and remember simple, obvious lessons about the psychology of design: we like beauty, simplicity, familiarity, and following our peers.

We should assume we're (partially) wrong

No matter what we design and build, we'll get some things wrong. A dose of humility in face of the vast complexity of human behavior is a good thing. It spurs us to test the real, quantifiable impact of our products, and test every major change we make to them.

Looking Ahead

Some pretty cool things are happening right now: Rapidly increasing power and resolution on smartphones and on tablets. Wearable computing. Smart thermostats and other gadgets. New research in behavioral economics and psychology on how our minds work.

Within this flurry of activity and innovation, we're seeing the emergence of a new generation of products that apply behavioral social science to the practical problems of people's everyday lives: helping people take action and change behavior. A few of these products already touch millions of lives and have the potential to profoundly change society for the better: by helping us get in shape; by helping us save for the future; and by helping us become active in our communities and in politics on the issues we care about. Other products shape our lives in more mundane, but still powerful, ways: by helping us manage our email better or organize our days.

No one knows what will come next. There's a wide-open field ahead of us. I look forward to what each of us discovers, designs, and builds.

[*Appendix A*]

Glossary of Terms

This book introduces many new concepts and terms, such as the "behavioral plan" and the "Create Action Funnel." This glossary provides definitions of those terms, for your convenience. For the sake of brevity though, many of the common behavioral economics terms referenced in the book (e.g., "implementation intentions") are not included here.

ability (per the Create Action Funnel): a stage in the Create Action Funnel when the user evaluates whether or not she can take the target action now. The ability to take the target action has four criteria: knowing logistically how to take the action, having the resources necessary to act, having the skills necessary to act, and having a sense of self-efficacy or belief in success. See *Create Action Funnel.*

actor (aka target actor): the person who takes action because of the product. When the *actor* takes the *action,* it causes the product's *outcome.* See *(target) action, (target) outcome.*

action (aka target action): the behavior that the design process seeks to engender. When the *actor* takes the *action,* it causes the product's *outcome.* Note: "action" and "behavior" are used as synonyms throughout the book. See *(target) actor, (target) outcome.*

action sequence: the sequence of small steps that the user is encouraged to take. The small steps lead up to a final, target action. The action sequence is the core narrative of the *behavioral plan.*

behavioral bridge: a description that links a behavior that the user already knows and is comfortable with to a new, unfamiliar behavior. For example, an appeal to users that describes the (unfamiliar) act of running a race as similar to the (familiar) running around the office they normally do.

behavioral persona: a stylized individual used to represent a group of users who are likely to respond similarly to an appeal to change their behavior. For example, the persona "active Jake" could represent users of the product who are active in their daily lives and would be likely to join a competition to see who exercises the most. See *persona*.

behavioral plan: a detailed "story" of how the user progresses from being a neophyte to accomplishing the action while using the product. The "story" can take many forms, such as a journey map, written narrative, or a simple list of actions. The behavioral plan provides the conceptual design for the product, providing its functional requirements. See *action sequence, conceptual design.*

behavioral strategy: a high-level strategy for changing behavior with a product. This book discusses three strategies: supporting the conscious choice to take the target action, building (or changing) habits, and "cheating."

behavioral tactic: a low-level technique for changing behavior in a product. For example: showing a peer comparison, highlighting loss aversion, or priming a particular mindset. See also *behavioral strategy.*

causal map: a diagram showing the intended effect that the user's actions within the product will have on the target outcome, along with additional, unintended factors that are likely to also impact the target outcome.

cheating (per behavioral strategies): a strategy for changing behavior in which the burden of work is shifted from the user to the product, and the user need only give consent for the action to occur on his behalf. See *behavioral strategy.*

company objective: what the company seeks to achieve, for itself, by building the product.

conceptual design: a set of documents or illustrations that indicate what the product should do (i.e., what functionality the product should provide) at a conceptual level. When designing for behavior change, the behavioral plan fulfills this role. See *behavioral plan.*

context (of action): the three factors that shape a user's decision whether or not to act. Namely, the *user* himself, the *environment* the user is in, and the *action* the user is deciding upon.

Create Action Funnel: a stylized model of how the mind makes the conscious decision to act. Once the mind detects a cue, it has an intuitive reaction, which may bubble up into conscious awareness for evaluation of the merits of action, and an assessment of whether the user has the ability and right timing to act. If all of these mental processes pass successfully without the user getting distracted or deciding against the action, the user will execute the action. Together, they spell the acronym "create." See *cue, reaction, evaluation, ability, timing.*

cue (per habits): something that causes a habit to occur. The cue can be something the person sees, hears, smells, or touches in the environment (an external cue) or an internal state like hunger (internal cue) that initiates the habitual routine.

cue (per the Create Action Funnel): the first stage in the Create Action Funnel when something first makes the user think about taking the target action. The cue can be something the person sees, hears, smells, or touches in the environment (an external cue) or an internal state like hunger (internal cue) that starts the process of taking action. For habitual actions, the cue alone can be enough to cause the behavior to occur. See *Create Action Funnel.*

data bridge: a mathematical relationship or statistical model that relates a target outcome outside of the product to behavior within the product. For example, "60% of the time that users indicate in the application that they will create a vegetable garden, they actually create one."

designing for behavior change: a four-stage process of designing a product with the specific purpose of changing user behavior. The four stages are: understanding how the mind makes decisions, discovering the behavioral goals of the product, designing the product around those goals, and refining the product over time.

design pattern for behavior change: a template that describes a class of similar behavior-changing products (or product features). Within that class, the general functionality and look and feel of the products are the same. For example, exercise trackers.

dual process theory(ies): a family of related theories in psychology that posit that the mind effectively has two independent decision-making processes: one deliberative, and one intuitive. The deliberative, or "System 2," process is associated with intentional conscious thought. The intuitive, or "System 1," process is associated with automatic, emotional reactions or implicit, "subconscious" behaviors.

environment (of action): one of the three parts of the decision-making context (along with the user and the action itself) that shapes a user's decision to act. The environment consists of the product that the person is interacting with and the physical environment surrounding the person when he decides whether or not to act. See *context.*

evaluation (per the Create Action Funnel): the third stage in the Create Action Funnel, when the user consciously evaluates the value of taking the target action, often considering its costs and benefits. See *Create Action Funnel.*

external cue: something in our environment that causes us to think about or take a certain action. See *cue, internal cue.*

extrinsic motivation: the desire to achieve a particular outcome, such as receiving a reward for it (like money or winning a competition). See *intrinsic motivation.*

habit: a repeated behavior that's triggered by internal or external cues. A habit is automatic: the action occurs outside of conscious control, and we may not even be aware of it happening. Habits can be formed through simple cue-routine repetition or can include a reward that becomes associated with the cue and encourages the user to repeat the behavior. See *cue, routine, reward.*

interface design: a set of documents or illustrations that says how the product should look and interact with the user.

internal cue: a prior thought or bodily state (like hunger) that leads us to think about or take a certain action. See *cue, external cue.*

intrinsic motivation: comes from the inherent enjoyment of the activity itself, without considering any external pressure or reward. See *extrinsic motivation.*

mindset: a mental mechanism for interpreting and responding to the world, which shapes how we act. Mindsets as facets of the mind, which are built up in different contexts. Here, the term is used to encompass a range of psychological mechanisms that guide our behavior in ambiguous contexts, including schemas and activated frames.

Minimum Viable Action (MVA): the shortest, simplest version of the target action that users can be asked to take, with which the company can still test whether the product has the desired impact on behavior. See *target action*.

outcome (aka target outcome): the real-world impact that the company seeks to have because of the product. A measureable change in the world that happens when the product succeeds in changing behavior. When the *actor* takes the *action*, it causes the product's *outcome*. See *(target) actor, (target) action*.

persona: in the user experience field, a persona is a stylized individual used to represent a group of similar users, usually based on a particular demographic profile. See *behavioral persona*.

reaction (per the Create Action Funnel): the second stage in the Create Action Funnel when the user has an automatic, System 1 reaction to the idea of taking action. That reaction renders an intuitive verdict (whether the action is interesting or not) based on prior associations with the action or similar experiences. It also activates thoughts about other possible actions the person could take. See *Create Action Funnel*.

reward (per habits): something that gives us a *reason* to repeat a behavior. It might be something inherently pleasant, like good food, or the completion of a goal we've set for ourselves, like putting away all of the dishes.

routine (per habits): the habitual action that a person takes when exposed to the habit's cue. For example, buying Starbucks coffee whenever a person sees the Starbucks sign next to her office at 9 a.m. in the morning.

self-narrative: how we label ourselves, and how we describe our behavior in the past.

small win: a feeling of accomplishment after a (relatively small) action is taken.

timing (per the Create Action Funnel): the fifth stage of the Create Action Funnel, in which the user determine *when* to act. See *Create Action Funnel.*

user story: A term used in product development (especially agile development) for a plain-English statement about what the user needs. It captures the "who," "what," and "why" of a product requirement. For example, "As a user, I want to <take an action>, in order to <reason for action>." See *http://en.wikipedia.org/wiki/User_story* for more information.

vision (aka product vision): *why the product is being developed,* at a high level.

[*Appendix B*]

Resources to Learn More

Resources on Behavior and Decision Making

This book provides an overview of the literature on behavior change and decision making. But it isn't comprehensive: the literature is simply too vast, and most of it doesn't apply when designing *products* for behavior change. If you'd like to learn more, though, here are some great resources to inspire your work and spur new ideas.

Resources on Applying the Mind's Shortcuts to Design

BJ FOGG'S PERSUASIVE TECHNOLOGY AND BEHAVIOR MODEL

BJ is the father of contemporary product-mediated behavior change. He founded the field of persuasive technology—the use of computers to persuade—in the 1990s (Fogg 2002). More recently, he's developed a model of what's required for intentional behavior to occur (the Fogg Behavior Model) and a method for building habits (Tiny Habits). There's a lot more out there, but his work is a good place to start thinking about these issues.

Here is a list of his writings and websites:

- Fogg Behavior Model (*http://behaviormodel.org/*): motivation, ability, and a trigger are needed for intentional behaviors.
- Behavior Grid (*http://behaviorgrid.org/*): a typology of 15 types of behaviors, with guides on how they can be changed, based on the frequency of the behavior, and whether it is to be started, stopped, increased, or decreased.

- Fogg's Persuasive Technology Lab at Stanford (*http://captology.stanford.edu/*), where Fogg is a half-time professor. The site has links to numerous videos and articles.
- Fogg's book, *Persuasive Technology: Using Computers to Change What We Think and Do* (Morgan Kaufmann, 2002).

STEPHEN ANDERSON'S SEDUCTIVE INTERACTION DESIGN

Stephen's book, *Seductive Interaction Design* (New Riders, 2011), provides thoughtful, powerful examples of how psychology can be used to affect behavior via product design. He groups these applications into a set of themes, which provides a useful structure to the otherwise overwhelming research literature.

He also has a set of cards for designers summarizing the key topics, called "Mental Notes" (*http://getmentalnotes.com/*).

DAN LOCKTON'S DESIGN WITH INTENT

Dan has developed a toolkit for "Designing with Intent," described in his PhD thesis.

- The toolkit (*http://www.danlockton.com/dwi/Main_Page*) is a set of 101 cards showing "patterns" for influencing behavior through design. They are organized under a set of eight "lenses" for thinking about, and designing for, intentional behavior change.
- The thesis (*http://architectures.danlockton.co.uk/phd/*) describes how the toolkit was developed, how it was tested in the field, and what other researchers are doing in the space
- His background research for the thesis spawned a number of working papers (*http://architectures.danlockton.co.uk/dan-lockton/#workingpapers*), which are the most detailed review of the field that I've seen.

SUSAN WEINSCHENK'S NEURO-WEB DESIGN AND 100 THINGS

Susan has two interesting books in this space, one on web design specifically, and one on the cognitive mechanisms and ways in which the mind works that affect web behavior. The latter book provides a valuable list of mechanisms but doesn't help to structure that list or give a method to select and target behavioral goals.

The web design book is called *Neuro-Web Design* (New Riders, 2009), and the book on mechanisms is called *100 Things Designers Need to Know About People* (New Riders, 2011). Her professional website, *http://www.theteamw.com/*, has more information about her work.

JEFF JOHNSON'S DESIGNING WITH THE MIND IN MIND

Jeff's book, *Designing with the Mind in Mind* (Morgan Kaufmann, 2010), applies research on visual perception and psychology to user interface design, in particular. He covers issues such as gestalt psychology and visual ambiguity, our visual system's ability to detect differences in color, how pattern recognition is built up, and how we scan web pages.

BLOGS

There are a handful of blogs on how psychology can be used in product design to help change behavior (send me an email if you know of any others):

- Anders Toxboe's *Persuasive Pattern Library* (*http://persuasive-patterns.com/*)
- David Royer's blog (*http://www.davidroyer.com/*)
- Kristian Tørning's *Persuasive Design Blog* (*http://www.persuasive.eu/*)
- Nir Eyal's blog (*http://www.nirandfar.com*) also covers product design and behavior change.
- Sebastian Deterding's *Coding Conduct Blog* (*http://codingconduct.cc/*) covers persuasive design, serious games, and gamification.

Design Trickery

There's only one site I know of that identifies the nasty tricks not-so-ethical designers sometimes use (and shames them for it): Dark Patterns. You can also see Jesse Snyder's write-up on Dark Patterns and a TechCrunch post specifically about Facebook.[161]

Chris Nodder's new book *Evil by Design* (Wiley, 2013) also covers "evil" design patterns and how they work.

Books on Decision Making

In recent years, there has been a rapid growth of research in behavioral economics and a rediscovery of solid work in the psychology of judgment and decision making. Much of it can be applied to product design and development, after some translation and experimentation. The following links are for books and sites intended for a general audience, not the academic journal articles.

EXPLICIT BEHAVIOR CHANGE APPROACHES IN BEHAVIORAL ECONOMICS

Most of the behavioral economics research is on how the mind works (and makes financial decisions, in particular), but here are a few works that explicitly look at behavior change:

- Richard H. Thaler and Cass R. Sunstein's *Nudge* (Penguin Books, 2009). This is one of the best general-audience books on behavioral economics out there. It introduces the concept of "Choice Architecture," or how our decision-making environment affects our choices. Check it out.
- Benartzi's *Save More Tomorrow* (Portfolio Hardcover, 2012). This describes one of the most effective financial interventions out there—having people commit to use their future income increases for savings.
- Karlan et al.'s paper "Getting to the Top of Mind," on the incredible power of simply reminding people to do what they said they want to do (this is an academic article).
- Kim Ly et al.'s *Practitioners Guide to Nudging* is a new ebook on how to use behavioral economics for behavior change.

GENERAL BEHAVIORAL ECONOMICS/JUDGMENT AND DECISION-MAKING BOOKS

- Kahneman's *Thinking, Fast and Slow* (Farrar, Straus and Giroux, 2013). I love this book. I don't love very many books, I must admit. I purchased a copy for everyone on my team. This is a wonderfully detailed and thoughtful analysis of how the mind works, from dual process theory to how various cognitive mechanisms and heuristics affect behavior. It's a long one, though.

- Dan Ariely's *Predictably Irrational* (Harper Perennial, 2010). A fun and well-told read that makes the underlying psychological and behavioral economics principles understandable and memorable. A good introduction for general audience.
- Malcolm Gladwell's *Blink* (Back Bay Books, 2007). An easy read, which is less thoroughly grounded in the research than other books, but still a useful summary of dual process theory and mental heuristics.

Also, a good list of resources on behavioral economics can be found on the Corporation For Enterprise Development website, *http://cfed.org/knowledge_center/research/behavioral_economics/*.

RESEARCH ON HABIT FORMATION

Habit formation has many names and was studied in much of the old behaviorist literature on conditioning. Most of the modern work I've seen is explicitly on addiction. But three works are bringing the study of habits into broader areas of application, including how to help people change their (nonaddictive) habits:

- Charles Duhigg's *The Power of Habit* (Random House, 2012). An overview of how reward-based habits form and how they can be changed. He also presents a metaphor about how habits function within organizations and companies. The anecdotes reach a bit too far, but he cites much of the research that's out there and provides excellent examples.
- Jeremy Dean's *Making Habits, Breaking Habits* (Da Capo Lifelong Books, 2013). He reviews the research on habit formation and change, and stays closer to the research than Duhigg's work. A solid, informative book. Also check out his very popular blog on psychology: *http://www.spring.org.uk/*.
- Neale Martin's *Habit: The 95% of Behavior Marketers Ignore* (FT Press, 2008), provides a cogent, detailed summary of the academic literature, and then applies that knowledge to the field of marketing.
- Nir Eyal's *Hooked* (forthcoming). Nir is currently working on this book, which will hopefully be out soon! Hooked focuses on habits and "the desire engine" as a core driver of behavior change, and on building a business model that uses it responsibly.

For the underlying research, see Neale Martin's great resource list on habits: *http://www.sublimebehavior.com/knowledge/habit-research/*.

HOW TO APPLY BEHAVIOR CHANGE CONCEPTS TO ONE'S OWN LIFE

In *Switch* (Crown Business, 2010), Chip and Dan Heath apply the psychology literature, especially dual process theory, to changing one's own behavior. It uses the metaphor of the rider (our conscious rational mind) and the elephant (our intuitive reactive mind) throughout, to explain what we need to do in our daily lives to align the rider and elephant and "switch" our behavior. Check it out.

BLOGS

Here are some blogs on behavioral social science, often with humorous applications in people's daily lives:

- Dan Ariely's blog (*http://danariely.com/*)
- Linked to the book *Nudge* by Thaler and Sunstein, *The Nudge Blog* (*http://nudges.org/*); it isn't active as of this writing, however.
- Jeremy Dean's *PsyBlog* (*http://www.spring.org.uk*)

Behavior Change Approaches from Marketing and Sales

Sales and marketing aren't my main interests, but they are fields we can certainly learn from, and apply to other domains.

- Robert B. Cialdini's classic *Influence: Science and Practice* (Pearson, 2008) details ways to influence people, especially for sales purposes. Despite his showmanship, Cialdini did some solid and important research on persuasion, and his book is justifiably a classic for its clear and practical presentation.
- Noah Goldstein, a protégé of Cialdini, and Steve Martin published *Yes!: 50 Scientifically Proven Ways to Be Persuasive* (Free Press, 2009), which includes a longer list of influence tactics. The core concepts are similar, but you may find this presentation more accessible for your work.
- The Marketing Sciences Institute's *Consumer Insights* covers 42 tricks that marketers use to influence buying decisions.

These two books don't give "how-to" instructions like the previous ones do, but they are useful summaries of the research used in sales and marketing:

- Martin Lindstrom's *Buyology* (Crown Business, 2010)
- Paco Underhill's *Why We Buy* (Simon & Schuster, 2008)

Where to Get the Latest List of Resources

An online and periodically updated version of this annotated list can be found at *http://actiondesign.hellowallet.com/about-the-research/*.

I also maintain a larger list of relevant books in the field on Shelfari at *http://www.shelfari.com/sawendel/shelf*.

Please feel free to shoot me an email (*http://about.me/sawendel*) or reach out to me via Twitter (*@sawendel*) with suggestions or corrections to this list.

[Appendix C]

Bibliography

Ajzen, Icek. "The Theory of Planned Behavior." *Organizational Behavior and Human Decision Processes* 50, no. 2 (December): 179–211. 1991.

Alba, Joseph W. *Consumer Insights: Findings from Behavioral Research*. Edited by Joseph W. Alba. Cambridge, MA: Marketing Science Institute. 2011.

Alexander, Christopher, Sara Ishikawa, and Murray Silverstein. *A Pattern Language: Towns, Buildings, Constructions*. Oxford: Oxford University Press. 1977.

Allcott, Hunt. "Social Norms and Energy Conservation." *Journal of Public Economics* 95, no. 9–10 (October): 1082–1095. 2011.

Allen, David. *Getting Things Done: The Art of Stress-free Productivity*. New York: Viking. 2001.

Anderson, Stephen P. *Seductive Interaction Design: Creating Playful, Fun, and Effective User Experiences*. Berkeley, CA: New Riders. 2011.

———. "Mental Notes." *http://getmentalnotes.com/*. 2013.

Ariely, Dan. *Predictably Irrational: The Hidden Forces That Shape Our Decisions*. New York: HarperCollins. 2008.

———. *The Upside of Irrationality: The Unexpected Benefits of Defying Logic*. New York: HarperPerennial. 2011.

Bandura, Albert. "Self-efficacy: Toward a Unifying Theory of Behavioral Change." *Psychological Review* 84, no. 2: 191–215. 1977a.

———. *Social Learning Theory*. Vol. viii. Oxford: Prentice-Hall. 1977b.

Bargh, John A., Mark Chen, and Lara Burrows. "Automaticity of Social Behavior: Direct Effects of Trait Construct and Stereotype Activation on Action." *Journal of Personality and Social Psychology* 71, no. 2: 230–244. 1996.

Baumeister, Roy F. "Choking Under Pressure: Self-consciousness and Paradoxical Effects of Incentives on Skillful Performance." *Journal of Personality and Social Psychology* 46, no. 3: 610–620. 1984.

Baumeister, Roy F., and John Tierney. *Willpower: Rediscovering the Greatest Human Strength*. New York: Penguin Press. 2011.

Bayer, Patrick J., B. Douglas Bernheim, and John Karl Scholz. "The Effects of Financial Education in the Workplace: Evidence From A Survey Of Employers." *Economic Inquiry* 47, no. 4: 605–624. 2009.

Bechara, Antoine, Hanna Damasio, Daniel Tranel, and Antonio R. Damasio. "Deciding Advantageously Before Knowing the Advantageous Strategy." *Science* 275, no. 5304 (February 28): 1293–1295. 1997.

Benartzi, Shlomo, and Richard H. Thaler. "Save More Tomorrow: Using Behavioral Economics to Increase Employee Saving." *Journal of Political Economy* 112, no. 1 (February). 2004.

Berridge, Kent C, Terry E Robinson, and J Wayne Aldridge. "Dissecting Components of Reward: 'Liking', 'Wanting', and Learning." *Current Opinion in Pharmacology* 9, no. 1 (February): 65–73. 2009.

Beshears, John, and Katherine Milkman. "Temptation Bundling and Other Health Interventions." Action Design D.C. Meetup, April 21. *http://www.slideshare.net/sawendel/temptation-bundling-and-other-health-interventions-addc-april-2013*. 2013.

Blackson, Thomas. "Plato A New Theory of the Human Soul." *Ancient Greek Philosophy From the Presocratics to the Hellenistic Philosophers. http://tab.faculty.asu.edu/toc.html*. 2013.

Bornstein, Robert F. "Exposure and Affect: Overview and Meta-analysis of Research, 1968–1987." *Psychological Bulletin* 106, no. 2: 265. 1989.

Bower, Bruce. "The Hot and Cold of PRIMING." *Science News* 181, no. 10 (May 19): 26. 2012.

Brass, Marcel, and Patrick Haggard. "The What, When, Whether Model of Intentional Action." *The Neuroscientist* 14, no. 4 (August 1): 319–325. 2008.

Brendryen, Håvar, and Pål Kraft. "Happy Ending: a Randomized Controlled Trial of a Digital Multi-media Smoking Cessation Intervention." *Addiction* 103, no. 3: 478–484. 2008.

Brignull, Harry. Dark Patterns. *http://darkpatterns.org/*. 2013.

Cagan, Marty. *Inspired: How to Create Products Customers Love.* Sunnyvale, CA: SVPG Press. 2008.

Chabris, Christopher, and Daniel Simons. *The Invisible Gorilla: How Our Intuitions Deceive Us.* New York: Broadway Books. 2009.

Chapman, Antony J. "Funniness of Jokes, Canned Laughter and Recall Performance." *Sociometry* 36, no. 4: 569–578. 1973.

Chatzisarantis, Nikos L. D., and Martin S. Hagger. "Mindfulness and the Intention-Behavior Relationship Within the Theory of Planned Behavior." *Personality and Social Psychology Bulletin* 33, no. 5 (May 1): 663–676. 2007.

Chatzky, Jean. *Pay It Down! Debt-Free on $10 a Day.* New York: Penguin. 2009.

Chopra, Paras. "Why Multi-armed Bandit Algorithm Is Not 'Better' Than A/B Testing." *Split Testing Blog.* *http://visualwebsiteoptimizer.com/split-testing-blog/multi-armed-bandit-algorithm/*. 2012.

Christakis, Nicholas A., and James H. Fowler. "The Spread of Obesity in a Large Social Network over 32 Years." *New England Journal of Medicine* 357, no. 4: 370–379. 2007.

Cialdini, Robert B. *Influence: Science and Practice.* 5th ed. Boston: Pearson. 2001.

Cialdini, Robert B., and N.J. Goldstein. "Social Influence: Compliance and Conformity." *Annual Review of Psychology* 55: 591–621. 2004.

Cialdini, Robert B., Carl A. Kallgren, and Raymond R. Reno. "A Focus Theory of Normative Conduct: A Theoretical Refinement and Reevaluation of the Role of Norms in Human Behavior." In *Advances in Experimental Social Psychology, Mark P. Zanna Ed.*, 24:1–243. San Diego: Academic Press. 1991.

Clear, James. "Identity-Based Habits: How to Actually Stick to Your Goals This Year." *James Clear* (blog). *http://jamesclear.com/identity-based-habits*. 2012.

Cohn, Mike. *Succeeding with Agile: Software Development Using Scrum*. Upper Saddle River, NJ: Addison-Wesley. 2010.

Cooper, Alan, Robert Reimann, Dave Cronin, and Alan Cooper. *About Face 3: The Essentials of Interaction Design*. Hoboken, NJ: Wiley. 2007.

Crum, Alia J., and Ellen J. Langer. "Mind-Set Matters: Exercise and the Placebo Effect." *Psychological Science* 18, no. 2 (February 1): 165–171. 2007.

Curtis, Dustin. "You Should Follow Me on Twitter." *Dustin Curtis* (blog). *http://dustincurtis.com/you_should_follow_me_on_twitter.html*. 2009.

Damasio, Antonio R, B.J. Everitt, and D Bishop. "The Somatic Marker Hypothesis and the Possible Functions of the Prefrontal Cortex [and Discussion]." *Philosophical Transactions: Biological Sciences* 351, no. 1346: 1413–1420. 1996.

Danziger, Shai, Jonathan Levav, and Liora Avnaim-Pesso. "Extraneous Factors in Judicial Decisions." *Proceedings of the National Academy of Sciences* 108, no. 17 (April 26): 6889–6892. 2011.

Davison, W. Phillips. "The Third-Person Effect in Communication." *Public Opinion Quarterly* 47, no. 1 (March 20): 1–15. 1983.

Dean, Jeremy. *Making Habits, Breaking Habits: Why We Do Things, Why We Don't, and How to Make Any Change Stick*. Boston: Da Capo Press. 2013.

De Bono, Edward. *Lateral Thinking: Creativity Step by Step*. New York: Harper & Row. 1973.

Deci, Edward L., Richard Koestner, and Richard M. Ryan. "A Meta-analytic Review of Experiments Examining the Effects of Extrinsic Rewards on Intrinsic Motivation." *Psychological Bulletin* 125, no. 6 (November): 627–668; discussion 692–700. 1999.

Deci, Edward L., and Richard M. Ryan. *Intrinsic Motivation and Self-Determination in Human Behavior*. New York: Plenum Press. 1985.

Demaree, David. "Google+ and Cognitive Overhead." *http://log.demaree.me/post/7845070213/google-and-cognitive-overhead*. 2011.

Deschene, Lori. "What Is Behavioral Targeting?" *CBS News Money Watch*. *http://www.cbsnews.com/8301-505125_162-51199800/what-is-behavioral-targeting/*. 2008.

Deterding, Sebastian. "Just Add Points? What UX Can (and Cannot) Learn from Games." Slide show presented at UX Camp Europe, Berlin, May 30. *http://www.slideshare.net/dings/just-add-points-what-ux-can-and-cannot -learn-from-games*. 2010.

———. *"Meaingful Play." http://codingconduct.cc/meaningful-play*. 2011.

Deterding, Sebastian, Dan Dixon, Rilla Khaled, and Lennart Nacke. "From Game Design Elements to Gamefulness: Defining Gamification." In *Proceedings of the 15th International Academic MindTrek Conference: Envisioning Future Media Environments*: 9–15. 2011.

Doyen, Stéphane, Olivier Klein, Cora-Lise Pichon, and Axel Cleeremans. "Behavioral Priming: It's All in the Mind, but Whose Mind?" *PLoS ONE* 7 no. 1 (January 18): e29081. 2012.

Drell, Lauren. "4 Ways Behavioral Targeting Is Changing the Web." *Mashable Digital Marketing Series*. *http://mashable.com/2011/04/26/behavioral-targeting/*. 2011.

Duhigg, Charles. *The Power of Habit: Why We Do What We Do in Life and Business*. New York: Random House. 2012.

Eldridge, Laura L., Donna Masterman, and Barbara J. Knowlton. "Intact Implicit Habit Learning in Alzheimer's Disease." *Behavioral Neuroscience* 116, no. 4: 722. 2002.

Ellsberg, Daniel. "Risk, Ambiguity, and the Savage Axioms." *The Quarterly Journal of Economics* 75, no. 4 (November 1): 643–669. 1961.

Eyal, Nir. "How To Manufacture Desire" *TechCrunch*. *http://techcrunch.com/2012/03/04/how-to-manufacture-desire/*. 2012.

———. "Hooked Workshop" April 7. *http://www.slideshare.net/nireyal/hooked-workshop-17974533*. 2013.

Fellowes, Matt. "The Retirement Breach in Defined Contribution Plans." HelloWallet Research Reports. 2013.

Fernandez, Eric. “Cognitive Biases—A Visual Study Guide.” *Scribd*. April 27. *http://www.scribd.com/doc/30548590/Cognitive-Biases-A-Visual-Study-Guide*. 2010.

Festinger, Leon. *A Theory Of Cognitive Dissonance*. Redwood City, CA: Stanford University Press. 1962.

Field, Matt, and W. Miles. “Attentional Bias in Addictive Behaviors: A Review of Its Development, Causes, and Consequences.” *Drug and Alcohol Dependence* 97, no. 1–2: 1–20. 2008.

Filiz-Ozbay, Emel, Jonathan Guryan, Kyle Hyndman, Melissa Schettini Kearney, and Erkut Y. Ozbay. “Do Lottery Payments Induce Savings Behavior: Evidence from the Lab.” Working Paper 19130. National Bureau of Economic Research. *http://www.nber.org/papers/w19130*. 2013.

Fisher, Robert J. “Social Desirability Bias and the Validity of Indirect Questioning.” *Journal of Consumer Research* 20, no. 2: 303–315. 1993.

Fogg, BJ. *Persuasive Technology: Using Computers to Change What We Think and Do*. San Francisco: Morgan Kaufmann. 2002.

———. [Graphic illustration of the Fogg Behavior Model]. *BJ Fogg's Behavior Model*. Retrieved from *http://behaviormodel.org/*. 2007.

———. “A Behavior Model for Persuasive Design.” In *Proceedings of the 4th International Conference on Persuasive Technology*, 40:1–40:7. Persuasive '09. New York: ACM. 2009a.

———. “The Behavior Grid: 35 Ways Behavior Can Change.” In *Proceedings of the 4th International Conference on Persuasive Technology*, 42:1–42:5. Persuasive '09. New York: ACM. 2009b.

———. *Keynote Address at Health User Experience Design Conference*. Boston. *http://www.youtube.com/watch?v=fqUSjHj IEFg*. 2012.

Fogg, B. J. and Jason Hreha. “Behavior Wizard: A Method for Matching Target Behaviors with Solutions.” In *Persuasive Technology*, edited by Thomas Ploug, Per Hasle, and Harri Oinas-Kukkonen, 117–131. Lecture Notes in Computer Science 6137. Springer Berlin Heidelberg. 2010.

Fogg, B. J., Jonathan Marshall, Othman Laraki, Alex Osipovich, Chris Varma, Nicholas Fang, Jyoti Paul, et al. "What Makes Web Sites Credible?: a Report on a Large Quantitative Study." *Proceedings of the SIGCHI Conference on Human Factors in Computing Systems*, 61–68. CHI '01. New York: ACM. 2001.

Freedman, Jonathan L., and Scott C. Fraser. "Compliance Without Pressure: The Foot-in-the-door Technique." *Journal of Personality and Social Psychology* 4, no. 2: 195. 1966.

Gallwey, W. Timothy. *The Inner Game of Tennis: The Classic Guide to the Mental Side of Peak Performance.* Rev Sub. New York: Random House. 1997.

Gamma, Erich, Richard Helm, Ralph Johnson, and John Vlissides. *Design Patterns: Elements of Reusable Object-Oriented Software.* Westford, Connecticut: Addison-Wesley. 1994.

Garner, Randy. "Post-It® Note Persuasion: A Sticky Influence." *Journal of Consumer Psychology* 15, no. 3: 230–237. 2005.

Gazzaniga, Michael S., and Roger W. Sperry. "Language after Section of the Cerebral Commissures." *Brain* 90, no. 1: 131–148. 1967.

Gerber, Alan S., and Todd Rogers. "Descriptive Social Norms and Motivation to Vote: Everybody's Voting and so Should You." *The Journal of Politics* 71, no. 01: 178–191. 2009.

Gilbert, Daniel, and Timothy D. Wilson. "The Social Psychological Narrative—or—What Is Social Psychology, Anyway?" *Edge*. *http://www.edge.org/conversation/social_psychological_narrative*. 2013.

Gladwell, Malcolm. *Blink: The Power of Thinking Without Thinking.* New York: Little, Brown and Company. 2005.

Gneezy, Uri, Stephan Meier, and Pedro Rey-Biel. "When and Why Incentives (don't) Work to Modify Behavior." *The Journal of Economic Perspectives* 25, no. 4: 191–209. 2011.

Goldstein, Daniel. "The Battle Between Your Present and Future Self." *http://www.ted.com/talks/daniel_goldstein_the_battle_between_your_present_and_future_self.html*. 2011.

Goldstein, Noah J., Steve J. Martin, and Robert B. Cialdini. *Yes!: 50 Scientifically Proven Ways to Be Persuasive.* New York: Free Press. 2008.

Gollwitzer, Peter M. "Implementation Intentions: Strong Effects of Simple Plans." *American Psychologist* 54, no. 7: 493. 1999.

Grier, Sonya, and Carol A. Bryant. "Social Marketing in Public Health." *Annual Review of Public Health* 26, no. 1: 319–339. 2005.

Haidt, Jonathan. *The Happiness Hypothesis: Finding Modern Truth in Ancient Wisdom.* Cambridge, MA: Basic Books. 2006.

Hamermesh, Daniel S., and Jeff E. Biddle. "Beauty and the Labor Market." Working Paper 4518. National Bureau of Economic Research. *http://www.nber.org/papers/w4518*. 1993.

Hanov, Steve. "20 Lines of Code That Will Beat A/B Testing Every Time." *Steve Hanov's* (blog). *http://stevehanov.ca/blog/index.php?id=132*. 2012.

Heath, Chip, and Dan Heath. *Switch: How to Change Things When Change Is Hard.* New York: Broadway Books. 2010.

Hershfield, Hal E, Daniel G Goldstein, William F Sharpe, Jesse Fox, Leo Yeykelis, Laura L Carstensen, and Jeremy N Bailenson. "Increasing Saving Behavior Through Age-Progressed Renderings of the Future Self." *Journal of Marketing Research* 48 (SPL) (November): S23–S37. 2011.

Hilgert, Marianne A., Jeanne M. Hogarth, and Sondra G. Beverly. "Household Financial Management: The Connection Between Knowledge and Behavior." *Federal Reserve Bulletin* 89: 309. 2003.

Hofmann, Stefan G., Alice T. Sawyer, Ashley A. Witt, and Diana Oh. "The Effect of Mindfulness-Based Therapy on Anxiety and Depression: A Meta-Analytic Review." *Journal of Consulting and Clinical Psychology* 78, no. 2 (April): 169–183. 2010.

International Council for the Control of Iodine Deficiency Disorders. "Iodine Deficiency." *http://www.iccidd.org/p142000263.html*. 2013.

Iyengar, Sheena S. *The Art of Choosing.* New York: Hachette Book Group. 2010.

Iyengar, Sheena S., Wei Jiang, and Gur Huberman. "How Much Choice Is Too Much? Contributions to 401 (k) Retirement Plans." 2003-10. Pension Research Council Working Paper. 2003.

Iyengar, Sheena S., and Mark R. Lepper. "When Choice Is Demotivating: Can One Desire Too Much of a Good Thing?" *Journal of Personality and Social Psychology* 79, no. 6: 995–1006. 2000.

Janz, Nancy K., and Marshall H. Becker. "The Health Belief Model: A Decade Later." *Health Education & Behavior* 11, no. 1 (March 1): 1–47. 1984.

Jenkins, G. Douglas, Atul Mitra, Nina Gupta, and Jason D. Shaw. "Are Financial Incentives Related to Performance? A Meta-analytic Review of Empirical Research." *Journal of Applied Psychology* 83, no. 5: 777–787. 1998.

Johnson, Jeff. *Designing with the Mind in Mind: Simple Guide to Understanding User Interface Design Rules*. Boston: Morgan Kaufmann. 2010.

Kahneman, Daniel, and Amos Tversky. "Choices, Values, and Frames." *American Psychologist* 39, no. 4: 341. 1984.

Kahneman, Daniel. *Thinking, Fast and Slow*. New York: Farrar, Straus and Giroux. 2011.

Kaptein, Maurits, and Dean Eckles. "Selecting Effective Means to Any End: Futures and Ethics of Persuasion Profiling." In *Persuasive Technology*, edited by Thomas Ploug, Per Hasle, and Harri Oinas-Kukkonen, 82–93. Lecture Notes in Computer Science 6137. Springer Berlin Heidelberg. 2010.

Kaptein, Maurits, and Aart van Halteren. "Adaptive Persuasive Messaging to Increase Service Retention: Using Persuasion Profiles to Increase the Effectiveness of Email Reminders." *Personal and Ubiquitous Computing* (July): 1–13. 2012.

Karlan, Dean, and Jacob Appel. *More Than Good Intentions: Improving the Ways the World's Poor Borrow, Save, Farm, Learn, and Stay Healthy*. New York: Penguin. 2011.

Karlan, Dean, Margaret McConnell, Sendhil Mullainathan, and Jonathan Zinman. "Getting to the Top of Mind: How Reminders Increase Saving." Working Paper 16205. National Bureau of Economic Research. *http://www.nber.org/papers/w16205*. 2011.

Kirby, Kris N. "Bidding on the Future: Evidence Against Normative Discounting of Delayed Rewards." *Journal of Experimental Psychology: General* 126, no. 1: 54. 1997.

Kolata, Gina. "How Fen-Phen, A Diet 'Miracle,' Rose and Fell." *New York Times*. September 23. 1997.

Kolko, Jon. *Thoughts on Interaction Design a Collection of Reflections, Second Edition*. Burlington, MA: Morgan Kaufmann. 2011.

Kolotkin, Ronette L., Martin Binks, Ross D. Crosby, Truls Østbye, Richard E. Gress, and Ted D. Adams. "Obesity and Sexual Quality of Life." *Obesity* 14, no. 3: 472–479. 2006.

Krug, Steve. *Don't Make Me Think!: A Common Sense Approach to Web Usability*. Berkeley: New Riders. 2006.

Kuang, Cliff. "In the Cafeteria, Google Gets Healthy." *Fast Company*, April. *http://www.fastcompany.com/1822516/cafeteria-google-gets-healthy*. 2012.

Kuran, Timur, and Cass R. Sunstein. "Availability Cascades and Risk Regulation." *Stanford Law Review* 51, no. 4 (April): 683. 1999.

Laibson, David. "Golden Eggs and Hyperbolic Discounting." *Quarterly Journal of Economics* 112, no. 2: 443–477. 1997.

Lally, Phillippa, Cornelia H. M. van Jaarsveld, Henry W. W. Potts, and Jane Wardle. "How Are Habits Formed: Modelling Habit Formation in the Real World." *European Journal of Social Psychology* 40, no. 6: 998–1009. 2010.

Levin, Irwin P., Sandra L. Schneider, and Gary J. Gaeth. "All Frames Are Not Created Equal: A Typology and Critical Analysis of Framing Effects." *Organizational Behavior and Human Decision Processes* 76, no. 2 (November): 149–188. 1998.

Lieb, David. "Cognitive Overhead, Or Why Your Product Isn't As Simple As You Think." *TechCrunch*. *http://techcrunch.com/2013/04/20/cognitive-overhead/*. 2013.

Lindstrom, Martin. *Buyology: Truth and Lies About Why We Buy*. New York: Doubleday. 2008.

List, John A., Sally Sadoff, and Mathis Wagner. "So You Want to Run an Experiment, Now What? Some Simple Rules of Thumb for Optimal Experimental Design." Working Paper 15701. National Bureau of Economic Research. 2010.

Lockton, Dan. "Design with Intent Toolkit." *http://requisitevariety.co.uk/design-with-intent-toolkit/*. 2010.

———. "Design with Intent: A Design Pattern Toolkit for Environmental and Social Behaviour Change." Thesis, Brunel University School of Engineering and Design. 2013.

Lusardi, Annamaria, and Olivia Mitchell. "Financial Literacy and Retirement Preparedness: Evidence and Implications for Financial Education." *Business Economics* 42, no. 1 (January 1): 35–44. 2007.

Lusardi, Annamaria, and Olivia S. Mitchell. "Financial Literacy and Planning: Implications for Retirement Wellbeing." Working Paper 17078. National Bureau of Economic Research. *http://www.nber.org/papers/w17078*. 2011.

Lyons, Angela C., Lance Palmer, Koralalage S.U Jayaratne, and Erik Scherpf. "Are We Making the Grade? A National Overview of Financial Education and Program Evaluation." *Journal of Consumer Affairs* 40, no. 2: 208–235. 2006.

Maier, Steven F., and Martin E. Seligman. "Learned Helplessness: Theory and Evidence." *Journal of Experimental Psychology: General* 105, no. 1: 3–46. 1976.

Mandell, Lewis, and Linda Schmid Klein. "The Impact of Financial Literacy Education on Subsequent Financial Behavior." *Journal of Financial Counseling and Planning Volume* 20, no. 1: 16. 2009.

Martin, Neale. *Habit: The 95% of Behavior Marketers Ignore*. Upper Saddle River, New Jersey: FT Press. 2009.

McAdam, Doug, Sidney Tarrow, and Charles Tilly. *Dynamics of Contention*. New York: Cambridge University Press. 2001.

McNeil, Barbara J., Stephen G. Pauker, Harold C. Sox, and Amos Tversky. "On the Elicitation of Preferences for Alternative Therapies." *New England Journal of Medicine* 306, no. 21 (May 27): 1259–1262. 1982.

McNeil, Donald. "In Raising the World's I.Q., the Secret's in the Salt." *The New York Times*, December 16, sec. Health. *http://www.nytimes.com/2006/12/16/health/16iodine.html*. 2006.

Milkman, Katherine L., John Beshears, James J. Choi, David Laibson, and Brigitte C. Madrian. "Using Implementation Intentions Prompts to Enhance Influenza Vaccination Rates." *Proceedings of the National Academy of Sciences* 108, no. 26 (June 28): 10415–10420. 2011.

Milkman, Katherine L., Julia A. Minson, and Kevin Volpp. "Holding the Hunger Games Hostage at the Gym: An Evaluation of Temptation Bundling." SSRN Scholarly Paper ID 2183859. Rochester, NY: Social Science Research Network. *http://papers.ssrn.com/abstract=2183859*. 2013.

Miller, George. "The Magical Number Seven, Plus or Minus Two: Some Limits on Our Capacity for Processing Information." *The Psychological Review* 63: 81–97. 1956.

Miltenberger, Raymond G. *Behavior Modification: Principles and Procedures*. Belmont, CA: Wadsworth Cengage Learning. 2012.

Murphy, Anne L. "Lotteries in the 1690s: Investment or Gamble?" *Financial History Review* 12, no. 2: 227. 2005.

Murphy, Michael J. "Can 'Men' Stop Rape? Visualizing Gender in the 'My Strength Is Not for Hurting' Rape Prevention Campaign." *Men and Masculinities* 12, no. 1 (October 1): 113–130. 2009.

Nessmith, William, Stephen Utkus, and Jean Young. "Measuring the Effectiveness of Automatic Enrollment." Working paper, Vanguard. 2007.

Newell, Allen, and Herbert A. Simon. *Human Problem Solving*. Englewood Cliffs, NJ: Prentice-Hall. 1972.

Nisbett, Richard E., and Timothy D. Wilson. "The Halo Effect: Evidence for Unconscious Alteration of Judgments." *Journal of Personality and Social Psychology* 35, no. 4: 250–256. 1977.

Noar, Seth M., Christina N. Benac, and Melissa S. Harris. "Does Tailoring Matter? Meta-analytic Review of Tailored Print Health Behavior Change Interventions." *Psychological Bulletin* 133, no. 4: 673. 2007.

Nodder, Chris. *Evil by Design: Interaction Design to Lead Us into Temptation*. Hoboken, NJ: Wiley. 2013.

Norman, Donald A. *The Design of Everyday Things*. New York: Basic Books. 1988.

Norton, Michael I., Daniel Mochon, and Dan Ariely. "The 'IKEA Effect': When Labor Leads to Love." SSRN Scholarly Paper ID 1777100, Rochester, NY: Social Science Research Network. *http://papers.ssrn.com/abstract=1777100*. 2011.

Northcraft, Gregory B, and Margaret A Neale. "Experts, Amateurs, and Real Estate: An Anchoring-and-adjustment Perspective on Property Pricing Decisions." *Organizational Behavior and Human Decision Processes* 39, no. 1 (February): 84–97. 1987.

Olivola, Christopher Y., and Alexander Todorov. "Elected in 100 Milliseconds: Appearance-Based Trait Inferences and Voting." *Journal of Nonverbal Behavior* 34, no. 2 (June 1): 83–110. 2010.

Opower. "Opower Results." August 10. *http://opower.com/utilities/results/*. 2013.

Ouellette, Judith A., and Wendy Wood. "Habit and Intention in Everyday Life: The Multiple Processes by Which Past Behavior Predicts Future Behavior." *Psychological Bulletin* 124, no. 1: 54. 1998.

Packard, Vance. *The Hidden Persuaders*. New York: David McKay. 1957.

Pariser, Eli. "Welcome to the Brave New World of Persuasion Profiling" *Wired Magazine*. *http://www.wired.com/magazine/2011/04/st_essay_persuasion_profiling/*. 2011.

Piacentini, John, Douglas Woods, Lawrence Scahill, Sabine Wilhelm, Alan Peterson, Susanna Chang, and Ginsburg Golda. "Behavior Therapy for Children with Tourette Disorder: A Randomized Controlled Trial." *JAMA* 303, no. 19 (May 19): 1929–1937. 2010.

Prochaska, James O., and Wayne F. Velicer. "The Transtheoretical Model of Health Behavior Change." *American Journal of Health Promotion* 12, no. 1 (September): 38–48 1997.

Ramsey, Dave. *The Total Money Makeover: A Proven Plan for Financial Fitness*. Nashville, TN: Thomas Nelson. 2009.

Ries, Eric. *The Lean Startup: How Today's Entrepreneurs Use Continuous Innovation to Create Radically Successful Businesses*. New York: Crown Business. 2011.

Rogers, Todd, Katy Milkman, Leslie John, and Michael I. Norton. "Making the Best Laid Plans Better: How Plan-Making Increases Follow-Through" (working paper). 2013.

Rolls, Barbara J. *The Volumetrics Eating Plan: Techniques and Recipes for Feeling Full on Fewer Calories*. New York: Harper. 2007.

Rubin, Kenneth S. *Essential Scrum: a Practical Guide to the Most Popular Agile Process*. Upper Saddle River, NJ: Addison-Wesley. 2012.

Ryan, Richard M., and Edward L. Deci. "Intrinsic and Extrinsic Motivations: Classic Definitions and New Directions." *Contemporary Educational Psychology* 25, no. 1: 54–67. 2000.

Saffer, Dan. *Designing for Interaction: Creating Innovative Applications and Devices.* Berkeley: New Riders. 2010.

Schultz, P. Wesley, Jessica M. Nolan, Robert B. Cialdini, Noah J. Goldstein, and Vladas Griskevicius. "The Constructive, Destructive, and Reconstructive Power of Social Norms." *Psychological Science* 18, no. 5 (May 1): 429–434. 2007.

Schwartz, Barry. *The Paradox of Choice: Why More Is Less.* New York: Harper Perennial. 2004.

Schwarz, Norbert. "Meta-Cognitive Experiences in Consumer Judgment and Decision Making." SSRN Scholarly Paper ID 532222. Rochester, NY: Social Science Research Network. 2004.

Shah, Anuj K., and Daniel M. Oppenheimer. "Heuristics Made Easy: An Effort-reduction Framework." *Psychological Bulletin* 134, no. 2: 207. 2008.

Shapiro, Shauna L., Linda E. Carlson, John A. Astin, and Benedict Freedman. "Mechanisms of Mindfulness." *Journal of Clinical Psychology* 62, no. 3: 373–386. 2006.

Shih, Margaret, Todd L. Pittinsky, and Nalini Ambady. "Stereotype Susceptibility: Identity Salience and Shifts in Quantitative Performance." *Psychological Science* 10, no. 1 (January 1): 80–83. 1999.

Simon, Herbert A. *Models of Bounded Rationality.* Cambridge, MA: MIT Press. 1982.

Spiegel, Alix. "Hotel Maids Challenge the Placebo Effect : NPR." NPR.org. 2008.

Steiner, Sheyna. "1 in 4 Americans Has No Emergency Savings." Financial Security Index, Bankrate.com. *http://www.bankrate.com/finance/consumer-index/1-in-4-americans-has-no-emergency-savings-1.aspx.* 2011.

Strack, Fritz, Leonard L. Martin, and Norbert Schwarz. "Priming and Communication: Social Determinants of Information Use in Judgments of Life Satisfaction." *European Journal of Social Psychology* 18, no. 5: 429–442. 1988.

Strauss, Valerie. "Mega Millions: Do Lotteries Really Benefit Public Schools?" *The Washington Post—Blogs*. *http://www.washingtonpost.com/blogs/answer-sheet/post/mega-millions-do-lotteries-really-benefit-public-schools/2012/03/30/gIQAbTUNlS_blog.html*. 2012.

Silver, Brian D., Barbara A. Anderson, and Paul R. Abramson. "Who Overreports Voting?" *The American Political Science Review* 80, no. 2 (June): 613. 1986.

Stead, Martine, Ross Gordon, Kathryn Angus, and Laura McDermott. "A Systematic Review of Social Marketing Effectiveness." *Health Education* 107, no. 2 (February 27): 126–191. 2007.

Stubblebine, Tony. Interview with Tony Stubblebine, Lift CEO. 5 March 2013.

Susi, Tarja, Mikael Johannesson, and Per Backlund. "Serious Games: An Overview." 2007.

Thaler, Richard H., and Cass R. Sunstein. *Nudge: Improving Decisions About Health, Wealth, and Happiness*. New Haven, Connecticut: Yale University Press. 2008.

Till, Brian D., and Michael Busler. "Matching Products with Endorsers: Attractiveness Versus Expertise." *Journal of Consumer Marketing* 15, no. 6 (December 1): 576–586. 1998.

Tufano, Peter. "Saving Whilst Gambling: An Empirical Analysis of UK Premium Bonds." *American Economic Review* 98, no. 2: 321–26. 2008.

Tversky, Amos, and Daniel Kahneman. "Availability: A Heuristic for Judging Frequency and Probability." *Cognitive Psychology* 5, no. 2 (September): 207–232. 1973.

———. "The Framing of Decisions and the Psychology of Choice." *Science* 211, no. 4481 (January 30): 453–458. 1981.

Underhill, Paco. *Why We Buy: The Science of Shopping—Updated and Revised for the Internet, the Global Consumer, and Beyond*. New York: Simon and Schuster. 2009.

Verba, Sidney, Kay Lehman Schlozman, and Henry E. Brady. *Voice and Equality: Civic Voluntarism in American Society*. Cambridge, MA: Harvard University Press. 1995.

Vohs, Kathleen D., and Roy F. Baumeister. *Handbook of Self-Regulation, Second Edition: Research, Theory, and Applications*. 2nd ed. New York: The Guilford Press. 2011.

Wansink, Brian. *Mindless Eating: Why We Eat More Than We Think*. New York: Bantam Books. 2010.

Wansink, Brian, and Koert van Ittersum. "Portion Size Me: Downsizing Our Consumption Norms." *Journal of the American Dietetic Association* 107, no. 7 (July): 1103–1106. 2007.

Webb, Thomas L., and Paschal Sheeran. "Does Changing Behavioral Intentions Engender Behavior Change? A Meta-analysis of the Experimental Evidence." *Psychological Bulletin* 132, no. 2: 249–268. 2006.

Wood, Wendy, and David T. Neal. "A New Look at Habits and the Habit-goal Interface." *Psychological Review* 114, no. 4: 843–863. 2007.

Wood, Wendy, Jeffrey M. Quinn, and Deborah A. Kashy. "Habits in Everyday Life: Thought, Emotion, and Action." *Journal of Personality and Social Psychology* 83, no. 6: 1281–1297. 2002.

Wood, Wendy, Leona Tam, and Melissa Guerrero Witt. "Changing Circumstances, Disrupting Habits." *Journal of Personality and Social Psychology* 88, no. 6: 918. 2005.

Weinschenk, Susan. *100 Things Every Designer Needs to Know About People*. Berkeley: New Riders. 2011.

Wilson, Timothy D. *Redirect: The Surprising New Science of Psychological Change*. New York: Little, Brown and Company. 2011.

Zajonc, Robert B. "Attitudinal Effects of Mere Exposure." *Journal of Personality and Social Psychology* 9 (2, Pt.2): 1–27. 1968.

Zichermann, Gabe, and Christopher Cunningham. *Gamification by Design*. Sebastopol, CA: O'Reilly Media. 2011.

[*Appendix D*]

Endnotes

1 *http://www.nike.com/us/en_us/lp/nikeplus-fuelband*; *http://www.nest.com/*; *http://www.vitality.net/glowcaps.html*; *http://call.barackobama.com/* as of summer 2012 (website discontinued); *http://www.nandahome.com/*; *http://blog.lift.do/*; *http://fb.me/QuitNow App/*.

2 Thaler and Sunstein (2008), Gladwell (2005), Ariely (2008).

3 See *https://www.gov.uk/government/organisations/behavioural-insights-team*.

4 Dan Lockton has a set of working papers (and published papers) that provide an extensive review of the various domains in which intentional behavior change has been applied. See *http://architectures.danlockton.co.uk/dan-lockton/#workingpapers*.

5 The Dark Arts have also been applied specifically to software user interfaces. Chris Nodder (2013) and Harry Brignull (2013) have a book and website, respectively, devoted to documenting intentionally deceptive user interface practices.

6 Social marketing entails using the techniques of marketing for beneficial behavior change and explicit social good. For example, Murphy (2009) talks about a social marketing campaign by the organization Men Can Stop Rape that features members of the D.C. United Soccer team stating, "My Strength is Not for Hurting," with the explicit behavioral goal of delegitimizing rape.

See Stead et al. (2007) for a recent review of the field and its effectiveness, and Grier and Bryant (2005) for public health applications of social marketing.

7 In addition, some of the lessons about behavior and behavior change reviewed in this book *haven't* been applied in fields such as sales and marketing (for either positive or negative applications). Neale Martin's book *Habit* (FT Press, 2008) describes how habits are often ignored in marketing efforts, even though they drive most of our purchasing behavior.

8 If you're in the D.C. area, even if you're just visiting, come check us out—information about the group can be found at *http://www.meetup.com/Action-Design-DC*. We also have an online forum (*www.actiondesigner.net/*) for sharing product ideas, research summaries, and more.

9 That's the "third-person effect" in communications research (Davison 1983). See *http://www.spring.org.uk/2010/08/persuasion-the-third-person-effect.php* for a recent write-up.

10 There is actually a family of theories, so dual process theories would be more accurate, but cumbersome. Dual process theories give a useful abstraction—a simplified but generally accurate way of thinking about—the vast complexity of our underlying brain processes.

11 There are great books about dual process theory and the workings of these two parts of our mind. Kahneman's *Thinking, Fast and Slow* (Farrar, Straus and Giroux, 2011) and Malcolm Gladwell's *Blink* (Back Bay Books, 2005) are two excellent places to start; I've included a list of resources on how the mind works (including dual process theory) in Appendix B for those who are curious.

12 For example, biases and heuristics in our decision-making process—the role of these mental slants and shortcuts is discussed further in this chapter.

13 This particular list of "A" words comes from Wikipedia at *http://en.wikipedia.org/wiki/List_of_biases_in_judgment_and_decision_making*. Their *partial* list of biases in judgment and decision making has 166 different mechanisms! Wikipedia obviously isn't authoritative, but it gives you an idea of the problem. The descriptions, examples, and citations are my own.

14 Dan Lockton's Design with Intent Toolkit organizes 101 design patterns for behavior change (Lockton 2010). In *Yes!*, Noah Goldstein lists 50 mechanisms for persuasion (Goldstein et al. 2008). The Marketing Science Institute lists 42 mechanisms that marketers use (Alba 2011). Eric Fernandez presents 104 in "A Visual Study Guide to Cognitive Biases" (2010). And there are many more.

15 The boundaries between "habit" and other processes ("intuition," etc.) are somewhat blurry; but these terms help draw out the differences among types of System 1 responses. See Wood and Neal (2007) for the distinction between habits and other automated System 1 behaviors; see Kahneman (2011) for a general discussion of System 1 behaviors.

16 I'm indebted to Neale Martin for highlighting the situations in which the conscious mind does become active. See his book *Habit* (2005) for a great summary of the literature on when intuitive and deliberative processes are at play.

17 This isn't to say that the rider is equivalent to the left side of the brain and the elephant to the right side. Our deliberative and intuitive thinking isn't neatly divided in that way. Instead, this is just one of the many examples of how rationalizations occur when our deliberative mind is asked to explain what happens outside of its awareness and control. Many thanks to Sebastian Deterding for catching that unintended (and wrong!) implication of the passsage.

18 I'm indebted to Sebastian Deterding for helping clarify and hone this section (among many other sections, but this one in particular).

19 The game is known as the Iowa Gambling Task and has been used in dozens of studies of cognition and emotion.

20 See Bargh et al. (1996) for a discussion of the four core characteristics of automatic behaviors, such as habits: uncontrollable, unintentional, unaware, and cognitively efficient (doesn't require cognitive effort).

21 There's a nice summary and video here: *http://newsinhealth.nih.gov/issue/jan2012/feature1*, *http://www.cbsnews.com/8301-18560_162-57423321/hooked-why-bad-habits-are-hard-to-break/*

22 There's an active debate in the field about how exactly the notion of a reward affects a person *after* the habit is formed. See Wood and Neal (2007) for a discussion.

23 See Berridge et al. (2009) on the difference between "wanting" and "liking." The difference between wanting and liking is a possible explanation for why certain drugs instill strong craving in addicts although taking them long stopped being pleasurable.

24 Duhigg's story also is an example of the complex ethics of behavior change. Hopkins accomplished something immensely beneficial for Americans and American society. He also was wildly successful in selling a commercial product in which demand was partially built on a fabricated "problem" (the fake problem of tooth film, which is harmless, rather than tooth decay, which is not).

25 This is one form of "motivated cueing," in which there is a diffuse motivation applied to the context that cues the habit (Wood and Neal 2007). There is active debate in the field on how, exactly, motivation affects habits that have already formed.

26 I'm using the term "frames of reference" to encompass the range of processes that show we have multiple potential reactions to the same stimulus, depending on our current context and what is top of mind. Schemas, priming, framing, and self-narratives all affect our choice set and salient associations and thoughts. Each process has distinct characteristics and research literatures. Priming, for example, is usually relevant for short-term changes in behavior, and self-narratives are (more) relevant for longer-term changes in behavior. But the lesson for product designers is the same—our moment-to-moment selves, and thus the actions we decide to take, are subject to cues in our environment.

27 There is considerable recent debate in psychology over the presence and interpretation of priming effects (Bower 2012), centering on another famous study by Bargh et al. (1996) with college students primed to think about ageing before walking down a hallway (those primed to think about ageing walked more slowly). More recent research by Doyen et al. (2012) argues that priming didn't influence the participants—but rather the expectations and subtle cues from the researchers themselves, who knew what the students had been primed with.

Here, I am not trying to wade into the debate over priming, but rather making the more general point that there are a variety of mechanisms by which our intuitive minds shape our behavior in response to selective activation (and interpretation) of our memories and internal concepts.

28 In fact, many of the hundreds of biases and heuristics that are discussed in the literature are redundant—special cases of general rules that our mind follows. See Shah and Oppenheimer (2008) for one way to organize and make sense of the literature on heuristics.

29 The original study is Strack et al. (1998); I first encountered the story in Kahneman (2011).

30 See Cialdini's *Influence* (HarperBusiness, 2001) for an overview of social proof.

31 Cialdini (2001)'s work provides a good practical overview. See Cialdini and Goldstein (2004) for a framework to understand various social conformity pressures.

32 See Roy F. Baumeister and John Tierney's book *Willpower* (Penguin Books, 2011) for a good general-public summary of the research into willpower, and Kathleen D. Vohs and Baumeister's *Handbook of Self-Regulation* (The Guilford Press, 2011) for the underlying academic research.

33 In this case, one could argue that limiting the search of movies is an optimal strategy from a global decision making perspective. True, and economists and game theorists subsequently have made that argument. But Simon's core finding holds—we don't try to find the optimal solution to problems.

34 That is, the natural "clustering" of positive and negative perceptions. See Kahneman (2011) for a discussion of this clustering. Stephen Anderson (2011) also gives some great examples of the importance of good visual design on behavior.

35 One such commonly used heuristic is the volume of the food—yes, how big it is. Barbara Rolls, head of the Penn State Human Ingestive Behavior Lab, developed a diet that leverages this heuristic to help people lose weight (see Rolls 2007 and *http://nutrition.psu.edu/foodlab/barbara-rolls*). Wansink (2010) has a humorous, readily accessible ("digestible"?), description of this research.

36 I'm thankful to BJ Fogg for stressing that behavioral prerequisites must occur at the same time. It's something he talks about in the Fogg Behavior Model (Fogg 2009a), and that sets his work apart from other models of behavior and intentional action—which too often focus on the raw materials of behavior (resources, motivation, etc.) but not the *timing* required for action.

37 These two models are particularly widespread and generalizable. Other major models on behavior include the Health Belief Model (Janz and Becker 1984) in health, and Social Learning Theory (Bandura 1977b).

38 Increasing the benefits of doing one's taxes early can (partially) counteract the tendency to procrastinate until the last minute, but that just muddies the conversation and makes costs (ability) and benefits (motivation) all-encompassing. Time pressure (urgency) is usually a separate consideration from the benefits of action in our minds.

39 For lack of a better term, I'm using "thinking" to refer to preconscious sensory processing and reactions and, later on, conscious thought.

40 I'm indebted to Nir Eyal for reminding me of the importance of internal cues, and showing me how products can move from relying on external cues to internal cues over time.

41 Many thanks to Keri Kettle and Remi Trudel for their feedback on an early draft of this chapter, and for bringing up the intuitive needs assessment and search for alternatives.

42 See Dean (2013) for a great overview.

43 In this general concept of "ability," I'm combining disparate elements from the self-efficacy literature (Bandura 1977a), work on goals and implementation intentions (Gollwitzer 1999), and "weak" rational choice models of resource constraints, like the Civic Volunteerism Model (Verba et al. 1995). You may be familiar with the term "ability" from Fogg's Behavior Model. I'm using it in a different way here—as the perceived and actual capability of the individual to take the action. Fogg uses the term for how "easy" or "simple" the action is, i.e. the lack of costs (Fogg 2009a).

44 Many thanks to BJ Fogg for introducing me to the concept of Kairos.

45 Many thanks to Nir Eyal for brainstorming on the action funnel. And, as he says in his workshops on the Hooked Model—it's an "acronym, so it must be true."

46 This concept of ever-present competition is found in social marketing (e.g., Grier and Bryant 2005), but is considered in few other behavior change perspectives.

47 There can be an interplay between the deliberative and intuitive minds, as our conscious attention shifts, potentially intervening in an automatic process, or relinquishing control back to automatic processes. See Wood and Neal (2007) for a discussion of some of these scenarios.

48 Many thanks to John Beshears and Katy Milkman for presenting the idea of basic cognitive barriers to action (procrastination, forgetfulness, and a lack of motivation), when they came to speak at the Action Design Meetup, April 2013 (Beshears and Milkman 2013).

49 We will talk about the other two elements (associations and shortcuts) later, but they are really tactics that can improve *any* other behavior change strategy—assuming you know enough about the population you're working with.

50 For many Americans, the behavior change isn't what our policy makers and companies intended—it's become a short-term savings vehicle. But the impact on savings is still amazing. See Fellowes (2013) for a discussion of the downsides of auto-enrollment and auto-escalation.

51 From McNeil (2006): *http://www.nytimes.com/2006/12/16/health/16iodine.html?fta=y&_r=0*. Though, to be fair, I found that citation from Wikipedia: *http://en.wikipedia.org/wiki/Iodised_salt*.

52 Legally, prize-linked savings is usually structured as a sweepstakes in the United States; no need to get into the legal definitions here though.

53 One could also point to state lotteries as examples of making a behavior, contributing money to schools, incidental. In California alone, they have funneled $24 billion to "education funding" since 1985 (Strauss 2012). But state lotteries are also a great example of how different the mind is from a conscious budgetary process.

In our minds, school contributions are a side-effect of our lottery purchases. No extra work. In reality, state budgeters consciously know that a dollar is a dollar, and move the money around from one budget category (schools) to another. Changing *lottery participant* behavior doesn't mean that you're also changing the behavior of accountants!

54 Another great example of making savings behavior incidental comes from the IDEO/Bank of America "Keep the Change" program. The program rounds up purchases made on debt cards to the nearest dollar, and takes the different between original cost and and the rounded version and automatically deposits it into the person's savings account. The person does nothing differently—savings is incidental. See *http://www.ideo.com/work/keep-the-change-account-service-for-bofa/* and *https://www.bankofamerica.com/deposits/manage/keep-the-change.go*.

55 The related tendency to create consistent (non-dissonant) stories about our own behavior has been in everything from North Korean gulags to the "foot in the door" technique of successive commitments in sales. See Cialdini (2001).

56 *http://lift.do/*; Stubblebine (2013)

57 This cue-routine-reward is a clearer presentation of the antecedent-behavior-consequent (ABC) model used in Rational emotive behavior therapy and applied behavioral analysis. See Miltenberger (2011) for one application of the ABC model.

58 In studies of classical conditioning with animals, you actually don't need to link the cue, routine, and reward beforehand. You can build a habit around simple trial and error. However, with us humans, and especially with *voluntary* behavior change, you can skip the trial-and-error part and tell people what's going on.

59 But where we expect a strong pattern, and don't get it, we're angry. Would you be happy if you went to Starbucks for your morning coffee, and some days the coffee was terrible, and other days it was great? That would be random reinforcement.

60 There's much more that one could say about designing habits, but my goal is not to exhaustively cover them here. Numerous books have been written about forming and breaking habits in different contexts; Duhigg (2012), Dean (2013), and Eyal (2013) are three

good places to start. In addition, BJ Fogg has developed a new hands-on approach to creating habits in one's own life; see *http://tinyhabits.com/*. For now though, my goal is to give enough of a foundation that a product team can make a solid product plan, and then learn what really works for them in their particular context.

61 And, in cases of chemical addiction, there are added layers of difficulty that make *defeating addiction beyond the scope of this book*. For example, drugs can cause brain's receptors for key neurotransmitters to change, requiring additional levels of stimulation to receive the same experiences that were had before the drug was used. While many of the techniques described here are also used for addiction, I don't try to cover the extensive research on addiction.

62 They're difficult to change on their own, and, of course, there are also other factors associated with the habit that make it more difficult to change—like peer pressure, chemical addiction, etc.

63 Changing circumstances is used widely beyond addiction counseling as well. See Wood et al. (2005) for research on this method.

64 *http://www.covenanteyes.com/services/filtering/*

65 See *http://www.changeTech.no*. Many thanks to Sebastian Deterding for mentioning this example.

66 *http://www.getsomeheadspace.com/*

67 *http://propellerhealth.com/*

68 *http://www.myfitnesspal.com/*

69 *http://thepaleodiet.com/*

70 See Kolata (1997) for the story of fen-phen and how it rose to prominence and was later pulled from the market (*http://www.nytimes.com/1997/09/23/science/how-fen-phen-a-diet-miracle-rose-and-fell.html?pagewanted=all&src=pm*).

71 See Vita on *http://brianwansink.com*; version as of publication date: *http://brianwansink.com/wansink_vita_11-09.doc*.

72 The size of our plates (and cups, popcorn buckets, etc.) has various effects on eating behavior. One effect is on how much food we put on our plate, another is on how much we eat, and yet another

is on how much we consider normal to eat (e.g., Wansink and van Ittersum 2007). See Wansink 2010 for a funny and very accessible account of the research in this space.

73 Wansink has numerous cartoons summarizing his research and available for teaching purposes. See *http://foodpsychology.cornell.edu/*.

74 *http://sunlightfoundation.com/about/*

75 In other words, this is a different distinction than the one I made in the Preface about behavior change affecting a behavior *within a product* or *outside of it*. In either case, a company could start with the benefit for user or the benefit for the company.

76 For example, that's common with advocacy websites that try to influence policy makers to change regulations (like on the cost of gasoline), which then change behavior in society to drive outcomes like lower greenhouse gas emissions. My thanks to the folks at ForumOne for pointing this out.

77 A lean startup approach can certainly help, but isn't required. In a new product development process, for example, there are steps in the waterfall that are explicitly devoted to testing out product ideas—early on. They just aren't iterative.

78 I intentionally place the process of coming up with possible actions *before generating user personas* because I want the idea-generation process to be free of strong self-censorship on what actions the users are likely to take. I'm sure there are good examples of when these should be reversed, though.

79 Since we were doing microtargeting, the end result of this process was a set of machine-learning models of the propensity of ActMore's members to respond to different product features, which we then field tested before rolling out the product for real. We used quantitative data from the organization and from third-party providers. But the core concept is the same in a less quantitative-data heavy environment. Who are the users, and how will they respond differently to appeals to change their behavior? At HelloWallet, we achieve this step primarily through qualitative user research.

80 Thank to Jim Burke for highlighting the importance of direct observation.

81 This technique, of rating potential actions, is inspired by a method I learned from BJ Fogg called "Priority Mapping," in which he rates behaviors based on ease of implementation and effectiveness. Also, on the example of learning languages: there's certainly a science to teaching people new languages, and I won't go into those methods here; this is just a stereotyped example.

82 This interacts with business considerations of course. Physically fit people might be easiest to serve, but the market might already be crowded. Look for the place you'll gain most traction with users from both a business and behavioral perspective.

83 This three-part design process has similarities to Sebastain Deterding's descriptions of game design (Deterding 2010), and differentiates it from a traditional UX process, where only the product (tool) itself is designed.

84 This tactic isn't unique to the Obama campaign and was somewhat controversial for trying to generate a sense of (extraordinary) support on the ground for the legislation. But it's a darn good example of helping people voluntarily take an action they wouldn't otherwise take.

85 A 1993 Roper Center survey estimated the percent of Americans *ever* calling into a talk show at any point in their lives at 11%; and roughly half of them had actually been on air. You can see a reprint at *http://www.ropercenter.uconn.edu/public-perspective/ppscan/46/46096.pdf*.

86 See Kolko (2011) for various examples of journey maps, touchpoints, and concept maps. Xplane(.com) developed the empathy map; see *http://innovationgames.com/empathy-map/* for an interactive example. Tools like the Touchpoint Dashboard (*http://www.touchpointdashboard.com/*) can be used, but a whiteboard or some sticky notes work well too.

87 When automation of the whole process is possible—something I strongly recommend—then commitment to the action is a real issue. For example, people that are automatically enrolled in a 401(k) without their real commitment are likely to cash out the money and use it for something else. But if your product isn't doing automation, and you can still make *everything* that the user needs to do easy, that's a nice, high-class problem to have.

88 While there are various forms of extrinsic motivation, there is always an element of external control; we feel intrinsically motivating things are things we "want to do," and extrinsically motivating things are things that we "need to do," even if it is to get a reward that we want and choose. When a "want to" is turned into a "need to" by adding extrinsic motivation, it's hard to go back to feeling that it's something we want to do.

The destructive sense of external control is lessened when the outcome we seek (the extrinsic motivation) is aligned with our other goals and desires. Such "integrated" motivations are less likely to undermine intrinsic motivations.

89 An activity can move from relying on an extrinsic motivation to an intrinsic one over time in stages. For example, consider a kid who plays the piano under the watchful eye of a parent. Over time, the kid can internalize the parent's wishes and hear her parents nagging voice in her head (an "introjected motivation"; Ryan and Deci 2000, with thanks to Sebastian Deterding.). Later, the kid might learn to really enjoy playing the piano—making it an intrinsic motivation.

90 They leverage loss aversion, the cognitive quirk in which we work much harder to retain the things we own (or otherwise feel to already belong to us) rather than to earn something of equivalent value.

91 Millennia, really. For example, Plato saw desires coming from three parts of the soul (Blackson 2013)

92 Understanding your users' landscape of motivations also allows for clever techniques like temptation bundling (Milkman et al. 2013)—in which you make something people really like, such as reading the *Hunger Games*, conditional on something people like but aren't as keenly motivated by, such as exercising at the gym. That doesn't mean you can hold the things that people love hostage to something they hate. Instead, the researchers focused on intentional, voluntary bundling—allowing people the option to get the book and exercise at the same time.

93 In economic terms, we "discount," or place less value on, things that are in the future. The further in the future they are, the less we value them.

94 By effective, I mean they engender more action that than not using them. This technique is really obvious, but there are actually experimental studies that show that they work. See *http://whichtestwon.com/* for some examples of optimizing these simple calls to action.

95 The quantified-self movement has brought rightful attention to feedback loops and their power to both inform and change behavior; check out *http://quantifiedself.com/* to learn more.

96 We talked about this briefly in Chapter 2—that at each stage of the Create Action Funnel, the action must *relatively* better than the other potential actions the person is thinking about undertaking.

97 We discussed this study briefly in Chapter 1, as an introduction to the idea of "self-concepts" or "self-narratives."

98 *http://www.moves-app.com*

99 James Clear (2012) expands upon this concept further in his Layers of Behavior Change model. He describes three layers of progressively increasing power over behavior: appearance, performance, and identity. See *http://jamesclear.com/identity-based-habits*.

100 On the other extreme, generating a supportive self-narrative may require overcoming what's known as learned helplessness (Maier and Seligman 1976). If people have failed repeatedly, and they believe they had no control over the outcome, they can simply stop trying. For example, a student that has repeatedly failed at math despite hard work may shut down and think he simply isn't smart enough to handle it. Learned helplessness is difficult to overcome; products have to find creative ways to reinterpret past events and have users develop other ways of explaining future ones. Show that the person does have control over their own future, and that the causes of past failures don't apply to the present situation.

101 When I was a professional software engineer, both in the early stages of HelloWallet and in prior gigs in the Bay Area of California, we used various sequential development methods. They've fallen out of favor in some camps but are still widely used in other companies. The suggestions here come from my own experiences, from discussions with other companies at the Action Design D.C. Meetup and from interviews conducted for this book.

102 The term "design patterns" is used frequently in the UI world for specific elements of interactions, like how to design form fields. See *http://ui-patterns.com* for one collection. UI design patterns are at a much lower level than the behavior change patterns discussed here—rather than a specifc UI element, behavior change patterns provide an overall approach to an application or feature.

103 See *http://requisitevariety.co.uk/design-with-intent-toolkit/* and *http://getmentalnotes.com/*. These two approaches focus on particular tactics to change behavior, and are most similar to a list of tactics I present in Chapter 9. Here, I focus on a higher-level UI approach. In addition, Chris Nodder (2013) provides a list of design patterns for behavior change—which he calls "persuasive design patterns" in his book *Evil by Design*. He takes a different approach, organizing the patterns around the particular "sin" that they appeal to, and focusing on the underlying psychology. The behavior change design patterns presented here provide common approaches to structuring the *overall* UI and application functionality. In Chapter 9, I present a list of particular psychological tactics for (beneficial, voluntary) behavior change that is somewhat similar to Nodder's list.

104 *http://www.hellowallet.com/*

105 *http://www.makeourway.com/*

106 See Susi et al. (2007) for an introduction to the field of Serious Games. See *http://gameswithpurpose.org/* for an annotated list of such games.

107 *http://keas.com/*

108 *http://www.motherearthnews.com/garden-planner/vegetable-garden-planner.aspx#axzz2W0kvVZrk*

109 *http://www.omnigroup.com/products/omnifocus/*; *http://www.nozbe.com/*

110 *http://runkeeper.com/*

111 *http://www.fitbit.com/one*; *https://jawbone.com/up*

112 See *http://quantifiedself.com/*.

113 *http://www.monkeysee.com/play/10009-how-to-grow-a-vegetable-g arden*

114 *http://opower.com/what-is-opower/reports*

115 See *https://content.sierraclub.org/sierra-club-programs*. As of this writing, one such active campaign could be found at *https://secure.sierraclub.org/site/Advocacy?cmd=display&page=UserAction&id=10119*.

116 *https://text4baby.org/*

117 *http://www.meetup.com*

118 Naturally, one could design and build an NRA Fitbit for Second Amendment-related protests. It could be done (and I'd love to see one, by the way). The point is that it wouldn't fit the existing expectations and product experience of most NRA members. It would be *foreign*, and that foreignness would make it more difficult to have an impact on user behavior (and make it more difficult to "sell" overall).

119 It's difficult to think up many other ways to structure a hygiene app, isn't it? That's part of the power of design patterns—they are reference points for design that lock us in to thinking about the product in a particular way. That's another reason why it's important that the design team has creative freedom to think about the look and feel of the app, before starting from the 'obvious solution' or using the behavioral plan as a reference point.

120 This can occur when the team fleshes out specification outlines into full product requirements, or when the design team digs into the user stories, depending on the development methodology employed.

121 Scrum is one form of agile development. See *http://www.mountaingoatsoftware.com/scrum/product-owner* for a description of the role.

122 See Levin et al. (1998) for a discussion of the various different types of framing changes occurring in this example and in other cases in the literature.

123 There are many more examples—both in the academic literature and beyond. The website *http://whichtestwon.com/* features examples of minor (and not so minor) changes like this, and their impact on behavior in consumer applications.

124 Dan Lockton provides a good (and unfortunately rare) example of systematically organizing these tactics—he discusses them as eight "lenses" for thinking about behavior change (2013).

125 This presentation in table form is inspired by a conversation with Nir Eyal and ideas42's Behavioral Map.

126 As long as the interaction designer gets a head start on designing the basic structure of the application. That's important to keep creative freedom, and avoid using the behavioral plan as a user interface template, as noted in Chapter 8.

127 For a good summary on the various ways in which making concrete plans affect behavior, and under what conditions, see Rogers et al. (2013).

128 But there's an obvious problem there—once that future time comes, then the pain and effort will be immediate, and the person won't want to do it. That's a core issue in procrastination. Look for ways to lock the person into the future effort: with public statements that they'll do it, with the potential to lose money if the person backs out of the deal, etc.

129 *http://www.lift.do*; *http://goalsponsors.com*

130 The engineering review may be as part of the specification process, directly afterwards, or after the initial user testing; it's not relevant exactly where it occurs.

131 Inspired by Neighborsations, *http://www.neighborsations.com/*.

132 There are a variety of perspectives on what makes a good metric, but no generally accepted and applied definition. These are characteristics that I've found to be important.

133 It may take an up-front investment (that's not cheap) to make reoccurring measurement cheap. We want to set up data collection that will be cheap and easy to check whenever there is a change to the application. Survey data, for example, is often "cheap" to measure the first time, but the cost usually remains the same with each iteration (and survey data is plagued with biases; discussed under the section "figure out how to measure"). Ideally, we want automatically gathered administrative data—that is collected from

the original source without the need for human intervention or extra costs. Asking people what they spend money on is a survey. Their actual credit card transactions are administrative data.

134 *http://www.contactually.com*

135 *https://www.kissmetrics.com/*; *https://mixpanel.com/*

136 *http://piwik.org/*

137 Most of us forget or don't even think about what we're eating. See Wansink (2010) and *http://www.mindlesseating.org/* for humorous and disturbing examples.

138 *https://www.dssresearch.com/KnowledgeCenter/toolkitcalculators/samplesizecalculators.aspx*

139 I like to use R, which is open source and extremely powerful. In R, you can use the functions `power.t.test()`, when working with average values, and `power.prop.test()`, when dealing with percentages.

140 In R, that's the `prop.test()` function for proportions and the `t.test()`, or a regression function for numerical values. If the outcome is ordinal (the possible values are in order, but the spacing between them may be irregular and they aren't directly comparable) things are a bit trickier. Get a good stats book, find a statistics person, or tweak the measurement so that the result is binary, floating point, or integer.

141 I can't just point you to the right function in R, sorry.

142 *http://vanity.labnotes.org/*. Vanity allows the sample size to grow until you observe a statistically significant difference, which can undermine the test and give false positives. A better way to handle an unknown number of users is described in "You don't know the users yet". My thanks to Katya Vasilaky for mentioning this problem.

143 *https://github.com/gregdingle/genetify/wiki.*

144 *https://www.optimizely.com/*; *https://www.google.com/analytics/*

145 My thanks again to Katya Vasilaky for the reference and description of the problem.

146 There are often many possible changes to the product you want to analyze—so focusing too long on features that don't appear to change behavior in practically significant ways means you're wasting time that could be used more valuably elsewhere. This is a difference from academic social science work—in that researchers usually devote a significant amount of time to a single question; because of a lack of data, they usually don't have a long list of alternative questions that can be explored immediately.

147 By the way, if the area is large, I imagine that the best way to do this would be access government or commercial satellite imagery. Professional geographers have worked out amazing algorithms to automatically detect vegetation cover, and even the type of vegetation. The GeoEye satellite that is used by Google Earth, for example, *measures down to increments of 16 inches.*

148 To clarify—at this point we're just talking about how to measure the real-world outcome. That forms half of the data you need in order to run an experiment, do a pre-post analysis, or build a statistical model of the relationship between the real-world outcome and user actions in the application. That process is what actually creates the data bridge, and is covered later on. But it helps to plan ahead for the *type* of analysis you will be running, to ensure you're gathering the right data you need when measuring the real-world outcome.

149 For example, you can use *http://easycalculation.com/statistics/population-confidence-interval.php* for calculating confidence intervals of proportions (percent of people creating vegetable gardens) and *http://easycalculation.com/statistics/confidence-limits-mean.php* for calculating confidence intervals of quantities (number of pounds lost after an exercise program). Penn State has a nice summary of the underlying math here: *https://onlinecourses.science.psu.edu/stat200/node/46.*

150 In the simplest case, you might look at the simple linear relationship between the real-world impact and user behavior in the product. But there's no reason to limit the analysis to a linear relationship. You want to build a model that most accurately describes the relationship between behavior in the product and outcomes in the real world.

151 Exactly how much additional improvement would occur would requires additional analysis, to separate out the self-selection into the program from the program's causal impact.

152 Many thanks to Jim Burke for noting that a similar process is used in mapping out an accident chain after major accidents, to determine root causes. Multiple supporting actions are analyzed that eventually lead to some significant outcome.

153 One example: the so-called Ikea effect (Norton et al. 2011). If you put together a lopsided, ugly bookshelf from Ikea, you'll think it's much more valuable than anybody else's identical, lopsided, ugly bookshelf from Ikea.

154 This approach is similar to the (much more detailed and thorough) diagnosis phase that ideas42, the leading behavioral economics consultancy in the United States, uses to start its design process.

155 This particular scenario is inspired by a company in the construction industry I worked with to apply this approach, called deconstruction.co. Many thanks to Brendon Robinson, the CEO of deconstruction.co, for his help writing up this example.

156 In addition to deconstruction.co, the inspiration for this example, there are quite a few of these companies. See *http://blog.softwareadvice.com/articles/construction/the-best-construction-management-apps-for-the-iphone-and-ipad-1082510/*.

157 Unlike my preceding assertion, this model proposes that there's a *single* pathway to action. But it's just not one that I see as generally applicable or true.

158 The concept of fluctuating environmental and social factors that create opportunities for action is a core concept of the Political Opportunity Structure tradition in political sociology (e.g., McAdam et al. 2001). BJ Fogg also models fluctuations in motivation with his concept of a Motivation Wave over time (Fogg 2012; see *http://www.youtube.com/watch?v=fqUSjHjIEFg*).

159 Where conscious reengagement is the end goal or a necessary stage until a habit is formed.

160 I'm a fan of the community blog Less Wrong (*http://lesswrong.com/*), to which I owe this phrase. I'm using it in a different context here, though.

161 *http://webdesign.tutsplus.com/articles/user-experience-articles/dark-patterns-in-ui-and-website-design/*; *http://techcrunch.com/2012/08/25/5-design-tricks-facebook-uses-to-affect-your-privacy-decisions/*

[Index]

Symbols

D

E

F

G

H

N

O

P

Q

R

S

T

U

V

W

[*About the Author*]

Stephen Wendel is a behavioral social scientist who serves as the Principal Scientist at HelloWallet, an independent financial guidance company. He conducts original research on financial behavior and coordinates the research efforts of HelloWallet's advisory board of leading behavioral economists and psychologists.

At HelloWallet, he's helped build an engaging product that helps users take control over their finances. The impetus for this book comes from the challenges he and the rest of the HelloWallet team faced along the way, as they learned to apply the behavioral literature to consumer products and consulted with companies similarly searching for effective ways to enable behavior change.

Prior to joining HelloWallet, Dr. Wendel co-founded two IT companies, and conducted research on the dynamics of political behavior. He's the co-founder of Action Design DC, a Meetup of over 800 practitioners and researchers applying behavioral science to their products, and serves as a mentor at 500 Startups and 1776 DC. He and his wife live in the DC area, with a small kid who loves to sing.